THE
HIDDEN
LIFE OF ART

Secrets and Symbols
in Great Masterpieces

THE
HIDDEN
LIFE of ART

Secrets and Symbols
in Great Masterpieces

CLARE GIBSON

BARNES & NOBLE

NEW YORK

ISBN-13: 978-0-7607-8301-6
ISBN-10: 0-7607-8301-2

Library of Congress Cataloging in Publication Data available.

Printed and bound in China

1 3 5 7 9 10 8 6 4 2

Page 1: *Some of the objects in Hans Holbein the Younger's portrait* The Merchant Georg Gisze *(see pages 184–86) are tools of the merchant's trade, while others convey symbolic meanings.*

Page 2: *Franz Marc rendered animals in vivid colors that represented their "essence" rather than their natural appearance, as in this arresting painting (see pages 162–63).*

Page 3: *Detail from* Matsya *(see pages 88–89).*

Below: *Paul Gauguin,* Portrait of Two Children, *1889. Gauguin's increasingly bold use of color marked the transition of his work from Post-Impressionism to Symbolism.*

EDITOR: Sara Hunt
ART EDITOR: Deborah Hayes

For Jack and Christeen Malan

CONTENTS

INTRODUCTION

"Art is a lie that makes us realize truth."

Pablo Picasso (1881–1973)

P ablo Picasso no doubt intended to shock and provoke when he stated, on September 21, 1958, that art is a lie, yet in adding that it makes us realize truth, was he also trying to open our eyes to reality? You may not think so if you consider this Spanish artist an attention-seeking *enfant terrible*, an anarchic trickster figure intent on shaking up the established order and challenging long-cherished beliefs for selfish purposes of publicity. But if you regard Picasso as a creative genius whose utterly original way of looking at the world marked him out as a giant among twentieth-century artists, you would probably find it difficult to think of anyone better qualified to comment on the nature, function and purpose of art.

EMBELLISHING THE TRUTH

In fact, there are many reasons why art may be termed a lie, not least because we always view a painting through a filter imposed by the artist, much as a photographer may choose a lens or filter to alter the viewer's perception of a subject, and typically for the most pragmatic of reasons. Indeed, just as wedding photographers may seek to please their clients —and thus obtain future work through word-of-mouth recommendation—by photographing

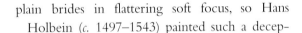

plain brides in flattering soft focus, so Hans Holbein (*c.* 1497–1543) painted such a deceptively attractive portrait of Anne of Cleves in 1539 that King Henry VIII of England eagerly solicited her hand in marriage. Yet on seeing his bride in the flesh, Henry was so disappointed to discover that she was no oil painting—he instead compared her to a "Flanders mare"—that he instantly determined to divorce his now fourth wife.

An impoverished or ambitious artist's desire to secure or keep a wealthy patron may likewise lead him or her to draw a gratifying parallel between the holder of the purse strings and an iconic figure of old, or to enlist the art of propaganda in order to give an unprepossessing subject a seductive aura of power or glamour. There is almost certainly a direct link to be made between the dashingly romantic images that Anthony van Dyck (1599–1641) conjured up of the actually somewhat weedy-looking King Charles I and the prestigious position of court painter and the knighthood that the English monarch bestowed on the Flemish artist in 1632, for example.

Art can similarly put an exaggerated spin on historical events, too, and it is especially rare for an action-packed history painting to present a neutral viewpoint: in martial scenes

Left: Paul Cezanne, Battle of Love, 1880: did the artist intend to convey literal or metaphorical violence in this dynamic scene? ***Above:*** *Holbein's comely portrait of Anne of Cleves scarcely resembled its subject.*

like Paolo Uccello's *The Battle of San Romano* (*c.* 1438–40), for instance, the warriors of one army usually stand out in appearing more heroic than their opponents, particularly if the picture was commissioned by a descendent—be it actual, political or ideological—or admirer of the victorious general. Indeed, when faced with any historical depiction, it is wise to ask oneself whether the artist has painted a "rosy picture" of the personality or event, and if so, why.

CODED COMMUNICATIONS

Other motives underlying an artist's decision to depict a rather different image from the reality may have nothing to do with patron-pleasing, however, but may instead be intended to send a message using art as a form of cryptograph. Continuing the tradition of the early Christians who were forced to worship in secret in pagan ancient Rome, and who used the apparently mundane, nonreligious—to non-Christians, at least—sign of the fish to identify the places where followers of Christ congregated, there have been occasions when artists have encrypted the true meaning of a painting using a symbolic code that is indecipherable to anyone who hasn't been initiated into its esoteric secrets. In his thriller *The Da Vinci Code* (2003), the U.S. author Dan Brown explores the notion that Leonardo da Vinci, the leading light of the Italian Renaissance, encoded heretical references to Mary Magdalene and the pagan Goddess in his masterpiece *The Last Supper* (1495–97, see pages 110–13) through the suggestion of the letter "M" and the downward-pointing triangle. According to Brown, da Vinci was the grand master of the Priory of Sion, a secret society devoted to protecting the Holy Grail at a time when the Roman Catholic Church (which disapproves of the

Above: *A dramatic detail from the eighth-century cave art at Dunhuang in western China, which graphically depicts conflict on the ancient Silk Road.*

notion of the divine feminine) had a tight grip on society,

Art historians have dismissed Brown's speculations as pure fantasy, but it is nevertheless a fact that centuries-old—if not really ancient—esoteric organizations like the Order of the Rosy Cross, or Rosicrucians, represented, disguised and disseminated their beliefs using the medium of art and such innocuous symbols as a rose at the center of a cross, which initiates would have recognized as signifying respectively secrecy and eternal life. They understood the mystical resonance and fascination of the symbol, for as the pioneering Austrian psychologist Carl Gustav Jung (1875–1961) explained: "What we call a symbol is a term, a name, or even a picture that may be familiar in daily life, yet that possesses specific connotations in addition to its conventional and obvious meaning. It implies something vague, unknown, or hidden from us." (*Man and his Symbols*, 1964.)

THE DEVELOPMENT OF SYMBOLISM

Artists may therefore "lie," or use symbolism, for a number of reasons, including trying to further their careers, to promote a person or a cause or to communicate covertly with like-minded individuals, so that a very different truth may lie beneath the surface. But why does humankind have an "inborn disposition to produce parallel images," in the words of Jung, that is, to think symbolically in the first place? Jung concluded that it is because symbols, in the form of archetypes representing aspects of the shared human experience that we have inherited from our ancestors, are hardwired into the section of the human psyche that he termed the collective unconscious.

Try to clear your mind of your twenty-first-century thoughts and distractions, and instead imagine that you are

Right and below: *Aside from being a great artist, Leonardo da Vinci (self portrait, c. 1512–15, below) was a visonary scientist with a particular interest in pure and applied geometry.*

one of your earliest forebears, a member of a primitive hunter–gatherer tribe whose pressing primary concerns are ensuring your survival, securing shelter from the elements and obtaining an adequate supply of food and water. In such circumstances, colors would assume great significance, for you would no doubt associate sunshine yellow with chill-banishing warmth and growth-encouraging energy; blue, with a clear sky and thirst-quenching water; green, with succulent, edible shoots; red, with the blood of a freshly slaughtered animal and the fire on which to cook its meat; and black, with rotting flesh and death. In the language of symbolism, these associations remain as pertinent today as they did millennia ago, which is why colors can be regarded as universal, archetypal symbols.

Early humans eventually learned to cultivate land and livestock, and it was their adoption of agricultural practices that brought the vital need to understand, and if possible, control, the cycles of nature and such natural phenomena as thunderstorms, which could, on the one hand, saturate the parched

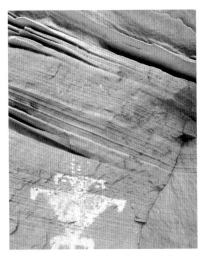

Above: Even the simplest of abstracted shapes can convey a complex object, as on this ancient petroglyph.

earth and encourage plant life to grow, and on the other, devastate crops and strike people dead with random bolts of lightning. And so it was that omnipotent, unpredictable, supernatural beings came to be credited with causing these awesome manifestations of natural energy: sky gods like the Vedic Indra, the Hindu Vishnu, the Greek Zeus, the Roman Jupiter, the Norse Thor and the Germanic Donar, all of whom were believed to hurl lethal lightning bolts at those who infuriated them, or if not properly worshipped or propitiated, their weapons being symbolized by, for example, a mace, a jagged arrow or a hammer.

Although there has certainly been some symbolic crossover between—and sometimes wholesale adoption of—sacred belief systems in various parts of the world throughout the ages, the striking similarity with which different cultures and civilizations have generally visualized their thunder gods, as well as other deities, such as those associated with the sun and moon (solar deities usually being thought of as masculine, and lunar deities, as feminine) attests to their archetypal symbolism.

ETERNAL ARCHETYPES

Indeed, certain pagan divine or cosmic archetypal images and symbols appear to resonate so powerfully and profoundly within the human collective unconscious that they were even incorporated into the iconography of religions that otherwise frowned on the so-called "barbaric" beliefs of the spiritual systems that preceded them, so that the holy figures of Christianity were depicted with the haloes that once denoted the rays of the sun, and thus solar deities, for instance, and the Virgin Mary was portrayed with attributes, and in attitudes, borrowed from the goddesses of the ancient Egyptian, Mesopotamian and Mediterranean pantheons. Nor are archetypal figures and symbols confined to systems of sacred and religious belief, for numerous examples may also be found in the world's treasure house of myths, legends, folklore, fairy tales, art and literature. And not only are such archetypes as the hero a constant presence, but they have endured remarkably unchanged over the millennia. Marduk (the hero of the ancient Babylonian poem *Enuma Elish* and the slayer of Tiamat), Perseus (the dispatcher of the sea monster and the rescuer of Andromeda in Greek mythology, *see* pages 56–57), Beowulf (the hero of the eponymous eighth-century Anglo-Saxon epic poem,

Below: Giorgio Vasari's Perseus and Andromeda *(1570) portrays Perseus in the role of the archetypal hero.*

who slaughtered the monstrous Grendel and its terrible mother), St. George (the valiant dragon-killer of Christian tradition, *see* pages 178–79) and Luke Skywalker (the wholesome hero and vanquisher of the monstrous Darth Vader in the 1977 movie *Star Wars*), are but a few examples that are identifiable as fundamentally the same character.

It is, in addition, significant that hero myths the world over tell of epic battles between the forces of good and evil, "good" typically being personified by the hero, unselfishness and light, and "evil" being represented by monsters, selfishness and dark. It is striking that belief in this duality of two dynamic, polar-opposite cosmic forces is both universal and most powerfully expressed through symbols, such as the Taoist t'ai chi circle that reconciles yang (the white, positive, masculine energy) and yin (the black, negative, feminine energy), and through symbolic, hybrid beings that do not exist in reality, but that humans that have found it necessary to invent in order to express complex concepts. These include angels, the radiant, winged embodiments of goodness, and demons or monsters, the horrible, repellent, unnatural personifications of evil.

An archetype is thus an incalculably ancient and universal symbol that, when activated, acts as a sort of light switch or tripwire in our brains by triggering a host of primitive, inherited unconscious associations and responses. An encounter with an archetypal symbol or pattern may explain why, halfway through a book or movie, you know how the story being told will end, or why you may occasionally experience *déjà vu* (the French for "already seen"), an uncomfortable, otherworldly feeling that increasingly tells you that although you know that you are setting eyes on something for the first time in your life, you have the strong, intuitive sense that you have seen it somewhere

Above: Raphael's St. Michael Victorious *(1518) portrays the archangel defeating evil, embodied in a hideous creature.* **Below:** *This medieval woodcut shows the devil brought to his knees by a magician. Secure within his protective magic circle, which the devil cannot penetrate (around which powerful symbols such as crosses and the signs of the zodiac are inscribed), and clutching his magic wand, the magician neutralizes the evil spirit with powerful words from his book of spells.*

before. Symbols are undeniably powerful, so it is small wonder that some—and particularly the most ancient, namely such shapes as pentagrams, hexagrams, crosses and circles—have been credited by many occult traditions with possessing supernatural powers.

TUNING INTO THE HIDDEN LIFE OF ART

Although archetypal symbols have deep significance when they take the form of characters and objects in humankind's collective library of sacred and cultural texts, they seem to come vibrantly to life when depicted in art. This is, perhaps, not surprising when you think that it is only in recent centuries that literacy became relatively widespread, and that certain concepts are far more difficult to express in words than to sketch. Indeed, there are still many parts of the world where the only stories that community members can "read" are those that are related visually, in pictures. Along with the archetypes, it consequently seems as though we have inherited humankind's instinctive preference for visual communication, and that these two ancient legacies are interdependent, as is their relationship with the sacred:

"Man, with his symbol-making propensity, unconsciously transforms objects or forms into symbols (thereby endowing them with great psychological importance) and expresses them in both his religion and his visual art. The intertwined history of religion and art, reaching back to prehistoric times, is the record that our ancestors have left of the symbols that were meaningful and moving to them. Even today, as modern painting and sculpture show, the interplay of religion and art is still alive."
—(Aniela Jaffé, *Man and his Symbols, ibid.*)

Aniela Jaffé, a colleague and collaborator of Jung's, was writing over forty years ago, at a time when Western populations were generally more observant of, and more willing to adhere to, the strictures of organized religions than they are today. We may be no less spiritual in the twenty-first century, and may, indeed, be far more aware of, and open to, the precepts and symbols of different systems of sacred belief, but may nevertheless lack the ingrained familiarity with the minutiae of Christian lore, for example, that comes of spend-

Above: *The identity of St. Mark, one of the four evangelists, is evident here because the lion is his symbol.*

ing every Sunday of one's life in church, unquestioningly absorbing its teaching and preaching and gazing at stories and symbols depicted all around the building, be it in stained-glass windows, in statues, in carvings or in paintings. In short, although we may understand the broad brushstrokes of many religious portrayals, the significance of their details may pass us by, which is why the first two chapters of this book are devoted to introducing the most prevalent of the world's mythological and sacred figures and symbols as depicted in art.

Because the sacred has been so closely intertwined with the secular in the Western societies of the past few millennia, many hidden religious allusions may furthermore be contained in paintings that may, on the surface, seem to be nothing more than portraits, landscapes or history paintings. The third chapter of this book, which focuses on allegorical figures and symbols, explains that not everything is therefore quite as it seems, and that what appears to be the most straightforward of images on the surface may, in fact, harbor the most profound symbolism—that is, if you know firstly what to look for, secondly, what you are actually looking at, and thirdly, some background details with which to put the painting into its proper context. Take, for instance, Jan van Eyck's *Portrait of Giovanni Arnolfini and his Wife ("The Arnolfini Portrait")*, which is reproduced and decoded on pages 187–89: on viewing it on its completion, the artist's fifteenth-century contemporaries would have taken in the rosary, the mirror, the dog and the discarded pattens, and would instantly have understood that this was both a double portrait and an allegory on the ideal Christian marriage. (And, incidentally, unlike most people today, they would not have immediately assumed that the lady in green was expecting a child.)

"How is it that in the so-called barbarian ages art was understood, whereas in our age of progress exactly the opposite is true?" bemoaned the French artist Pierre-Auguste Renoir (1841–1919). The answer may be that we have increasingly lost touch with symbolic associations that our ancestors unthinkingly understood, especially now that so many of us no longer live in rural surroundings, but in industrial or urban environments instead, where we are so cut off from nature that we have become completely unfamiliar

Left: *Renoir's* Dance at Le Moulin de la Galette *(1876) conveys the carefree atmosphere of Montmartre, Paris, in a single glance.*

Above: Vincent van Gogh said of his Night Café *(1888), "I have tried to express the terrible passions of humanity by means of red and green. ...I have tried to express, as it were, the powers of darkness in a low drink shop."*

with growing cycles, and with the behavior of the birds and the beasts. If you aren't privileged to see a swallow's forked tail flitting though the air on its reappearance after a long winter absence each year, how would you instinctively recognize that this bird symbolizes the arrival of spring, and also, in Christian iconography, resurrection? Many symbols and archetypes have multiple meanings, depending on the cultures that generated them, and may, in addition, be used in a variety of contexts in art, which is why you'll find a detailed index at the back of this book that will alert and direct you to further information and examples.

EVERY PICTURE TELLS A STORY

Every piece of art has meaning, be it because its creator consciously intended to convey a certain message or because the artist unconsciously projected and incorporated his or her emotions into the work. We know that Edvard Munch (1863–1944) suffered a "complete mental collapse," as he himself described it, in 1908. Was *The Scream* (1891), part of his "Frieze of Life" series, a conscious expression of his emotional anguish or an unconscious cry for help? Researching an artist's background, and looking into his or her personal situation at the time that the image that interests you came into being, may well prove satisfying, for you may discover a symbolic parallel between the subject and its creator's circumstances that may in itself tell a fascinating tale.

"The more minimal the art, the more maximum the explanation," said U.S. cultural critic Hilton Kramer; bear this in mind when next you are tempted to dismiss, perhaps, a painting by Mark Rothko (1903–70) as being little more than a few unimaginative daubs of color. "I'm interested only in expressing basic human emotions—tragedy, ecstasy, doom and so on," said Rothko, continuing, "The people who weep before my pictures are having the same religious experience as I had when I painted them." It is interesting that Rothko mentions "religious experience" in connection with his work, especially in view of the parallel that Jaffé draws between religion, art and symbolism. It is also noteworthy that the last works that Rothko painted before committing suicide were black—in color symbolism, the shade of death.

Take a little time to browse through the pages of this book and familiarize yourself with the basic building blocks that make up language of symbolism, and you will reap huge, thought-provoking, knowledge-enhancing and emotion-enriching rewards. Switching yourself on to symbolism is like flipping a switch that transforms dull, black-and-white graphics into vibrantly colored images, or like turning on the lights in a dark room—in other words, it will truly open your eyes to a whole new world. For if you understand a symbol's hidden meaning, you will understand the secrets that underpin a painting, and will join the ranks of the select few who can appreciate what a work of art is *really* about. And once your eyes have been opened in this way, you will never pass by a painting unheedingly again, but will instead scour it for the symbols that you can be certain are present, and will soon be deciphering the secret story that it relates as a result.

"We see nothing truly until we understand it."
—John Constable (1776–1837)

MYTHOLOGICAL FIGURES & SYMBOLS

Left: *Hermes (Mercury), messenger of the Greco–Roman gods, is depicted carrying the infant Dionysus to safety in this third-century mosaic; his winged feet can be seen clearly, but his caduceus has suffered damage.*
Far left: *The ancient Egyptian mother goddess Hathor was often depicted with the head or headdress of the nurturing cow.*
Opposite: *Mengardi's Minerva Competing with Neptune for the Possession of Attica, 1780 (see pages 46–49).*

Both art and symbolism have always, it seems, been linked with the sacred. For ever since humans first began to try to make sense of their world—their surroundings, the heavenly bodies, the weather, their supplies of sustenance and, indeed, the cyclical nature of life itself—by associating each and every aspect of earthly existence and experience with various deities, they have sought to depict these supernatural beings. Such portrayals may have had many purposes: they may have expressed veneration; they may have been wish-fulfillment requests made to gods and goddesses whose benignity or wrathfulness could spell life or death; or they may have served as educational tools in societies whose populations were largely illiterate. And what would be more natural, or easily grasped, than representing a moon goddess with a lunar crescent adorning her head, for example? Over the generations, people became so familiar with individual deities' attributes that they were used alone to symbolize their divine "owners." Although this innate understanding of the symbolic language of mythology has, to some extent, now been lost, Jungian psychologists believe that many mythological symbols have endured as archetypes in humankind's collective unconscious.

It is a tribute to the power of the mythologies of the early Mediterranean civilizations—most notably those of ancient Egypt, Greece and Rome—and the later European pantheons that they inspired, that we remain familiar with their leading deities thousands of years after the decline of their active worship. This is due partly to the rich legacy of documentation and vivid pictorial images that has survived, but also reflects the enduring fascination of colorful, immortal lives. Thus we see the deities and myths of ancient Greece and Rome in particular being reinterpreted with relish by the Christian Renaissance artists of fifteenth- and sixteenth-century Europe, thereby initiating a revival that has continued to this day.

ANCIENT EGYPT

Two natural features dominated the Egyptians' physical world: the scorching sun and the mighty River Nile, whose annual flooding brought fertility to the parched land. Both the sun and the Nile were vital for the preservation of life. Thus there evolved at Heliopolis a cult of the sun god, Re. This belief system was intended to placate these natural powers and came to dominate the Old Kingdom—and the art of its people, which is redolent with its symbols.

THE ENNEAD

Above: An illustration of Nut being held aloft by her father Shu (god of the air), with Geb (the earth god), below.

Although, as elsewhere, a vast number of lesser deities—each of which protected the particular locality with which its veneration was associated—figured prominently in the sacred beliefs of ancient Egypt, during the period of the Old Kingdom (c. 2686–2181 BC) a pantheon of nine "state" gods whose worship became general emerged. Known collectively as the Ennead, this divine family included the following.

Below: A symbol-filled scene from the Egyptian Book of the Dead, depicting Re (center) and other deities riding in his solar boat.

Atum/Re The sun and creator god Atum, or Re, crossed the sky in his solar boat as a young man in the morning, becoming adult at noon and an older man at night. During the hours of darkness, he traveled through the underworld (often in the form of a ram-headed man), keeping evil at bay before rising to the sky again at dawn. In symbolic art, Re was sometimes depicted in human form, but his most powerful symbols were aniconic: the stone obelisk, worshipped as a petrified ray of sunshine, which also represented the *axis mundi* that linked the earth with the heavens; and the solar disk, often flanked by a pair of falcon's wings (*see* page 18), signifying Re's mastery of the heavens, whose numerous rays often culminated in human hands. The solar disk is prominent in Egyptian iconography, frequently appearing as part of the headdress of the gods, or incorporated into amulets with positive symbolism: the scarab, or dung beetle, which, because it laid eggs in dung, came to represent regeneration; the scavenging vulture, which symbolized purification; and the cobra, or *uraeus*, which signified rebirth and protection.

Tefnut Child of Re, goddess of moisture, dew and rain, she represented the relief brought to the arid land by the moisture that she embodied. Yet despite her aqueous associations, which may be depicted by her jar of life-giving water, her symbolism primarily proclaims her status as the daughter of the sun god, for she was personified as having the head of a lion (a solar attribute) and wearing the solar disk (which some also associate with the world egg) as a crown.

Nut Child of Shu and Tefnut, goddess of the sky. It was said that after she had given birth to Osiris, Set, Isis and Nephtys, she was raised to the sky by Re, her body thus forming the vault of the heavens over which Re sprinkled the stars (hence her appellation "starry one"). She was most often depicted in this athletic, arched stance, with Shu, her father, supporting and separating her body from Geb, and with the Milky Way—representing the milk that she produced as the celestial cow—adorning her torso. She was regarded as the protectress of the dead, and her image was painted on the inner lids of sarcophagi.

Osiris Child of Geb and Nut, god of the underworld. The pre-eminence of Re was rivaled by that of a triad comprising Osiris, Isis and their son, Horus. Egyptian mythology tells how the evil Set, jealous of his brother, dismembered Osiris, scattering the remains throughout the world. The inconsolable Isis reassembled Osiris's body by magical means, and was able to conceive their son, Horus, the divine infant who, under the fierce protection of his mother, would eventually avenge his father's murder and become pharaoh of Egypt. Thus it was that Osiris, originally worshipped as a god of vegetation because of his mythical role in bringing agriculture to Egypt, became the lord of the underworld and a symbol of resurrection and immortality. He was depicted as a mummy, symbolizing his death, wearing the white crown of upper Egypt and carrying the scepter (leadership) and flail (judgment). *See The Hall of Judgment*, pages 36–37.

Above: Osiris, lord of the Egyptian underworld, is generally represented as a crowned and mummified figure holding a scepter and flail, the symbols of his authority. Here he is accompanied by the regal Isis, whose thronelike headdress is a hieroglyph of her name. Below: The sandstone Temple of Horus is the best preserved of all the ancient Egyptian temples. Its entrance is guarded by two magnificent granite statues of Horus in his guise as a falcon.

OTHER MAJOR DEITIES

Hathor Hathor was a deity of ancient origin who became closely associated with Isis during the period of the New Kingdom (*c.* 1567–1085 BC). She, too, was worshipped as a mother goddess and depicted as the celestial cow, who was often represented suckling the infant pharaoh. The solar disk that she bore between her horns has particular significance in this context, for she was sometimes termed "the golden egg of the sun," or "the Nile Goose" who laid the cosmic egg. Hathor's body was sometimes represented as spangled with stars, and the Milky Way was said to flow from her breasts. She was also envisaged in a sevenfold form, as the Hathors—protectresses of newborn children and nourishers of the deceased. In common with other Egyptian mother goddesses, Hathor's attributes included many symbols of natural abundance, including the lotus and the sycamore tree.

Set/Seth Child of Geb and Nut, god of the desert and storms, and of other forces of death, destruction and chaos. He was symbolized by the Set animal, a doglike creature with square ears, a curved muzzle and a pointed tail, or by its head on a human body.

Isis Child of Geb and Nut, mother goddess. *See* overleaf.

Nephtys Child of Geb and Nut, goddess of the moon. She was regarded as Isis's darker side, yet this association was not by any means negative, for she, too, was perceived as a benevolent protector of the dead, and was thus, like Isis and many other Egyptian goddesses, symbolized by the vulture, as well as by her primary attribute, the moon. Nephtys was crowned with the hieroglyph that denoted a house (*see* page 18)—symbolizing both the divine pantheon and the ancestral dynasty of the pharaohs.

Horus The primary symbol of Horus, the divine child of Osiris and Isis and master of the skies, was the *wedjat*—the eye of Horus—depicted either as the right eye, representing the solar power of Re, with which he was associated and whose winged sun disk he shared as a symbol, or the left, signifying lunar power. He could also be represented with the head of a falcon—a bird that dominates the skies. *See also The Hall of Judgment*, pages 36–37.

Isis

Above: Isis extends the kite's wings with which she flew in search of Osiris's dismembered body, and which fanned life into him.

Isis sits on her throne, feeding her infant son, Horus. Ancient Egyptian statues like this are said to have inspired similar depictions of the Madonna and child, or Christianity's Virgin Mary cradling the baby Jesus. Here, Isis's cow-horn headdress identifies her as a mother goddess.

Isis was the most powerful goddess of ancient Egypt. It was told that the evil Set murdered his brother, Osiris. The distraught Isis eventually recovered the corpse of her brother/husband, but Set discovered and dismembered it, scattering its parts all over Egypt. With the help of Thoth, the god of wisdom and magic, who tutored her in magical powers, Isis assumed the shape of a kite and flew ceaselessly over the land until she had eventually located all of Osiris's body parts. She reassembled them with the help of her sister, Nephtys, as well as Nephtys's son, Anubis, the jackal-headed god of embalming. By fanning his body with her kite's wings, Isis resurrected Osiris just long enough to conceive a son, Horus. Having thus demonstrated her qualities as an exemplary wife, Isis now dedicated her formidable energies to protecting her son against Set. When grown, Horus avenged his father's murder in battle, after which Osiris became the ruler of the underworld and judge of the dead, and Horus, the lord of the sky.

It was as the devoted mother of Horus, who was regarded as the mythical ancestor of the pharaohs, that Isis was especially celebrated, and numerous depictions showed her tenderly nursing her son in her lap (an archetypal image that was later applied to the Christian Madonna and infant Jesus). In reflection of her maternal role, Isis was also symbolically personified as a white sow or cow (whose head, some said, Thoth gave her after Horus decapitated her in his anger that she had shown mercy to Set after his defeat). She was also depicted bearing the solar disk between her cow-horn headdress. Because she had resurrected Osiris from the dead, she was accorded such life-giving symbols as the basket within which she placed Osiris's body parts, the grain whose growth represented Osiris's resurrection, or a jar from which, like Tefnut, she poured water on the land; indeed, the tears that she shed on Osiris's death were said to cause the annual flooding of the Nile. She was also sometimes shown wearing the vulture headdress, which represented her function as bearer of the dead, and also—through the bird's habit of scavenging—purification. In this headdress, the vulture was frequently combined with the cobra, a dual symbol of rebirth and protection. Her importance as Osiris's consort was underlined by the ankh that she sometimes carried as the key to eternal life. As consort of the lord of the underworld, she was represented crowned with a throne (the hieroglyph of her name) or in association with the crescent moon.

Anubis During the weighing of the deceased's heart in Osiris's Hall of Judgment (*see* pages 36–37), Anubis, the jackal-headed god of embalming, who had helped Isis and Nephtys, his mother, embalm their murdered brother, manipulated the scales, which held the heart in one basket and the white ostrich feather—symbol of Ma'at, the goddess of truth, justice and divine order, *see* page 18—in the other.

Thoth Thoth was the god of wisdom, the moon and magic. He was represented with either a baboon's or an ibis's head, the curved beak of the latter signifying both the quest for knowledge and the crescent moon. The inventor of writing and patron of scribes, he wrote down the results of the weighing of hearts in the Hall of Judgment (*see* pages 36–37) to pass to Osiris.

Above: Anubis, the son of Nephtys, helped his mother and aunt embalm the body of Osiris. He is identifiable by his jackal's head; this animal was associated with the realm of the dead.

Amun-Re The pharaohs believed that they were the divine sons of Re, linked to him by a lineage traced back through Horus and Osiris to Geb, the first earthly king. When the Theban princes assumed the rulership of Egypt, they merged the characteristics of their own patron god of Thebes—Amun—with those of Re, thus creating the god Amun-Re. He was worshipped at the vast temple complex of Karnak.

The Aten The sun was worshipped in the form of the solar disk, the Aten, during the reign of the "heretical pharaoh," Amenhotep IV, who took the name Akhenaten. The Aten was portrayed as a circular sun disk from which emanated solar rays that turned into human hands.

Khons/Chons/Khonsu Khons, the son of Amun-Re and Mut, was worshipped at the temple complex at Karnak. Khons was venerated as the god of the moon, and was also believed to have healing powers. As the child of the two other members of the Theban triad of deities, he was represented in art as a young man, with a side lock of hair, carrying such symbols of divine authority as the flail and adorned with lunar symbols.

Left: This Eighteenth Dynasty statue of Khons was created for his temple at Karnak. The moon god is portrayed with his distinctive side lock of hair.

For **The Apis Bull** *see The Destruction of the Golden Calf*, pages 98–99.

Min As a god of male fertility who was invoked during the coronation rites of the New Kingdom in the hope that the new pharaoh would be blessed with sons, and thus heirs, Min was portrayed with an erect penis, which he typically grasped in his left hand, while wielding a flail in his right hand. In ancient Egyptian art, Min is also often identifiable on account of his tall, feathered headdress and wide collar. As well as representing masculine virility, Min was regarded as having the power to encourage the growth of vegetation. His protection was sought by travelers as their caravans of camels wended their way slowly across the desert, perhaps because this god was associated with the constellation of Orion.

Sekhmet Lions—and lionesses—are fearless and brutal predators, which is why Sekhmet, the ancient Egyptian goddess of war, was portrayed as either this ferocious African feline or with the body of a woman and the head of a lioness. Sekhmet acted as the Eye of Re, when she represented the bloodthirsty and vengeful aspect of the goddess, seeking out and stalking her prey from her high vantage point in the sky before swooping down to earth and pouncing on her victims for the kill.

Right: This sculpture (c. 1400 BC) represents the fearsome, lion-headed Sekhmet, whose symbolism reflects her status as a war goddess.

Bast Although she had a martial aspect, the moon goddess Bast, or Bastet, whose cult centered on Bubastis, was an ambiguous deity, for she was also celebrated as a goddess of pleasure. She was represented in the form of the cat, whose characteristics are similarly ambivalent, an association underlined by the fact that the dilation and contraction of feline pupils appears to mimic the waxing and waning of the moon.

Ma'at The goddess of truth, whose responsibility was maintaining divine order, was a deity with strong connections to the underworld, for she played a crucial role in the judgment of the souls of those who had recently died. In Osiris's Hall of Judgment, the heart of the deceased would be weighed against the ostrich feather that symbolized truth, and that also personified the goddess herself. *See The Hall of Judgment*, pages 36–37.

THE OGDOAD OF HELIOPOLIS

There may have been an Ennead of nine leading deities in Heliopolis (*see* pages 14–15), but many lesser gods and goddesses were worshipped, too, including the Ogdoad, or the eight deities that were believed either to have inhabited the chaotic primordial waters before Atum/Re created cosmic order or to have themselves created the primordial mound from which the sun god emerged. Comprising four gods— Nun, Amun, Kek and Heh—and four goddesses—Naunet, Amaunet, Kauket and Hauhet—the males were envisaged as frogs, and the females as snakes (or, later, baboons). The eight members of the Ogdoad were furthermore arranged in male–female pairs, each representing the masculine and feminine aspect of the four elements that were the essence of the primordial chaos, namely water, or the ocean (Nun and Naunet); air or invisible power (Amun and Amaunet); darkness (Kek and Kauket); and infinite space or eternity (Heh and Hauhet). The Ogdoad could also be represented as men and women, with symbolic attributes.

Above: The Great Sphinx of Giza is a limestone sculpture around 66 feet high and 240 feet long. Created in about 2620 BC, its face is thought to have been modeled on that of Pharaoh Khafra.

SIGNIFICANT SYMBOLS

Pyramid The pyramid was a royal edifice with profound sacred symbolism. It represented both the primordial cosmic mountain and, through its ascending structure and alignment with the stars, a bridge between earth and the heavens.

Sphinx The combination of the sphinx's leonine body and pharaoh's head embodied the union of natural and spiritual power, and this hybrid creature was thus simultaneously a symbol of perfection, protection and the pharaoh's might.

Ankh In combination with the oval of Isis, the *tau* cross became the ankh—a potent symbol that represented such unions of opposites as masculinity and femininity, heaven and earth, air and water; its keylike shape symbolized immortality through its ability to unlock the doors of the underworld.

Djed pillar The djed pillar—essentially a vertical pillar with four crossbars—is an aniconic depiction of the backbone of Osiris. This symbol represented stability.

Winged Solar Disk The winged sun disk, the primary symbol of the sun god Atum/Re (*see* page 14), combined the solar circle and a pair of wings, symbolizing respectively the might of the sun and mastery of the skies. The *uraeus*, the protective cobra that was said to decimate its enemies by breathing fire on them, was often depicted emerging from the solar disk.

Above: The winged sun disk of Egypt, sometimes used to represent Atum/Re and also Horus. Below: Isis and Nephtys, wearing throne and house headdresses respectively, encourage the sun to rise from the djed pillar that represents Osiris's spine. An armed ankh holds aloft the solar disk, venerated by baboons.

In Caravaggio's Jupiter, Neptune and Pluto *(c. 1599–1600), Jupiter is accompanied by an eagle, Neptune, by a seahorse, and Pluto, by the three-headed dog, Cerberus.*

ANCIENT GREECE AND ROME

Most citizens of ancient Greece and Rome worshipped the national pantheon of gods. Through trade and conquest, each of these mighty civilizations was exposed to the gods of other traditions, too, some of whom were absorbed into their own sacred beliefs—the Romans, for example, adopting the Greek pantheon virtually wholesale.

Although the gods were responsible for ensuring that humans followed the moral system of *ethike*, punishing any transgressions with natural disasters, they generally held themselves aloof from humanity. However, they demanded worship from humans, who erected sanctuaries (*temenos*) containing statues of their chief gods where they offered placatory sacrifices in homage.

Not surprisingly, there are conflicting versions of most Greek myths, but it was Hesiod, writing in the eighth or seventh century BC, who first recorded the theogonies ("birth of the gods") that personified creation and the forces of nature as deities. In the beginning, he said, there was the primeval vacuum, Chaos, whom Hesiod regarded as female. From Chaos's womb emerged Gaia (also called Ge), goddess of the earth, and then Eros, god of love, closely followed by the goddess Nyx (the deity of the night, personified with black wings and wearing a dark robe studded with stars) and her brother Erebus (darkness), the pair who brought day and space into being. Gaia alone created the sea, Pontus, and then Ouranos, god of the sky, whom she took as her husband, giving birth as a result to three sets of children, known as the Titans, Cyclopes and Hecatoncheires.

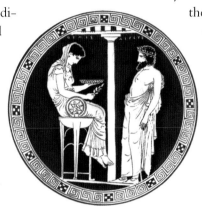

Above: *The Delphic Oracle was the outlet for the prophetic voices of Gaia and her Titan daughters before it was usurped by Apollon/Apollo, who replaced Gaia's python guardian with his own priestess, the Pythia or "Pythoness."* ***Below:*** *The Titan Rhea, daughter of the earth goddess Gaia and mother of the Olympian deities Zeus, Hera, Hades, Poseidon, Demeter and Hestia, was widely venerated as a powerful mother goddess.*

Gaia bore many children and was credited with powers of prophecy, and the oracle at Delphi, which was guarded by her python son, was originally hers. Gaia was the great mother whose attributes include all of the symbols of natural abundance sacred to so many other earth goddesses, but she was also specifically associated with the sickle (whose shape resembles that of the crescent moon), and the serpent, a symbol of fertility.

THE TITANS

The twelve Titans were the first group of children of Gaia and Ouranos (called Uranus in Rome). They were Oceanus, Tethys, Iapetus, Clymene, Hyperion, Theia, Coeus, Phoebe, Themis, Rhea, Mnemosyne and Kronos (equated with Saturn in Rome).

Theia, goddess of light and sister/wife of Hyperion, gave birth to the god Helios (the sun), Selene (goddess of the moon) and Eos (dawn). Themis, the guardian of the law whose symbol was a pair of scales, was said to have been a wife of Zeus and mother of the Horae, Eunomia, Dice, Eirene, of Astraea, the three Moirae and also of the Hesperides. Mnemosyne, too, took Zeus as her husband, their union producing the nine Muses. Phoebe mated with her brother Coeus, by whom she had Asteria and Leto. With her brother/consort Oceanus, Tethys was the ruler of the sea and mother of the innumerable river deities, collectively termed the Oceanids. Rhea (whose Roman counterpart was Ops) mated with Kronos and gave birth to Hestia, Demeter, Hera, Hades, Poseidon and Zeus. The identity of

Rhea as a mother goddess was often fused with that of Gaia (whose scythe she carried as Rhea Kronia, and whose adjunctive name, "Pandora," and sacred vase, she shared). Rhea was also identified with Demeter and Cybele, who, like Rhea, was frequently depicted riding in a chariot drawn by lions.

Ouranos/Uranus feared the size and strength of his children and locked them in Tartarus, the deep underworld, to keep himself safe from them. Furious about the containment of her children, Gaia descended to the underworld and persuaded her youngest Titan child, Kronos/Saturn, to rebel against his father. Gaia provided the scythe with which Kronos castrated his father. Kronos was the father of Gaia's later children, the Furies, Giants and Meliads.

Having supplanted his father, Kronos freed his siblings from their confinement in Tartarus and apportioned to each of them some share of his domain. There followed a time in which Kronos ruled wisely and well; this was known as the Golden Age, a time when humans did not suffer from sickness or disease, and fertility bloomed on the planet.

A curse that Ouranos had passed down haunted Kronos, however, and as each of his own children appeared, he devoured them, seeking to avoid being supplanted by a stronger offspring. Rhea, his sister and wife, concealed her sixth child, the baby Zeus, and gave Kronos a stone wrapped in cloth. Kronos devoured the package and forgot about Zeus, whom Rhea sent to the island of Crete, where he grew to adulthood in secrecy, raised by nymphs and nursed by the goat Amaltheia.

Above: Goya's Saturn Devouring One of His Children *(1821–23) is a nightmarish vision of the cursed Kronos/Saturn's doomed precaution.*

THE OLYMPIANS

The twelve Olympians, also known as the Dodekatheon, were the principal gods of the Greek pantheon, residing atop Mount Olympus. There were, at various times, seventeen different gods recognized as Olympians, though never more than twelve at one time. Zeus, Hera, Poseidon, Ares, Hermes, Hephaestos, Aphrodite, Athena, Apollon and Artemis are always considered Olympians. Hebe, Helios, Hestia, Hades, Demeter, Dionysus and Persephone are the variable gods among the twelve. The Olympians became the greatest Greco–Roman deities and the objects of universal worship.

Zeus/Jupiter Once he had attained maturity, Zeus (Jupiter in Rome) revealed himself to Kronos. After a short, but terrible, battle, Kronos was overthrown, exiled from Mount Olympus, and forced to disgorge the five children that he had swallowed. He retired to Italy and presided there as the Roman god Saturn, ruling wisely as a chastened lawgiver.

Some of the Titans accepted Zeus's dominance, but others resisted, and a prolonged war was fought in Thessaly; Zeus and his fellow gods fought from Mount Olympus, while the Titans occupied Mount Othrys. Zeus won only through the gift of thunderbolts, given to him by the Cyclopes. After defeating the enormous monster, Typhon, he retained mastery of the sky, dividing the remainder of the cosmos between his brothers Hades, who received the underworld, and Poseidon, who became master of the sea.

As the ruler of the sky, his primary attribute was the thunderbolt, or staff; he was also depicted with the soaring eagle (*see* page 49) and the powerful bull; the oak tree, which was thought to attract lightning; and the laurel leaf, the symbol of victory.

Zeus was also a lover of mortal women, and in this capacity assumed many symbolic forms to seduce the objects of his passion: the white bull that carried off Europa, resulting in the birth of Minos, king of Crete; the shower of gold that impregnated Danaë with Perseus; or the white swan to which Leda succumbed, giving birth to Helen as a result. *See The Creation of the Milky Way,* pages 38–39.

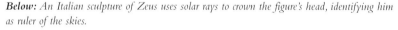

Below: An Italian sculpture of Zeus uses solar rays to crown the figure's head, identifying him as ruler of the skies.

Above: Aphrodite/Venus and Ares/Mars were lovers, and Botticelli's Venus and Mars *(c. 1485) personifies the disarming effect that love can have on war.*

Hera/Juno Hera (Juno in Rome) was the child of Kronos and Rhea. She was sheltered by one of the Titan couples during the war between Zeus and the Titans and afterward moved into a place of honor on Mount Olympus. She became the bride and lasting queen of Zeus.

Hera was the Olympian "first lady," regarded as the protector of women, goddess of marriage (*see The Judgment of Paris*, pages 54–55) and a maternal deity. The nurturing cow, many-seeded pomegranate and cornucopia of abundance were among her primary symbols, as was the lily with which she was said to have conceived Ares. Although the cuckoo was sacred to her, perhaps the bird that best personified Hera was the peacock. *See The Creation of the Milky Way*, pages 38–39, and page 45, detail.

Ares/Mars Ares (Mars in Rome) was the first child of Zeus and Hera, and god of war. The one true love of his life was Aphrodite: their passionate relationship is thought to have symbolized the divine reconciliation of opposites. Once Ares's martial blood was stirred, he would throw himself into the fray with little thought. This got him into serious trouble on several occasions.

Ares was usually represented bearing his accouterments of war—helmet, breastplate, spear, sword and shield (*see Apollo and Mercury*, pages 44–45). As Mars, he was the object of devout worship in the martial Roman Empire, where he was also especially revered as the father of Romulus, the founder of Rome, and Remus. The wolf that suckled the twins and the woodpecker that fed them, both symbolized their father.

Poseidon/Neptune Poseidon (Neptune in Rome) was the god of the oceans and rivers. Even Zeus could not command Poseidon to do his bidding when it came to the tides and waves. The Greeks saw him as a moody god, one who supported the Greeks during the Trojan War, but then turned against Odysseus and increased the time that it took him to return home after the war ended. He was symbolized principally by the trident with which he directed the water, but all of the sea creatures under his command could also represent him. *See The Union of Water with Earth*, pages 40–41, and *Minerva Competing with Neptune for the Possession of Attica*, pages 46–49.

Below: The horses that pulled Poseidon's chariot could gallop through deep waters. This French sculpture shows Triton (see page 34) announcing the sea god's arrival with his sea-shell trumpet.

Hermes/Mercury Hermes (Mercury in Rome) was the cunning son of Zeus by Maia, whose ingenuity and mediating skills caused him to become his father's messenger. In artistic representations, Hermes wears a pair of winged sandals (*talaria*), symbolizing his fleet-footedness, and a winged cap (*petasos*), and carries the *kerykeion* ("herald's wand") or caduceus—the snake-entwined, winged staff with the power to convert strife into harmony (in the hands of Asclepius, it may represent medicine). *See Apollo and Mercury*, pages 44–45; and pages 49 and 55, details.

Left: The Forge of Vulcan, *1630, by Diego Velázquez, depicts Apollo (the god of light, which radiates from his head) telling the shocked Vulcan that his wife is conducting an affair with Mars. Apollo as the god of light was sometimes known as Phoebus. Vulcan is identified by the tools of his trade, or by fire. He is sometimes deformed or, as here, not standing straight—an allusion to his lameness.*

Hephaestos/Vulcan   Hephaestos (the Roman Vulcan) was the god of fire and metalwork and the lame son of Hera and Zeus. He married Aphrodite. Hephaestos was trained as a blacksmith by the Oceanids, and toiled in his fiery volcanic workshops to create Zeus's thunderbolts. His primary symbols were those of fire and the anvil.

Aphrodite/Venus   Aphrodite was the goddess of love, beauty and sexual pleasure, and the mother of Eros (Amor, or Cupid), whose arrows could inflame the heart with love. She was often depicted astride a sea goose or swan, or shown with the attributes of the pearl and scallop shell. All of these evoke the universal Goddess in her aqueous, lunar aspect, as do the fish, the fecund turtle and the dolphin, called "the woman of the sea," whose name derives from the Greek for "womb." *See The Birth of Venus, pages 52–53.*

Below: Aphrodite/Venus was proud of her beauty. In Velázquez's The Toilet of Venus *(1647–51), her son Eros/Amor/Cupid holds the mirror that is one of her symbols, because of its association with vanity.*

Although married to Hephaestos, Aphrodite led a promiscuous immortal life, her favored lover being Ares, god of war. Notoriously vain, one of her major attributes was the mirror with which she admired herself (from which is derived the modern botanical and zoological symbol of femininity). The planet Venus—the Morning Star—was named in her honor. Her multitude of natural symbols—primarily the rose and dove, but also the myrtle and swallow, as well as the violets that garlanded her head—are mainly those that were admired for their beauty and that came to symbolize love. But the apple testifies to her vanity: *see The Judgment of Paris, pages 54–55.*

Athena/Minerva   Athena (or Athene, and Minerva in Rome), the goddess of reason, learning and crafts, yet also of war, was venerated for her cerebral qualities. In her martial aspect (*see page 54*), she was symbolized by her helmet, spear and the shield known as the aegis, which together represented *epheboi*, or adulthood. The aegis, whose frame was fashioned by Hephaestos, was covered with the skin of the goat that had nurtured Zeus. After Perseus decapitated Medusa with the assistance of Athena's reflective shield, he gave the Gorgon's head to the goddess, who placed it in the center of the aegis. Confusingly, the aegis was also referred to as the serpent-fringed cloak that Athena sometimes wore, the snakes associating her with the Minoan and the Mycenaean goddess. Perhaps the most popular of Athena's attributes was the owl: wisdom was ascribed to it through its ability to see in the dark, in symbolic terms, penetrating the murky depths of ignorance. She was the patron goddess of Athens. *See Minerva Competing with Neptune for the Possession of Attica, pages 46–49, and Pallas Athene, pages 50–51.*

Above: Pollaiuolo's Apollo and Daphne *(c. 1432–98) depicts the moment when the amorous Apollon/Apollo catches up with Daphne, and finds her turning into a laurel tree.*

Apollon/Apollo Twin of Artemis and son of Zeus, Apollon (Apollo in Rome) was the god of light, healing and poetry, and presided over the nine Muses of the arts. He was often depicted wielding a bow and arrow as a symbol of his power. As the lord of the arts, he could be represented with a lyre, demonstrating his mastery of music. After killing the python of Delphi, Apollon established his own oracle at the site, transmitting his prophecies through the Pythoness—the high priestess of the Delphic Oracle—who was widely consulted as she sat on her sacred tripod, itself a symbol of Apollon's wisdom. Further emblems of Apollon include sheep and their shepherds, for Zeus forced his son to work as a herdsman as penance for murdering the Cyclopes.

A popular myth of Apollon was that concerning his infatuation with the nymph Daphne, who scorned him. His love was caused by an arrow from Eros, who was jealous because Apollon had mocked his archery skills, while Daphne's scorn was the result of another of Eros's arrows, this one bearing hate. Following a spirited chase, Daphne prayed to her father—a river god—to help her, and he changed her into a laurel tree.

In later times, Apollon became partly confused or equated with Helios/Sol, god of the sun; however, they remained separate beings in literary and mythological texts.

See also Apollo and Mercury, pages 44–45, and Apollo and the Muses, pages 172–73.

Artemis/Diana *See* overleaf.

Hebe/Juventas Hebe (Juventas in Rome) represented the freshness of youth. Daughter of Zeus and Hera, she was the cup-bearer of the other deities. When Herakles was granted immortality, Hera gave him Hebe's hand in marriage. She is usually depicted wearing a sleeveless dress.

Helios/Sol In Greek mythology, Helios (Sol in Rome) was the sun god who predated Apollon. He was the son of the Titans Hyperion and Theia. Helios drove his chariot of fire across the sky each day, drawn by his four horses. The Colossus of Rhodes, one of the seven wonders of the ancient world, was a statue of him.

Hestia/Vesta The oldest of the six children born to Kronos and Rhea, Hestia (the Roman Vesta) ceded her position as the twelfth Olympian to Dionysus (Bacchus) after the fifth century BC. She was regarded as the keeper of the flame that burned on the Olympian hearth, and was thus the guardian of harmonious family life. Her protective function assumed a civic aspect, and in most towns her image was placed in the temple—called the Prytanitis—dedicated to her, in conjunction with her perpetually burning flame, a symbol of harmony, continuity and life. As the Roman Vesta, this goddess was similarly regarded as the protector of the public "hearth," whose symbolic fire was tended in her temple by the six vestal virgins—for she had sworn to preserve her chastity.

Demeter/Ceres Demeter (Ceres in Rome) was sister to Hera and shared much of her symbolism as a mother goddess. She, too, was represented by the cow and the cornucopia, but also by the pig and grain, for her domain was that of agriculture and the earth.

Despite her primary association with natural fertility, Demeter was also regarded as a goddess of death, for she transformed her mortal lover, Mecon, into a poppy—a flower that became sacred to her.

Below: Francisco de Goya's The Sacrifice to Vesta, *1771.*

Artemis/Diana

Above: *Fragonard's eighteenth-century portrayal of a languorous Diana (Artemis) reflects the ambiguity of the lunar goddess's dual role as virgin deity of the hunt and the mother goddess who presided over childbirth. Three of Diana's symbols appear here: the crescent moon behind the reclining goddess; the animal skin in which she is draped; and the quiver of arrows that lies within her reach.*

When Artemis, the twin sister of Apollon, daughter of Zeus and Leto, was introduced into the society of gods on Mount Olympus, she was deluged with requests for her hand in marriage. She went to her father and asked if she could always remain single, a huntress, living in the woods. Zeus reluctantly concurred, and she became the symbol of the free female god.

Paralleling Apollon's association with the sun, his sister Artemis (Diana in Rome) was identified with the moon, its crescent form being her primary attribute. Each evening, she mounted her moon chariot and drove across the heavens. After the night journey was over, she took her bow and arrow and, accompanied by her maidens (all of whom were virgins), went into the woods to hunt for wild beasts. Though she was beautiful, she had a cool heart and could, like her brother, be terrifying in anger. Her arrows caused swift and sudden death to those who opposed her.

Perhaps more than that of any other Greek goddess, the mythological lineage of Artemis can be traced directly back to the ancient "mistress of the animals" depicted on Minoan seals. The crescent moon (and the scythe) were Artemis's primary symbols. Because she was also regarded as the goddess of wild animals and their human hunters, her other important attributes were the bow (curved, like the crescent moon), the arrow (symbolizing illumination) and such game animals as the stag (into which she transformed Actaeon), boar (whose killers she punished) and bear (the form into which Zeus changed her companion Callisto). Also sacred to her were dogs (ancient symbols of healing) trained for the hunt. As the lunar huntress, she was a virginal, vengeful figure, yet identification with the objects of other goddess cults sometimes credited her with more benevolent characteristics. As Diana of Ephesus, for example, whose temple was counted among one of the seven wonders of the ancient world, she was sculpted as an elegant figure from whose form many breastlike orbs were suspended, symbolizing fertility. This depiction of Artemis as a mother goddess was compounded by her function as the deity of childbirth, for it was said that, as the first-born, she had helped Leto to deliver Apollon. In common with many other such goddesses, including Demeter and Athena, Artemis could be represented by the (queen) bee, who was served by female *melissae* (bees) and castrated male *essenes* (drones). Her other attributes included fish (through her lunar association) and the fir tree (as an evergreen, a symbol of immortality), in whose groves she liked to roam. *See Diana and Endymion*, pages 42–43, *and Minerva Competing with Neptune for the Possession of Attica*, detail, page 48.

Actaeon, a hunter, is known in Greek mythology as the grandson of Cadmus, king of Thebes. One day, when out hunting with his hounds, he chanced across Artemis/Diana, bathing in a spring. Horrified lest he tell that he had seen her in the flesh, she threw water on him, turning him into a stag. The transformed Actaeon fled and was brought down and devoured by his own beloved hounds. In art, the goddess is often depicted in this scene with the mortal, most notably, perhaps, in Titian's Diana and Actaeon, *1556–58. Actaeon is often shown under attack by his hounds, as right, in the process of changing into the hunted.*

Artemis Clues

crescent moon

scythe

bow

arrows

dog

bear

boar

stag

fish

bee

fir tree

As Featured In:

Titian, *Diana and Callisto,*
    1556–59

Renoir, *Diana*, 1867

Persephone (Kore)/Proserpina It was believed that Demeter's adored daughter, Persephone (or Kore, "maiden"), was gathering flowers when Hades saw and desired her, and abducted her to his shadowy kingdom. Demeter was maddened by grief and withdrew her gift of fertility from the earth, bringing drought and famine wherever she wandered before she finally reached Eleusis. Needing Demeter's help to fertilize the earth, Zeus agreed to intercede. But Persephone had already eaten six small seeds of a pomegranate—the food of the dead—and therefore could not return entirely to the upper world. Hades decreed that Persephone might return to the surface for six months each year. This explained the agricultural "death" of winter, and the "rebirth" of nature in spring.

Along with the pomegranate, Persephone's symbolic attributes were the keys to the underworld and the mint plant into which she and her mother transformed the nymph Mintha, the clandestine lover of the dreaded Hades. In Greek art, Persephone is often portrayed robed, carrying a sheaf of grain or a poppy and smiling demurely.

Dionysus/Bacchus Dionysus (Bacchus in Rome) was the focus of a powerful *mysteria,* or mystery cult. In traditional Greco–Roman belief, Zeus had rescued the unborn Dionysus from the flaming body of his mother, Semele, and subsequently gave birth to the infant from his thigh. Brought up in India in order to protect him from the jealousy of Hera, Dionysus learned the art of wine-making from Silenus and then returned to Greece with the Maenads to introduce his cult at Thebes. He was symbolically represented by both the vine, whose grape causes intoxication, and the thyrsus—the pine-cone-topped staff entwined with vine and ivy leaves—all symbols of fertility, as were the goats and bulls that were sacrificed to him. *See also Minerva Competing with Neptune for the Possession of Attica, detail, page 49, and The Witches' Sabbath, pages 174–75.*

Hades/Pluto Lord of the underworld, Hades (Pluto) ruled from a throne set deep below the earth, where he welcomed the dead. The cypress tree and narcissus were sacred to him, and he is symbolized by a helmet, scepter, staff, Cerberus (his dog) and keys.

Right: As the god of wine and natural fecundity, Dionysus/Bacchus was typically portrayed—as here by Caravaggio—with wine, vine leaves and grapes or other fruits.

OTHER DEITIES & DEMIGODS

Eros/Amor/Cupid *See* overleaf.

Pan/Faunus Portrayed as having the horns and legs of a billy goat, Pan was hale and hearty, but quite unsociable; he was the god of the fields and woods, and of shepherds and their flocks. Pan stood for all that was wild and untamed in the world, indeed, for all that was not human. He was also a patron of drama, music and intoxication.

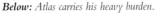
Below: Atlas carries his heavy burden.

Atlas Zeus punished Atlas for taking the Titan side in the war by making him carry the vault of heaven, or the sky, on his shoulders.

Atlas drew some comfort from the prophecy that two sons of Zeus would come his way eventually (he hoped that one of them might relieve him of his burden). Herakles was the first; he stole the golden apples of the Hesperides and failed to relieve Atlas of his burden. Therefore, the task fell to Perseus, who, after he slew the Gorgon Medusa, passed Atlas as he was flying back to Greece. Atlas begged the hero to show him the dreaded face of Medusa, which turned viewers to stone, so that he might be freed from his burden. Perseus obliged, and Atlas was immediately frozen into stone where he stood, thereby creating the Atlas mountain range of northwest Africa.

Eros/Amor/Cupid & Psyche

The son of either Chaos, or, more usually, of Ares and Aphrodite, typically depicted as a beautiful, winged boy equipped with a bow and arrows, Eros (called Amor or Cupid in Rome) had the ability to shoot his arrows in a way that inflamed the hearts and passions of both gods and humans. Not even Zeus was immune to his arrows. He was known to foster friendship between men and boys, and the Spartans paid homage to him before battle. Eros flew on missions to execute the will of his mother, the love goddess Aphrodite.

Psyche ("The Soul") was one of the three daughters of a Greek king. Her two sisters were fair to look upon, but she was beautiful beyond compare. Eros was smitten by his own arrows and fell completely in love with her. He brought her far away from her family and surrounded her with love and comfort, with only one proviso: that she should never look at him. Tempted by her two sisters, who were extremely jealous of her good fortune, Psyche dared once to look on Eros while he was sleeping and spilled a few drops of oil on him. He awoke immediately, understood that she had broken her word and fled to Olympus, where his mother, Aphrodite, tended to him.

Aphrodite laid numerous curses on Psyche, making her life utterly miserable. When Psyche gathered up her nerve and actually approached Aphrodite, the goddess of love laid enormous tasks upon her. Finally, Eros came back to himself, found Psyche and persuaded Zeus to allow him to marry her. Her story became the foundation for understanding the trials that the soul undergoes in its search for true love.

Above: Caravaggio's Amor Victorius (c. 1602–03) portrays Amor clutching his arrows in an allegorical image whose message is that love conquers all. *Right:* Goya's Cupid and Psyche (c. 1803). Worn out by her work for the jealous Aphrodite, Psyche fell into a deathlike coma, but was revived and made immortal by Zeus and then married Eros.

Eros Clues
bow
arrows
wings
blindfold

Psyche Clues
butterfly

As Featured In:
Anthony van Dyck, *Cupid and Psyche*, 1640
John William Waterhouse, *Psyche Opening the Door into Cupid's Garden*, 1904
William-Adolphe Bouguereau, *Cupidon*, 1875
François Gérard, *Cupid and Psyche*, c. 1798

Above: In Botticelli's Primavera (c. 1482), Flora can be seen in the flowery dress on the right, beside her Greek incarnation, Chloris, who is being abducted by Zephyros.

Prometheus Prometheus (whose name means "he who thinks in advance") was given the power to create the first men and women out of clay. He nourished a love for humankind and asked Zeus to give fire to the first humans. Zeus curtly refused: fire was to be a tool only for the gods. Prometheus then took a glowing ember from the sacred fire of Olympus, concealed it in a hollow stalk of fennel and brought it down from heaven as his gift to humankind.

Zeus was furious about the deceit. He ordered that Prometheus be chained to the top of the Caucasus Mountains (in present-day Georgia). Every day, an eagle would swoop down and peck at his liver until it was nearly gone. Then, at night, the liver would grow back. The eagle would come again the next day and resume the awful cycle, which kept Prometheus in perpetual agony. Prometheus was finally freed by the hero Herakles, who shot the eagle with an arrow. He is depicted chained to a rock, clearly suffering, usually with an eagle tearing at his liver.

Harmonia/Concordia A Roman goddess, the personification of harmony. The Romans dedicated shrines to her after major civil disputes were settled. She was portrayed as a matronly woman who held an olive branch in her left hand and the cornucopia (horn of plenty) in her right.

Below: Charon the ferryman is identified by the pole or oar with which he conducts his boat to the underworld.

Charon The son of Nyx (Night) and Erebus, this Greek deity ferried the souls of the dead across the dreaded River Styx. Charon would only do so if the person had been properly buried and his or her relatives had placed a gold coin in the dead person's mouth as Charon's fee.

Flora The Roman goddess of flowers and springtime. She commanded the vegetative power that made trees blossom, and it was said that her breath became petals and her footprints became flowers.

Janus A Roman god who had no counterpart in Greek mythology. He had two faces, looking either forward and backward or east and west. The god of beginnings, gates and avenues, he was always the first god to be evoked in Roman ritual. The doors of his temple in Rome were closed only in times of peace. His tools were a set of keys and a janitor's staff.

Fortuna The Roman goddess associated with fortune and luck. Often depicted as blind, she was shown with a cornucopia (the horn of plenty) and a rudder (symbolizing her ability to turn the direction of men's lives). After the Roman Republic was replaced by the Roman Empire, each Roman emperor had his own personal "Fortuna" goddess to guide him.

Hygeia The Greek goddess of health. One of the daughters of Asclepius, she was shown holding a cup of water in one hand, a snake in the other, and feeding the water to the snake.

Iris The Greek goddess of the rainbow and first messenger of the gods (prior to Hermes). A winged deity, she traveled between the earth and the heavens on a rainbow and attended to Hera's needs when not delivering communications. *See also The Creation of the Milky Way*, pages 38–39.

Theseus A Greek hero who had many adventures. Perhaps his most famous feat was killing the Minotaur with the help of Ariadne, the daughter of King Minos of Crete. He is usually depicted with the Minotaur (*see* page 34).

For **Zephyros/Zephyrus** *see The Birth of Venus,* pages 52–53. *For* **Eris/Discordia** *see The Judgment of Paris,* pages 54–55. *For* **Nike/Victoria** *see Pallas Athene,* pages 50–51. *For* **Hecate** *see The Witches' Sabbath,* pages 174–75. *For* **The Muses** *see Apollo and the Muses,* pages 172–73.

Achilles A Greek hero, the son of Thetis, a Nereid, and King Peleus of Phthia. Thetis tried to make Achilles invulnerable to wounds by dipping him in the River Styx, but neglected to immerse the heel by which she held him. With his friend Patroclus, Achilles later joined the Greeks in the war against Troy. After Patroclus's death at the hands of Hector, Achilles exacted terrible revenge on the Trojans, including killing Hector. Achilles died when an arrow from Paris's bow penetrated his "Achilles heel."

Herakles/Hercules The greatest hero of ancient Greece, and the only human to earn his way to immortality, Herakles (or Hercules, as the Romans called him) was the son of Zeus and the mortal Alcmena (or Alcmene). (*See The Creation of the Milky Way*, pages 38–39.) Jealous of her husband's amours, Hera sent two serpents to kill the baby Herakles in his cradle. He awoke and quickly strangled the snakes. Growing to manhood, he was recognized everywhere as the strongest human. His success in life seemed certain until he again aroused the anger of Hera, who drove him temporarily insane. In a fit of rage, he killed his own wife and children. To repent for this, he needed to perform twelve heroic labors for his cousin, King Eurystheus of Tiryns.

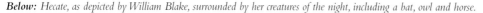

Below: Hecate, as depicted by William Blake, surrounded by her creatures of the night, including a bat, owl and horse.

The twelve labors were as follows. Herakles killed the Nemean lion (1) and the Hydra (2). He captured the Cerynitian hind (a stag with golden horns that was sacred to Artemis) (3) and took the Erymanthian boar alive (4). He cleaned the filthy stables of Aegeas, the king of Ellis, by diverting a river to wash out the muck and mire (5) and chased away the Stymphalian birds (6). Herakles captured the Cretan bull and brought it to King Eurystheus (7) and fetched the man-eating mares of Diomedes, the king of Thrace (8). Herakles went to the land of the Amazons and took the magic belt of Queen Hippolyta (9). He fetched the cattle of King Geryon of Erytheia (10) and stole the golden apples of Hera from the Hesperides (11). His last and most formidable task was to capture and bring Cerberus, the three-headed hound of hell (*see* page 34), to the light of day. Terrified by the appearance of the monster, King Eurystheus had Herakles return Cerberus to Hades. He may be identified in paintings by any of these twelve scenes.

It was Herakles's fate to fall at the hands of trickery. He fatally wounded the centaur Nessus with one of his arrows. In his dying moments, the centaur gave a poison mixture to Herakles's second wife, Deianira, saying that it would keep the hero in love with her. Years later, she rubbed the mixture into a cloak and gave it to her husband. The cloak brought Herakles close to death, whereupon he built a funeral pyre on Mount Oite in Thessaly. Herakles mounted the pyre, resigned to death. But Zeus sent thunder and lightning to bring the hero to Mount Olympus and gave him a place among the immortals.

Helen of Troy   Daughter of Leda by Zeus/Jupiter, the wife of Spartan king Menelaus and reputed to be the most beautiful woman in the world, her abduction by Paris brought about the Trojan War. Led by Agamemnon, the king of Mycenae, the Greeks launched a great fleet to reclaim the queen and humble the Trojans. She is depicted as a beautiful woman, sometimes shown with an apple, dove, Trojan Horse, pyramids, obelisk, lily, swan, the moon or the sea. *See also The Judgment of Paris, pages 54–55.*

Asclepius   A son of Apollon and the mortal Coronis, who came to surpass his father in the healing arts; he is depicted with a caduceus.

Above: Raphael's portrayal of the three Graces. Favored companions of Aphrodite, they hold the apples that show their link to the goddess.

The Three Graces   Also known as the Charites in Greece, the Three Graces were Aglaea ("Radiance"), Euphrosyne ("Mirth") and Thalia ("Blooming"). They were the daughters of Zeus and Eurynome and the goddesses of charm, beauty, nature, creativity and fertility.

Below: The Farnese Hercules *is a third-century Roman or Athenian copy of a sculpture by Lysippos or one of his circle of fellow artisans, in the fourth century BC.*

The Horae (The Hours)   The three nature goddesses that presided over weather and the change of seasons. Eunomia ("Good Order"), Dice (Justice) and Eirene (Peace) were their names. They were the daughters of Zeus and Themis.

The Graeae   Three old, blind, toothless Greek goddesses. Sisters to the Gorgons, their names were Dino, Enyo and Pemphredo. They shared one eye and one tooth and lived in a cave in the Atlas Mountains. Despite their poverty and loneliness, they were privileged to know all living matters. The Greek hero Perseus approached them and stole their one eye. He blackmailed them into telling him where the Gorgons resided and how to obtain the winged sandals, helmet and wallet that would allow him to reach the land of the Gorgons and slay Medusa.

Castor and Pollux Castor and Pollux were brothers and Roman heroes, sons of Zeus and Leda and brothers of Helen and Clytemnestra. Castor was famed for his skill in taming and managing horses; Pollux was renowned for his boxing skill. These activities often identify the brothers in paintings. The brothers embarked on three great adventures: an expedition against Athens, the voyage of the Argonauts in search of the Golden Fleece, and their battle with the sons of Aphareus. Castor was killed in the last adventure, and Zeus gave Pollux the alternatives of being made immortal alone, or sharing with Castor the experience of being in the underworld every other day and then living in Olympus every other day. Pollux chose the later course, and the brothers remained together.

Romulus and Remus The twin sons of Mars and Rhea Silvia, in Roman mythology, who were cast out at birth and found and fed by a she-wolf. Famed for their bravery in adulthood, after Remus died through misadventure, Romulus founded the city that became Rome.

For **Perseus and Andromeda** see *Andromeda*, pages 56–57. For **Psyche** see page 26. For **Paris** see *The Judgment of Paris*, pages 54–55.

MYTHOLOGICAL MORTALS

Adonis A beautiful youth with whom Aphrodite fell in love and with whom the Greek goddess had two children. Adonis was killed while hunting a wild boar. Aphrodite grieved to such an extent that Zeus allowed him to return from the underworld for a portion of each year. Adonis may be symbolized by the anemones that sprang from his spilled blood.

Odysseus/Ulysses The Greek hero Odysseus provoked the anger of both Athena and Poseidon for outrages that the Greeks committed in their sack of Troy. He managed to escape alive from the terrific storm that Athena sent to wreck the Greek ships on their way home, but Poseidon made certain that his voyage was difficult and dangerous. He encountered one danger after another. He outwitted the giant Polyphemus, a son of Poseidon, escaped from the spells of Circe (*see* page 33), and lived to be the only man to claim that he had heard the songs of the Sirens (he ordered his men to tie him to a mast so that he would not jump overboard, lured by the beautiful singing). He spent years with the sea nymph Kalypso, who promised to grant him immortality if he would remain with her. He finally arrived in Ithaca a long, weary ten years after the fall of Troy. There, he had to outwit a great number of suitors for the hand of his ever-faithful wife, Penelope. He is usually portrayed in a ship at sea.

Below: In Del Piombo's The Death of Adonis *(1511–12), Eros is depicted breaking the news of her beloved's demise to Aphrodite.*

Penelope The wife of Odysseus, who was assumed to have died during his long absence from Ithaca following the fall of Troy, prompting many suitors to vie for Penelope's hand in marriage. Penelope said that she would make her choice once she had finished weaving a shroud for Laertes, Odysseus's aged father. She wove by day, and undid her day's work at night. By this means she was able to hold her suitors at bay until Odysseus returned and killed them.

Jason A Greek hero who was tricked by King Pelias of Iolcus into setting sail with his followers, the Argonauts, in search of the Golden Fleece. His return with the fleece, and a wife, Medea (*see* page 34), spelled Pelias's doom.

Leda The wife of King Tyndareus of Sparta, in Greek mythology, Leda caught the lustful eye of Zeus, who assumed the form of a swan in order to seduce her. Their union produced an egg, from which hatched Helen, the beauty who grew up to marry King Menelaus of Sparta.

Daedalus and Icarus Greek mythology tells that Daedalus was an Athenian architect who killed his nephew, Talus, and was forced to seek refuge in Crete. There, on the orders of King Minos, he built the labyrinth that held the Minotaur (*see* page 34) captive, before himself being imprisoned. Thinking that he and his son might fly to freedom, he designed and constructed two pairs of wings from feathers and wax. On launching themselves into the air, the two found themselves able to fly across the Aegean Sea. Daedalus ended up in Sicily, but Icarus flew too close to the sun, which melted the wax in his wings, causing him to fall into the sea and drown.

Midas A king of Phrygia, whose wish that everything that he touched should turn to gold was granted by Dionysus. When the food that he hungered for turned to inedible gold, he realized that his dearest wish was, in fact, a curse. Midas may be portrayed with the ears of an ass, or wearing a Phrygian cap to hide them.

Above: In Narcissus *(c. 1597–99), Caravaggio has perfectly captured the handsome youth's total self-absorption.*

Narcissus In Greek mythology, a good-looking young man who was so obsessed with his appearance that he spent all of his time admiring his reflection in a pool, oblivious to the love of the wood nymph Echo (*see* page 32). Eventually, he pined away and was transformed into a narcissus flower.

Hector and Andromache Hector was the eldest son of King Priam of Troy and Hecuba. A brave warrior who led the Trojan army, Hector was also a faithful husband to Andromache. He was killed by Achilles during the Trojan War. After the fall of Troy, Andromache was given as war booty to Neoptolemus (or Pyrrhus), Achilles's son, but later married Helenus, Hector's brother.

Oedipus The son of King Laius and Queen Jocasta of Thebes, Oedipus was rejected by his parents and later unwittingly killed his father and married his mother. When he learned of his true identity, he gouged out his eyes.

Pygmalion According to Greek mythology, Pygmalion was a king of Cyprus who was so repulsed by the women of his island that he fashioned his ideal female figure from ivory. So entranced was he by this image that he begged Aphrodite to give it life. Aphrodite obliged, whereupon Pygmalion married his creation (Galatea) in a ceremony attended by the goddess. The couple went on to have children and lived happily ever after.

Above: The tale of Arachne inspired Velázquez's painting The Spinners *(c. 1657).*

Arachne The daughter of Idmon of Colophon in Lydia, Arachne challenged Athena to a weaving contest, and flawlessly, though disrespectfully, depicted several scenes of Zeus's infidelities. Enraged, Athena struck Arachne, who fled and hanged herself. Taking pity, Athena sprinkled her with the juices of aconite and loosened the rope, which became a cobweb, while Arachne herself was changed into a spider who, some said, spun the web of fate.

Sibyls In both Greek and Roman mythology, the Sibyls were prophetesses who had received the ability to foretell the future from a divine source, usually Apollon/Apollo. The Cumaean Sybil was said to be the author of the Sibylline books, sacred oracles that were lodged in Rome.

NYMPHS, DAEMONS, HYBRID CREATURES & OTHER BEINGS

Echo A wood nymph whose duty was to attend Hera, who cursed her so that she could only repeat the last words that others said. Echo later fell in love with Narcissus (*see* page 31). After he failed to respond to her affection, she pined and faded away, becoming nothing more than a distant echo.

Centaurs Centaurs were half-man and half-horse. They were tempestuous and often violent. Two important exceptions were Cheiron (*see* below), a teacher and healer, and Pholus. *See also Minerva Tames the Centaur,* pages 180–81.

Below: Michelangelo's Sistine Chapel portrait of the Delphic Sibyl.

Cheiron/Chiron The son of Kronos and Philyra, Cheiron was a centaur (*see* above), but unlike most of his kind, he was wise, gentle and learned. He tutored most of the great Greek heroes: Achilles, Herakles, Jason, Aeneas and Peleus. A tragedy occurred when Herakles accidentally wounded him with a flaming arrow; Herakles was aiming for a group of riotous centaurs that Cheiron was seeking to control. Being immortal, yet receptive to pain, Cheiron was therefore condemned to suffer unbearable agony for eternity. Seeing a possible solution, some say that Cheiron asked Zeus to exchange his immortality for the mortal pains of Prometheus. Zeus agreed and Cheiron died.

Pegasus The winged horse upon which Bellerophon rode to defeat the chimaera in Greek mythology. Born from the blood of the severed head of the Gorgon Medusa (*see* opposite), Pegasus also created the Hippocrene Spring dedicated to the Muses, and thus became associated with intellectual and poetic inspiration. Pegasus symbolizes humankind's capacity for attaining higher spirituality and for transforming evil into good. *See also Andromeda,* pages 56–57.

Chimaera/Chimera A creature of complicated hybrid form, the Greek chimaera, which dates back to the fifth century BC, was said to have a lion's head, a goat's body and the tail of a dragon or snake; each part could also have its own head. Like many hybrid animals, its symbolism is that of chaotic, dark and uncontrolled forces and of natural disasters (particularly of storms and volcanic eruptions) on land and sea.

Sirens The Siren can assume two forms: a bird-woman or a fish-woman, sometimes with two tails. Both forms entice male passersby to their deaths by singing songs of irresistible sweetness. They symbolize dangerous worldly temptation along the spiritual path of life. Originally represented as three beautiful, winged women, the malevolent sea nymphs of ancient Greece could also summon winds to cause storms on land and whirlpools at sea.

Cyclopes/Cyclops A group of children born to Gaia and Ouranos. Their names were Arges (Brightness), Brontes (Thunder) and Steropes (Lightning). Sometimes they number more than three, and include Polyphemus. They were giants with one eye in the center of their foreheads. (Occasionally, they are depicted with three eyes.)

The Three Moirae/Parcae (Fates) Three sisters: Lachesis ("Disposer of the Lots") measured out the thread of each individual's life, Klotho ("The Spinner") spun the thread, and Atropos ("The Inflexible") severed it with her enormous, deadly shears. Like the Fates of many other traditions, the primary symbols of this trio were thread, spinning and shears (representing the creation, course and culmination of mortal life) and the web of destiny.

The Erinyes/Furiae (Furies) Also hopefully termed the Eumenides, or "Kindly Ones," in an attempt to curry their favor, the Furies lived in the underworld, but emerged to wreak punishment. Known as the avenging goddesses, they relentlessly pursued Orestes after he murdered his mother, Clytemnestra. They agreed to abandon their pursuit after he was acquitted by the Areopagus (an Athenian council, presided over by Athena). *See also The Judgment of Paris,* pages 54–55.

The Gorgons The terrifying Gorgon sisters (Euryale, Stheno and Medusa—of whom Medusa was chief) had snakes instead of hair and were said to turn men into stone just by looking at them. In Greek mythology, Medusa was the only mortal of the trio: once a beautiful girl, she angered Athena by behaving disrespectfully in her temple and was transformed into a Gorgon who preyed on men. She was finally killed by Perseus, and Pegasus is said to have sprung from Medusa's blood. Medusa's severed head became the emblem of Perseus, and, when depicted on amulets, it was believed to protect against thunderstorms. A symbol based on the Gorgon's head, the gorgoneion, was said to have been placed on the protective shield of Zeus and Athena (the aegis). Similar images were often placed in Greek temples to ward off evil. The gorgoneion can represent the terrible Great Mother, is a symbol of fear (particularly for men of women) and also signifies the fearful union of opposites, such as beauty and dread. *See also Pallas Athene,* pages 50–51.

Above: Caravaggio's Medusa, *her severed head crowned with snakes.*

The Harpies Aello, Celaeno and Ocypete were the winged daughters of Thaumus and Electra. Rapacious, long-clawed, birdlike women, they were instruments of divine vengeance. They were also messengers of the underworld, to which they transported the souls of the dead. Harpies are symbolic of death, windstorms and destructive feminine power.

Satyrs and Fauns Forest spirits. Satyrs attended Dionysus, god of wine, in his drunken revels, possessed the legs and hindquarters of a goat, budding horns and goatlike ears, and symbolized lustful behavior and profanity. By contrast, fauns, which shared the satyrs' physical characteristics, were identified with the god Pan, god of the pastures and forests, and were benevolent spirits. *See also The Judgment of Paris,* pages 54–55.

Circe In Greek mythology, Circe was a sorceress who lived on the Island of Aeaea, surrounded by people whom she had transformed into felines and wolves. When Odysseus (*see* page 30) landed on her island, she turned his companions into pigs by giving them poisoned wine.

Below: Burne-Jones's The Wine of Circe *(1863–69) portrays Circe pouring poison into a flask of wine.*

Medea An enchantress and priestess of Hecate who fell in love with the Greek hero, Jason (*see* page 31). After helping him to obtain the Golden Fleece, she traveled to Iolcus as Jason's wife and bore him children, which she later killed when Jason abandoned her. She is usually depicted with two children, holding a knife.

The Minotaur A man with a bull's head, said to be the offspring of a white bull and Queen Pasiphäe, was imprisoned by King Minos of Crete in the labyrinth below his palace. It was fed on girls and boys sent as tribute from Athens. Theseus was destined for this fate, but was saved by Ariadne, who gave him a ball of string with which to find his way out of the maze once he had despatched the Minotaur. This hybrid creature is the emblem of Crete and represents man's dark, bestial side that can be defeated by divine guidance. *See also Pallas Athene*, pages 50–51.

Above: Cerberus represents the irrevocability of death and, in psychology, the self-defensive instincts of the unconscious. **Below:** *Cezanne's Medea, 1880, was based on Eugène Delacroix's depiction, the mother poised to kill her own children.*

Triton Triton is the most famous of all mermen, who were half-men and half-dolphins and consorts of mermaids. He directed the waters by sounding a horn or conch shell, heard by humans as the roaring of the ocean. In Greco–Roman mythology, Triton was the son of the god of the sea, Poseidon/Neptune, and was also the herald of his father. Unlike many fabled sea creatures, Triton is generally a positive symbol of control and power (although he was on occasions believed to lose control, making the shores dangerous). *See* page 21 *and The Union of Water with Earth*, pages 40–41.

Orpheus & Eurydice Orpheus, according to Greek mythology, was a superb musician. When his wife, Eurydice, was killed by a venomous serpent and descended to the underworld realm of the dead, Orpheus followed her, and played such sweet music that Hades was moved to let Eurydice return to the land of the living, as long as Orpheus did not look back at her. Alas, he did, so there she remained.

Pandora In Greek mythology, the first mortal woman, whom Hephaestos fashioned from clay and Zeus then sent to earth with a box (her symbol) full of gifts from all of the gods. When the curious Pandora opened the box, all of the gifts flew away, leaving only hope.

Lamia In Greek and Roman mythology, Lamia was a Libyan queen who was robbed of her children by the jealous Hera/Juno. Driven insane by this, she vowed vengeance on all children and became a demonic child-devourer. She had the head and breasts of a woman, but the body of a serpent. As well as threatening children, she could share the predatory symbolism of the Sirens.

Cerberus Cerberus guarded the entrance to the Greek underworld and was usually portrayed as a dog with a serpent's tail and three heads (representing the infernal trinity), although it could have up to fifty. Its fangs dripped with poison. Although friendly to deceased entrants, Cerberus allowed no dead soul to leave the underworld or living person to enter. Some heroes, however, outwitted him.

NORSE AND GERMANIC BELIEF

The deities of the pre-Christian Norse and Germanic sacred traditions shared many characteristics with those of the Greco–Roman pantheon. The outstanding feature of both of these northern European belief systems was the veneration of nature. Their ferocious gods were frequently depicted in the midst of battle, too. Thus Norse and Germanic sacred beliefs comprised a potent mixture of mystical communion with nature and martial conflict.

NORSE & GERMANIC COSMIC SYMBOLS & DEITIES

Yggdrasil Yggdrasil, the cosmic tree, was watered by the eternal spring Urd, which was protected by the three Norns (Fates). As well as supporting the heavens, Yggdrasil contained nine worlds. The most important realm was that of the gods (aesir)—a fortress known as Asgard; humans inhabited Mitgard.

Ragnarök Having been created from the body of the giant Hymir, the aesir and humans shared a common origin, and both were constantly threatened by frost giants. The final, apocalyptic confrontation came at Ragnarök ("doom of the powers"), when, after a time of bitter cold and chaos, the vengeful Loki led an army of frost giants to attack Asgard.

Odin/Wotan The supreme Norse god was Odin (the Germanic Wotan or Wodan), a deity associated with both military prowess and wisdom. A great fighter, his spear was believed to ensure victory, and this weapon was one of his most important symbols. Others were the eight-legged steed Sleipnir, which carried him into battle (*see* page 134); the pair of wolves, Sköll and Hati (representing hatred and repulsion), which accompanied him; and the two information-gathering ravens that sat on his shoulder—Hugin ("Thought") and Munin ("Memory"). Upon their death in battle, human warriors and kings whose bravery had been outstanding would be conducted by the Valkyries (Odin's female warrior maidens, who were often symbolized by ravens, crows or swans) to Valhalla, "hall of the slain,"

Above: The three Norns replenish the well of Urd or Urdrbrunnen, the water of life. In the background is the tree of life, Yggdrasil, surmounted by its eagle, while the four stags of the cardinal directions and winds nibble at its leaves.

to enjoy a happy afterlife of fighting and feasting. However, Odin was not only the god of war, but also the god of knowledge, for he had drunk from the stream of Mimir, losing an eye for the privilege.

Thor/Donar The Norse god Thor (the Germanic Donar) was a sky god whose primary attribute was his lethal, double-headed hammer, called Mjöllnir, which he hurled in anger and which symbolized the thunderbolt. As well as bringing storms, Thor was the guardian of law and order. But his primary representation was as a wild, auburn-bearded warrior driving his goat- or ram-drawn chariot across the sky (thus causing thunder). *See Thor Battling the Mitgard Serpent, pages 58–59.*

Frigg/Frija Frigg (the Germanic Frija) was the Norse goddess of childbirth through her dual role as Odin's wife and mother of his children. Her symbols were those that expressed motherhood and natural fecundity.

Freyja The Norse Freyja and her brother, Freyr, were vanir, or fertility deities. They were collectively symbolized by golden boars—fecund animals—and by ships. The prolific hare was also a symbol of Freyja, whose chariot was pulled by cats. The beautiful Freyja, who was married to Odur, had a magical necklace named Brisingamen.

Below: Frigg, the Germano–Norse mother goddess and wife of Odin, was said to spin sun rays with her golden spindle. Here, she is surrounded by symbols of natural fertility: the stork that was believed to deliver children, a baby, a ram and dragonlike serpents.

FRIGGA

The Hall of Judgment   artist unknown

1550–1196 BC (New Kingdom), paint on papyrus, Museo Egizio, Turin, Italy

This representation of Osiris, the ancient Egyptian god of the underworld, presiding over the Hall of Judgment, is taken from a book of the dead, a collection of intricately illustrated texts inscribed on papyrus scrolls that contain incantations and prayers to the gods. They were intended to serve as guides to the underworld for the spirits of the recently departed, with whose mummies they were entombed.

When a person died, the ancient Egyptians believed that his or her spirit, or *ba*, descended to the underworld on a perilous journey that would end in either eternal life or total extinction. When it reached the Sixth Gate, the *ba* appeared before Osiris to be judged either worthy of immortality or fit only for obliteration. While the *ba* recited the "negative confession" (an assertion of innocence of certain wrongdoings) before forty-two assessor gods, taking care to address each by name, Anubis, the jackal-headed god of embalming, weighed the deceased's heart against the feather of Ma'at, the attribute of the goddess of truth. The ibis-headed deity Thoth, the god of scribes and writing, as well as of the moon and magic, stood ready to commit the result to writing before presenting it to Osiris. If the weight of sin caused the heart to prove heavier than the feather, he would condemn it to instant annihilation in the jaws of the terrible goddess Ammit, "Devourer of the Dead."

Ancient Egyptian mythology explains why Anubis and Thoth played such important roles in the Hall of Judgment. When Osiris, once a living pharaoh, was murdered and dismembered by his evil brother Set, it was Thoth who helped Isis, Osiris's sister–wife, to assume the form of a kite in order to seek out his body parts, and it was Anubis who reassembled and embalmed them, thus resurrecting Osiris long enough for Isis to conceive their son, Horus.

See also **The Ennead** (pages 14–15).

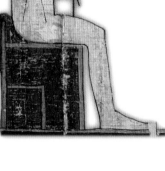

The fearsome, ever-hungry Ammit has the head of a crocodile, a lion's front quarters, and a hippopotamus's hindquarters.

According to one of the principles of ancient Egyptian art, the larger a figure in relation to others, the greater its status, and Osiris, who is portrayed sitting on a *naos* shrine, is clearly the most important character in this scene. Having been mummified by Anubis before descending to the underworld, his body is tightly swaddled in his grave clothes, a white shroud. His *atef* crown, which is enclosed by a pair of ostrich feathers, is an attribute of the pharaoh and consequently a symbol of the highest royal authority, as is the scepter that he holds, along with a shepherd's crook and flail, respectively symbols of guidance and discipline.

As well as being shown in ibis-headed form standing poised to record the result of the heart's weighing, Thoth makes a second appearance in this scene as a baboon (in whose form he was worshipped at Hermopolis, now al-Ashmunayn) perched on top of the scales, both holding them steady and supervising proceedings.

The goddess Ma'at is also portrayed twice: as a feather counterbalancing the deceased's heart, and as a goddess wearing an ostrich-feather headdress.

Anubis is almost always depicted as having both the head of a jackal and black skin.

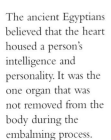

The canopy above the Hall of Judgment is supported by two lotus (water-lily) stems. The lotus (Nymphaea lotus) symbolizes rebirth because it grows and flowers spectacularly beautifully amid dark and stagnant waters, which are equated with chaos and death.

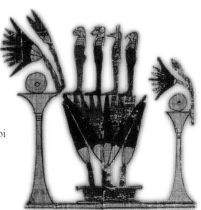

The forty-two assessor gods are represented sitting in two rows of twenty-one.

The ancient Egyptians believed that the heart housed a person's intelligence and personality. It was the one organ that was not removed from the body during the embalming process.

Pictured flanked by lotus blossoms, denoting rebirth, are the four sons of Horus: Imsety (guardian of the south and the deceased's liver); Quebsennuef (the west and the intestines); Duamutef (the east and the stomach); and Hapi (the north and the lungs).

The Creation of the Milky Way

Peter Paul Rubens

1636, oil on canvas, Museo del Prado, Madrid, Spain

The Creation of the Milky Way is one of a number of paintings focusing on scenes drawn from Greco–Roman mythology that King Philip IV of Spain commissioned from the Fleming Peter Paul Rubens, one of the most sought–after artists of his day. No wonder that Rubens's works were in such demand, for this image is typical in combining the dynamic composition, dramatic use of color and sure touch of a master of his art with a compelling scene portraying larger–than–life characters interacting on a vast, cosmic stage.

According to the ancient Greek and Roman writers, Zeus (the supreme Greek god who was venerated as Jupiter in the Roman Empire) and his wife Hera (Juno) were locked into a rocky relationship, partly on account of his insatiable libido and countless infidelities, and partly due to her nigh–insane jealousy and tendency to launch vicious vendettas against the objects of Zeus's lust, as well as against any offspring that his often blameless victims consequently bore. The hero Herakles (Hercules) was one of those whom the goddess persecuted from birth to death, despite her unwitting collusion in ensuring that he would then join the divine ranks. For when Hera learned that Alcmena, a mortal granddaughter of Perseus, was on the verge of bearing a child sired by Zeus (who

had disguised himself as Alcmena's future husband, Amphitryon), she sent her daughter Eileithyia (Ilythia), goddess of childbirth, to block his passage from the womb. She could not do so indefinitely, however, whereupon Herakles preceded his twin Iphikles (Iphicles), who was Amphitryon's child, into the world. One version of the tale says that Zeus then tricked Hera into breastfeeding Herakles, knowing that her milk would make him immortal, and that the baby sucked so hard that she pulled away in pain, causing her milk to spurt into the sky to create the cloudy belt of stars that we call the Milky Way.

See also **The Olympians** (pages 20–25), **Herakles/Hercules** (page 28), *The Judgment of Paris* (pages 54–55).

Having employed sly subterfuge in persuading Hera—who, until this moment, has remained blissfully unaware of his deception—to breastfeed his baby son, Zeus has literally taken a back seat as he watches Herakles greedily swallow the milk of immortality. He may have assumed an unobtrusive position, but the rays of golden light that crown his head, as well as the proximity of his lightning-bearer, the powerful eagle that grips a bundle of Zeus's punitive thunderbolts in its lethal talons, leave the discerning viewer in no doubt that this is a supreme deity and a mighty ruler of the skies.

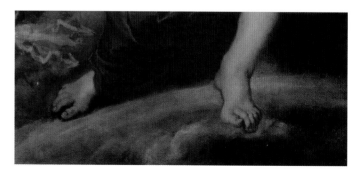

The rainbow is both the joint symbol of Zeus and Hera as king and queen of the heavens, when it may be equated with a throne, and an attribute of Hera alone. When she was not acting as a messenger between the immortal and mortal realms, Iris, the divine daughter of Thaumas and the Titan Elektra, and, with her delicate, shimmering, iridescent wings (or mantle), the personification of the rainbow, served as Hera's handmaid.

The peacocks that pulled Hera's chariot across the heavens were not only her favorite birds (which is apt, for they give the impression of being as vain, proud and majestic as the goddess herself), but symbolized the sky on account of the jewel-like "stars" that stand out against their velvety dark, richly hued plumage when they strut along, displaying their semicircular tails. It is told that Hermes (Mercury) lulled the all-seeing giant Argus Panoptes to sleep while he was supposed to be keeping many of his hundred eyes on the heifer Io, another of Zeus's conquests, on Hera's orders. When Hermes then killed him, Hera set the giant's eyes in the peacock's tail in his memory.

As a mother goddess, as well as the patron of marriage, married women and mothers, Hera's breasts were the source of a never-ending supply of magical milk. When this divine substance spilled onto the earth, milky white lilies were said to grow from it.

The Union of Water with Earth

Peter Paul Rubens

c.1618, oil on canvas, State Hermitage, St. Petersburg, Russia

Despite being Flemish, and having painted this canvas in Antwerp, Rubens would have been familiar with the myths of Rome, having lived and worked in Italy between 1600 and 1608. That said, although the characters depicted are drawn from the Greco–Roman pantheon, being named as Neptune (the Roman god of the sea whose Greek counterpart was Poseidon) and Cybele (originally a Phrygian, or Anatolian, earth goddess who was later also venerated by the ancient Greeks and Romans), there are no primary-source stories attesting to the harmonious union between these deities. Nor do any of the symbolic attributes with which Rubens has surrounded Cybele match those of ancient tradition, which included a mural crown, a tambourine, a libation dish and a pair of lions.

Because she was an "adopted," rather than a home-grown, deity, and because aspects of their characters, concerns and cults were similar, Cybele was often equated in Greece with the Titan Rhea (whose Roman equivalent was Ops), the wife of Kronos (Saturn), another earth goddess and *magna mater* ("great mother" in Latin), being the mother of the Olympian gods Zeus (Jupiter), Neptune (Poseidon), Hades (Pluto), Hera (Juno), Demeter (Ceres) and Hestia (Vesta). Both Cybele and Rhea were similarly confused with Demeter, too, the goddess of corn and agriculture. While there are no tales of Neptune having coupled with either Cybele or Rhea, there is one that relates that he did so with Demeter. For the ancient Greeks told that when Demeter was grieving for the loss of her daughter, Persephone, Poseidon made unwanted advances toward her, prompting her to change into a mare to elude him. He, however, transformed himself into a stallion and forced himself upon her in a water meadow at Onceium, in Arcadia. Yet there is no equine imagery in this painting, nor any hint of corn or unwillingness. Rather than being true to Greco–Roman mythology, Rubens's painting is therefore an allegory, with the voluptuous figure of Cybele representing all of the goddesses of the earth, fertility and abundance rolled into one.

See also **The Olympians** (pages 20–25), **Poseidon/Neptune** (page 21).

The figure blowing into a conch shell is Triton, Neptune's dolphin-tailed, merman son by his Nereid wife, Amphitrite, who trumpets his approval of his father's union with Mother Earth.

Cybele was a Near Eastern goddess whose feline companions were lions. The dangerous creature pawing gently at the cornucopia by her side signifies that Cybele's ferocious aspect is in abeyance, or else denotes her awesome ability to tame the wildest of beasts in her role as "Mistress of the Animals."

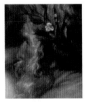

The earth goddess has placed her hand on Neptune's, denoting her willingness to give herself to him. Their conjoined hands rest on a terra-cotta urn from which water gushes. Terra cotta ("baked earth" in Italian) is clay that has been dug from the earth before being fired, and is therefore obviously a symbol of the goddess of the earth, while the urn's shape represents the womb and the flowing water symbolizes Neptune, as well as ejaculate. This centrally placed device suggests that this union of water with earth will be fruitful. An urn from which water flows is also a classical symbol of water gods.

The starfish and shells depicted here are the fruits of the sea that Neptune has laid at his bride's feet as a wedding gift.

The goddess's fruitfulness, or fecundity, is symbolized by a cornucopia of fruits of the earth, including figs, grapes, berries, peaches and pomegranates, juicy, life-sustaining foodstuffs whose seeds have the potential to provide an abundant harvest in the year to come.

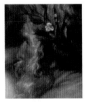

In art, Neptune is nearly always portrayed as a powerful older man with a long, gray beard. His trident—a three-pronged spear traditionally used to hunt fish in Mediterranean regions—is a symbol of his power and authority over the sea.

In Roman times, brides and grooms were crowned with wreaths, symbols of celebration and victory.

Rubens's inclusion of a pair of cherubic children indicates that they will soon be joined by Neptune and Cybele's divine offspring, not least because they appear to be bathing in the water flowing from the terra-cotta urn.

Diana and Endymion

Giambattista Pittoni

1723, oil on canvas, State Hermitage, St. Petersburg, Russia

So dynamic is Venetian artist Giambattista Pittoni's composition and rendition of his Greco–Roman subject that you can almost hear the "whoosh" as you regard the energetic female. She has clearly pulled her vehicle up short before sliding down to earth on a passing cloud in order to inspect more closely the sleeping young man who has captured her attention.

Pittoni's painting portrays a key scene from the myth of Diana and Endymion, which tells of the rather one-sided love affair between the Roman virgin goddess of the moon, hunting, flocks and childbirth (whose Greek equivalent was Artemis) and Endymion, a handsome young huntsman. Driving her chariot across the sky one night, Diana looked down as she passed over Mount Latmos, in the region of Caria, and was enraptured by the sight of the slumbering Endymion's beautiful body. Swooping down from the heavens to the hillside where he lay, the goddess caressed him chastely, reserving her final, enchanting kiss for his eyes to ensure that he would remain perpetually asleep, and thus eternally, and exclusively, hers.

Some versions of this Greco–Roman myth say that Endymion was a shepherd, and others that the moon goddess was not Diana, but Luna (or the Greek Selene). Yet more assert that Endymion was the king of Elis (an ancient Greek city-state), the son of Calyce and Aethlius, who grew up to lead a double life, conceiving fifty daughters with Luna on the hillside by night (who can still be seen as stars), and fathering sons with a mortal woman by day. And still further variations relate that Endymion was either so entranced by his Luna-induced dreams, or so desperate to spare his looks the ravages of old age, that he begged Jupiter (Zeus) to let him sleep forever, and that it was the chief god, not the goddess, who transformed him into a sleeping beauty.

See also **Artemis/Diana** (page 24), **Apollon/Apollo** (page 23).

Classical artists often depicted the goddess with a crescent moon nestling in her hair.

Diana wears short, practical garments that enable her to chase her prey and roam through woodland groves unimpeded by her clothing.

Her blue cloak both underlines her status as a heavenly goddess and provides a parallel with the Virgin Mary.

Her bow and arrows signal that she is a huntress. In addition, her bow may symbolize the moon on account of its crescent shape, while her arrows can signify light, or illumination.

By exposing her breasts, Pittoni may have intended to underline her Amazonian qualities, to hint at the erotic nature of her encounter, or simply to titillate the viewer.

Pittoni has allowed himself some artistic licence in his portrayal of Diana's lunar chariot. Strictly speaking, it should match the moon's hue in being silver, rather than gold, and should be pulled by heifers, mares, or stags, reflecting her status as goddess of flocks and the hunt. In classical art, it is Apollon, the god of the sun, whose (solar) chariot is gold and may be pulled by swans, which were sacred to him.

However, Diana and Apollon were twins, and it is said that when Leto gave birth to them, swans flew round their island birthplace seven times. In addition, because the pure-white swan is sometimes associated with the Virgin Mary, a Roman Catholic artist could, perhaps, be forgiven for linking this Christian symbol of chastity with a pagan maiden deity.

Diana is traditionally depicted accompanied by dogs, partly because they were her faithful hunting companions, and partly because, like the moon, they are an ancient symbol of healing.

It is apt that Pittoni has portrayed Endymion sleeping invitingly by a stream in a wooded area, for such natural surroundings were regarded as being sacred to, and favored by, Diana.

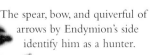

The spear, bow, and quiverful of arrows by Endymion's side identify him as a hunter.

Apollo and Mercury

Francesco Albani

c.1635, oil on copper, Musée national du Château, Fontainebleau, France

The Bolognese artist Francesco Albani was noted for setting scenes from mythology amid sweeping landscapes, which is why he must have seized upon a snippet of a pastoral story concerning Apollon, the Greco–Roman god of light, and Hermes (or Mercury, as he was called in Rome, the divine messenger of the gods) as being an ideal subject for his brush. Although his depiction is a broadly faithful interpretation of the myth—whose details in any case vary, depending on the teller—Albani has clearly indulged his imagination by incorporating a few flights of fancy (the divine spectators' gallery, for example), probably in order to add interest to an otherwise somewhat featureless background.

The tale told by the Roman poet Ovid, in his epic work *Metamorphoses* (Book II, lines 678–709), relates that when Apollon was miserably regretting his vengeful killing of Coronis, his unfaithful lover, he wrapped himself in a cloak and withdrew to Elis and the fields of Messenia, where, with a crook in one hand and a set of panpipes in the other, he watched over his cattle. So preoccupied with his rueful thoughts was he that he failed to see that his herd had wandered into the fields of Pylos. Neither the straying cattle nor his half-brother's negligence went unnoticed by Mercury, however, who seized the opportunity to steal the herd and hide the beasts in a nearby wood. Other versions of the myth state that Mercury was only a few hours old when he stole Apollon's cattle, and that he then slaughtered two of them and used their guts to make strings for the lyre that he had just invented. Given away by the blabbermouth Battus, he made amends to Apollon by presenting him with the lyre, thereby charming him and prompting him to give the young trickster his golden crook, or staff, in return, along with the job of guarding the gods' livestock. Thereafter, the two deities—now firm friends—were especially associated with these attributes, both being venerated in the Greco–Roman world as the protectors of flocks.

See also **The Olympians** (pages 20–25),
Apollo and the Muses (pages 172–73).

Mercury and Apollon have already exchanged attributes in Albini's portrayal. Mercury's identity is confirmed by his traveler's cloak and the wings on his *petasos*, or voyager's hat, and Apollon's, by his golden, sun-kissed beauty and shepherd's crook, a symbol of pastoral authority. Apollon's golden lyre, which is a relatively sophisticated kithara, signifies his love of music and virtuoso musicianship, while Mercury's snake-entwined staff, the caduceus—the sign of a herald and ambassador in ancient Greek times—supplies the power of flight, as well as the ability to give or withhold sleep.

Hercules (the Greek Herakles) wields the club with which he bludgeoned the Nemean lion (the first of his labors), whose pelt he wears as a trophy loincloth. On assuming godlike status, Hercules wed Juventas (Hebe), the lovely goddess of youth, who caresses her heroic husband here.

Mount Helicon is one of the homes of the Muses, goddesses of the arts and human knowledge who frequently make sweet music with Apollon.

Venus (Aphrodite) is identified by her nudity and her playmate Cupid (Eros), whose bow and arrow she has confiscated. Cupid's father, Vulcan, the god of the fire and the forge, sits next to his wife. Mars (Ares), the warrior god, looks lingeringly at his lover, Venus.

The winged horse Pegasus alights by the Hippocrene ("Horse Spring" in Greek), the fount of inspiration that he opened up by stamping his hooves on Mount Helicon, in Boetia.

Their respective birds, the eagle and peacock, are depicted by the sides of their master and mistress, Jupiter and Juno (Hera), the leading Olympians who are both children of Saturn (Kronos). Before being deposed by Jupiter, Saturn was the supreme deity, as well as a god of agriculture, which is why he leans on his reaper's sickle or scythe as he contemplates his powerful son.

Minerva (Athena), the patron deity of knowledge and the martial arts, is identifiable by her armor and shield, while the crescent moon decorating her companion's hair distinguishes the lunar goddess Diana (Artemis) as such.

Minerva Competing with Neptune for the Possession of Attica

Giovanni Battista Mengardi

1780, oil on canvas, Palazzo Priuli-Manfrin, Venice, Italy

This character-packed painting by Italian artist Mengardi portrays the moment when the Greek city of Athens gained its patron deity, its name and the first of the many olive trees that flourish in its soil today, providing its inhabitants with shade, olives and olive oil.

Greco–Roman myth explains that when King Cecrops of Attica began building a city-state, the project excited the interest of the gods, each of whom believed that being exclusively associated with this promising-looking venture would increase his or her personal power and prestige. After much bickering and bargaining, the number of claimants to the position of patron had been reduced to two, namely Poseidon (the Roman Neptune), the god of the sea, and Athena (who was worshipped as Minerva in Rome), the goddess of wisdom and learning, crafts and the martial arts. Because neither would give way to the other, Zeus (Jupiter), the chief god, decreed that they should compete for the honor, the stipulation being that each should create an innovation that would enhance the lives of the fledgling city-state's citizens, with the prize going to the originator of the one that was considered to be the most useful.

With their fellow gods sitting in judgment, so it was that Poseidon and Athena descended to the Acropolis, a huge, barren rock. Poseidon went first, smiting his trident against the rock and causing a stream of water (although some say a horse) to spring up. When the gasps had died down, Athena pointed to the olive tree that she had caused to grow on the rock, which the panel of divine judges saw would benefit the local populace in many more ways. Thus Athena was pronounced the winner, to the eternal benefit of its citizens, in whose welfare she subsequently took a keen interest, teaching them valuable cultural skills, as well as fortifying the Acropolis, on which the Parthenon, a temple dedicated to Parthenos, "the Virgin," as she was also called, was erected in the fifth century BC.

See also **The Olympians** (pages 20–25), **Pegasus** (page 32).

Poseidon's crown symbolizes his status as ruler of the sea.

Another symbol of his authority over the sea, his three-pronged trident was said to have a number of awesome powers, including causing floods, tempests, earthquakes and rock falls, as well as bringing springs of water into being.

Aphrodite (Venus), the goddess of erotic love, is distinguished by her youth and beauty, as well as by the white doves that are her avian attributes.

The lunar goddess Artemis (Diana) is recognizable on account of the crescent moon above her head. She leans on her twin brother, Apollon, who carries a golden lyre, a symbol of his musical prowess.

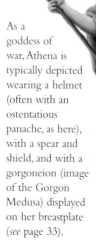

As a goddess of war, Athena is typically depicted wearing a helmet (often with an ostentatious panache, as here), with a spear and shield, and with a gorgoneion (image of the Gorgon Medusa) displayed on her breastplate (*see* page 33).

The soon-to-be Athenians are clearly awestruck by the sight of the first olive tree that any mortal has ever set eyes on (*see also* page 132).

Their personal attributes reveal the identities of the divine adjudicators. Peacocks are the birds of Hera (Juno), who sits by her husband, Zeus, whose pre-eminence is signaled by a halo and who is accompanied by an eagle, a symbol of his mastery over the skies. Their crowns proclaim the couple to be king and queen of the heavens.

The conspiratorial-looking trio are Dionysus (Bacchus), whose grape-and-vine-entwined tresses mark him out as the god of wine; Demeter (Ceres), the goddess of agriculture, whose hair is decorated with ears of corn; and Hermes (Mercury), the messenger god, whose winged helmet increases his speed of travel.

Pegasus, the winged horse and offspring of Poseidon by the Gorgon Medusa, may have given his father a helping hoof, for when the sea god created horses, he gave them the ability to produce water by stamping their hooves on the ground.

Pallas Athene

Gustav Klimt

1898, oil on canvas, Wien Museum, Vienna, Austria

Even if you don't know the identity of the impressive figure portrayed in this striking image, or the meaning of the symbols that can be discerned as peripheral details, your initial reaction to this painting may well be that it conveys both power and triumph, and in a startlingly—even disturbingly—original manner. If so, the Austrian artist Gustav Klimt has succeeded in his aim, behind which there lies a story.

Pallas Athene was painted in the year after Klimt, along with a group of like-minded individuals, broke away from Vienna's dominant Künstlerhausgenossenschaft (Cooperative Society of Artists), which they considered stuffy and stagnant, to set up their own, more idealistic and progressive, organization, the Vereinigung bildender Künstler Österreichs (the Association of Austrian Artists), better known as the Vienna Secession. From their 1897 viewpoint, winning success would certainly be a struggle, so they would need to invoke the psychological support of a powerful patron, while a symbol was required to represent the Secession in, for example, its magazine, *Ver Sacrum* ("Sacred Truth"). In Klimt's opinion, Athena (the Greek goddess of reason, war and the crafts, and protectress of heroes, whose Roman equivalent was Minerva) met these requirements perfectly, particularly in her emphatically martial aspect, when she was known as Pallas Athene. (Ancient Greek sources give two explanations for Athena's epithet of Pallas, which means "brandisher" in Greek. The first is that it was originally the name of a girlhood friend of hers, whom she accidentally killed, whereupon the devastated goddess took Pallas's name as an act of atonement and remembrance. And the second is that it was the name of the Titan Pallas, whom she slaughtered in battle, after which she flayed his skin and draped it over herself, thereby assuming his spear-brandishing strength, and with it, his name.)

By 1898, it seemed as though the battle of minds had been won, and that the members of the Secession had overcome the opposition of the reactionary representatives of the Künstlerhausgenossenschaft, which why the victorious Pallas Athene stares unflinchingly out at us with a distinct air of satisfaction.

See also **The Gorgons** (page 33), **Owl** (page 139), **Herakles/Hercules** (page 28).

The painting's dark background signifies an unenlightened past, which the radiant goddess of reason has turned her back on and put behind her.

Klimt depicts the culmination of an epic struggle, possibly between the hero Herakles (Hercules) and Antaeus, the Titan wrestler, or else between either Herakles or Theseus and the Minotaur (*see* page 34). The hero symbolizes a rational and civilizing force, and his vanquished opponent, instinctive, bestial and barbaric qualities.

Not everything in the past was primitive or uncivilized, however, which is why Klimt has included a musician, as well as deliberately adopting the style seen on ancient Greek artifacts in homage to art's classical roots.

A pair of round eyes gazes owlishly at us. The owl was an attribute of Athena, partly because these birds were commonly seen in Athens, and partly because its ability to see in the dark caused it to symbolize the ability of reason to penetrate the darkness of ignorance, hence its association with wisdom.

Pallas Athene holds out the miniature figure of the goddess Nike, daughter of the Oceanid Styx and the Titan Pallas, who often accompanied the gods in their battles. She was always depicted as being tiny, more like a talisman than a deity, naked or in armor and sometimes holding aloft a laurel wreath or palm branch, both symbols of victory.

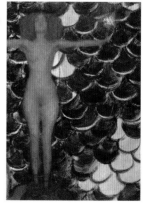

The implacable goddess's breastplate is the gorgoneion, the Medusa's severed head, for Perseus presented the hideous trophy to Athena after she had assisted him in decapitating the Gorgon. As the centerpiece of the aegis, the monstrous Medusa petrified Pallas Athene's enemies.

The serpentine coils that fringe the goddess's chain-mail garment are decorative devices drawn from the Art Nouveau stylebook, as well as allusions to the serpents with which the aegis (*see* page 22) was edged. In classical times, serpents denoted wisdom and knowledge.

The Birth of Venus

Sandro Botticelli

c.1482, tempera on canvas, Galleria degli Uffizi, Florence, Italy

Her nakedness apart, from looking at Botticelli's Venus (the Greek Aphrodite), it would be difficult to deduce that this willowy figure was worshipped by the ancient Romans as the goddess of erotic love. Rather than depicting her flaunting her sexuality, as might be expected of a deity who encouraged the indulgence of carnal appetites, the artist has portrayed her attempting to cover her breasts and genitals by adopting the *Venus pudica* (the Latin for "chaste Venus") pose.

There are a number of explanations for Botticelli's relatively unconventional representation of Venus, one being that having opted for a Classical female subject rather than a Christian one, such as the Virgin Mary—a daring step for an Italian artist in the fifteenth century—he considered it prudent to evoke a virginal impression. Another is that although Venus always signified love, symbolically speaking, she had both a "profane" and a "sacred" aspect, depending on her origin. As the child of the supreme god Jupiter (Zeus) and the Titan Dione, who gave birth to her in the normal manner, she was known in Greece as Aphrodite Pandemos ("Aphrodite of All People") and was associated with earthly, sexual or "profane" love. As the daughter of Uranus (Ouranos) and the sea foam (*aphros* in Greek), however, she was Aphrodite Urania ("Aphrodite of Uranus"), the goddess of divine, pure or "sacred" love, for not only was no sexual contact involved in her conception, but she was the lovely living embodiment of the union of heaven and water. Here, Botticelli has painted Venus as Aphrodite Urania, or, perhaps more accurately, as Aphrodite Anadyomene ("Aphrodite Risen From the Waters," as the Greek poet Hesiod calls her in his *Theogony*), that is, as the beautiful being who was created when the severed genitals of the sky god Uranus fell into the sea. Having subsequently been born from the sea foam, Venus raised herself above the waves and was blown first toward the island of Cythera, and then to that of Cyprus, where she stepped ashore at Paphos.

See also **Venus/Aphrodite** (page 22).

Zephyr (known as Zephyros in Greece, and as Favonius or Zephyrus in Rome), the winged god of the west wind, flies across the sea blowing Venus toward dry land.

Because the west wind brings warm weather to Mediterranean regions in spring, he was associated with this season, as were both Venus and the beautiful female who has entwined herself around him in a tight embrace. This is Flora, the Roman goddess of flowers (or Chloris, a nymph of the meadows in Greece), Zephyr's wife. This couple encourages new life to grow and flourish once winter is over.

The fluted, fan-shaped scallop shell is an attribute of Venus, for, like the goddess, the bivalve mollusks—*Pectinidae*—that a pair of such shells encloses originate in a marine environment. The scallop shell is furthermore a symbol of femininity, partly because its appearance recalls female genitalia, and partly because it performs the same function as the womb in sheltering and protecting vulnerable life forms within it.

Roses are the symbol of Venus (and love) on account of their beauty, fragrance and the pleasure that they give to humankind. The red rose also represents sexual maturity and Venus's carnal incarnation as Aphrodite Pandemos; the white rose denotes innocence and Aphrodite Anadyomene; and the pink rose suggests qualities lying somewhere between those indicated by the red and white rose, including sexual awakening.

That the attendant who has rushed to the shore to wrap a robe around Venus is dedicated to the service of this goddess is signaled by the cornflowers (whose blueness recalls the color of the Virgin Mary's mantle) embroidered on her white gown (denoting innocence), the roses encircling her waist and the myrtle garland around her neck. Myrtle, a plant that was dedicated to Venus, was a symbol of ideal wedded love in ancient times, being aromatic (sweet), fruit-bearing (fertile) and evergreen (always fresh and vital). She is also young and attractive, as were the three Graces (the three sisters called the Charities in Greece and the Gratiae in Rome) and the Horae, or the goddesses of the seasons, all of whom were counted among Venus's favorite companions.

The Judgment of Paris

From the workshop of Peter Paul Rubens

After 1632, oil on oak, Gemäldegalerie, Alte Meister, Dresden, Germany

Rather than *The Judgment of Paris*, this painting should more properly have been entitled *Paris Pondering a Momentous Decision*, but then a faithful depiction of his judgment itself would have deprived the viewer of the sight of three female nudes striking enticing poses, which must have been especially unusual—and titillating—during the seventeenth century. Indeed, stepping inside the painting and anticipating events a little, the moment that Paris utters his judgment, two of the three voluptuous ladies will be covering up at lightning speed, all the while hurling insults and spitting venom, which would have made a far less pretty picture (which was created in Rubens's Antwerp workshop before being reworked by the Old Master himself).

Paris is the young man depicted seated at right, clutching a golden apple. This is the apple of discord, which the spiteful Greek goddess Eris (whose Roman equivalent was Discordia), miffed because the gods had not invited her to the wedding feast of Thetis and Peleus, inscribed with the words "For the Fairest" and threw into the midst of the festive gathering. Hera (Juno) and Aphrodite (Venus)—respectively the goddesses of marriage and erotic love and both equally vain—instantly claimed it, as did Athena (Minerva), the goddess of wisdom and warfare, so setting a vicious squabble in motion. The rival goddesses appealed to their leader, Zeus (Jupiter), but he prudently refused to pass judgment and instead referred them to Paris, a mortal prince of Troy who still believed himself to be a mere herder of animals, who was deemed the best qualified to preside over this divine beauty contest, partly on account of his reputation for fairness and partly because he himself was outstandingly handsome. As well as displaying their charms to Paris, each goddess offered him an incentive to award her the golden apple. It was the combination of Aphrodite's beauty and her promise of the love of the most beautiful woman in the world that proved irresistible to Paris. He pronounced her the winner, thereby initiating a sequence of events that, according to Greek mythology, would lead to him eloping with Helen, provoking the Trojan War.

See also **Hera** (page 21), **Athena** (page 22), **Aphrodite** (page 22).

The pearls and rose that decorate her golden hair are attributes of Aphrodite, the former symbolizing the goddess's watery birth and lustrous loveliness, and the latter representing her fragrant beauty and her love of love, especially in its romantic and carnal forms.

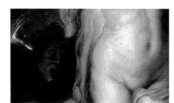

The shield propped up beside the goddess at left bears the gorgoneion (*see page 33*), identifying its owner as Athena, who has disencumbered herself of her weapons and armor so that Paris may admire her better. Athena has offered Paris the opportunity to become famous for his martial prowess in return for choosing her.

The bow that enhances Hera's hairstyle may refer to "tying the knot" or marriage, this goddess's particular responsibility. The peacock at her feet is her traditional companion, its majesty complementing her own as the chief goddess of the Olympian deities. Hera has promised Paris wealth, power and land in return for presenting the apple to her.

Tree spirits, perhaps fauns, or maybe satyrs, are agog as they watch the proceedings from their lofty vantage point.

The sheepdog may help his master to keep his sheep in line, but may also symbolize loyalty unto, and beyond, death.

Hermes (Mercury), who is recognizable on account of his winged helmet, is present to stiffen Paris's backbone and ensure that he makes a decision. The inharmonious entanglement of the snakes that wind themselves around the caduceus, his staff, emphasizes the strife inherent in this tense situation.

Impending doom is the unmistakable message conveyed by the frightful figure that hovers above the otherwise sylvan scene. She is probably one of the three Erinyes, or Furies, infernal sisters, hideous spirits of vengeance and foul harbingers of terrible fates, who have snakes instead of hair and brandish serpents (symbols of death in their hands) and burning torches that they use to cast light on their dark, underworld home.

The flaming torch has special significance in relation to Paris, for before he was born, Hecuba, his mother, dreamed of a firebrand that transformed Troy into an inferno, an omen that her unborn child would be the cause of the fiery destruction of her family's fortunes (which indeed proved to be the case).

Andromeda

Joachim Wtewael

1611, oil on canvas, Musée du Louvre, Paris, France

As unlikely as it may seem, Pegasus was the offspring of Poseidon (the Greek god of the sea) and Medusa, the fearsome Gorgon whose gaze could turn any living being to stone. Both of the winged horse's parents had an indirect hand in creating the mythological scene that Dutch painter Joachim Wtewael portrayed so dramatically in 1611.

Wtewael has depicted the moment when the Greek hero Perseus first set eyes on Andromeda, his future wife, and in the most desperate of circumstances, for she was about to pay the ultimate price for her mother's boastful vanity. Cassiopeia, wife of Cepheus, king of the Ethiopians (Libyans), can't have been blessed with a modest or prudent temperament, or maybe she was just not very smart, for in an age when the proud gods were quick to punish human presumptuousness, bragging that she was more beautiful than the Nereids was asking for trouble. Not only did these sea nymphs have the sympathetic ear of the sea god, but they also included Amphrite, his wife, among their number, so had little difficulty persuading Poseidon to avenge this insult, which he did, firstly by flooding Cepheus's kingdom, and then by sending a sea monster to terrorize the local shipping. On consulting the Oracle of Ammon, the frantic mortals learned that the only way of restoring order was sacrificing Andromeda to the sea monster, which is why Perseus, who was returning astride Pegasus to Seriphos from Cisthene, where he had decapitated Medusa, espied the naked Andromeda hopelessly awaiting her fate while chained to a rock near Joppa. As soon as Perseus had established the facts of the situation, the sea monster appeared, whereupon the hero quickly asked Andromeda's parents for her hand in marriage, and, on obtaining their consent, bravely slaughtered the monster. And once he had dealt with the small matter of her possessive and aggressive fiancé Phineus, Perseus and Andromeda were free to live happily ever after.

See also **Poseidon/Neptune** (page 21), **Pegasus** (page 32).

Focus hard on the section of rock above Andromeda's heavy iron chain, and you may be able to make out the Latin inscription *Joachim Wtewael fecit Anno 1611*, which means "Joachim Wtewael made this in AD 1611."

Terrified people cower in the background. The couple nearest to Andromeda may be her parents, who, the Roman poet Ovid tells us in *Metamorphoses* (Book IV), stood near their doomed daughter, lamenting her predicament.

We can't be certain whether the skeletons, skulls and bones at Andromeda's feet were victims of the ravening sea monster or are simply the remains of shipwrecked seafarers. What is clear, however, is that this coastal spot, where dry land merges with Poseidon's watery realm, may be a place of darkness and death for humans, but is rich in marine life. By surrounding the nubile Andromeda with a number of suggestively shaped, pink-hued shells, Wtewael may also have been alluding to her sexual attraction and potential fertility, for as well as being symbols of the sea, such mollusks may refer to female genitalia and fecundity. (Andromeda and Perseus went on to have eight children.)

Some ancient Greco–Roman sources say that the sea monster was called Cetus, and that it was set among the stars after its death (and Cetus, "The Whale," is indeed one of the eighty-eight constellations, as are Pegasus, Andromeda and Perseus, Cassiopeia and Cepheus).

Perseus is wearing the helmet of Hades (Pluto), which grants invisibility, and is wielding the diamond sickle or sword of Hephaestos (Vulcan), with which he is about to kill the sea monster. The severed head of Medusa can be seen in profile, mounted on his shield—the gift of Athene (Minerva)—and while some say that the gorgoneion turned the seaweed below into coral, others assert that it transformed Cetus into a stony reef. Pegasus is absent from some versions of this myth, Perseus instead gaining the power of flight from the winged sandals of Hermes (Mercury). In Renaissance times, the winged horse symbolized fame. Its white coat, celestial wings, heroic riders and evil opponents also denote goodness, nobility and such "higher" qualities as spirituality.

Thor Battling the Mitgard Serpent

Henry Fuseli

1790, oil on canvas, The Royal Academy of Fine Arts, London, England

This powerful image portrays the climax of the epic struggle between Thor, the Norse god of law and order and hurler of thunderbolts, and Jörmungand (also known as the Midgard, or Mitgard, Serpent, or the World Serpent), the monstrous child of the trickster Loki and the giantess Angrboda. Having ordered that the vicious, venomous serpent be brought from Jotunheim (the land of the giants) to Asgard (the realm of the Aesir, or gods), Odin, the chief god, then flung it into the sea surrounding Mitgard (the world of humans), where it grew and grew, until it encircled the Earth, plotting vengeance while biting its tail.

The (Prose) *Edda* tells how Thor, having assumed boyish form in order to travel incognito through Mitgard, coerced the giant Hymir into taking him on a fishing trip. Having procured the strongest line that he could find and cut off the head of the giant's prize ox to use as bait, Thor proceeded to fish for Jörmungand. When the serpent took the bait, a ferocious battle ensued, causing Hymir to cower in terror in his heaving boat as Jörmungand thrashed around in agony. Thor, however, held firm, bracing his feet so strongly that they pushed through the boat to rest on the ocean floor. Raising his hammer, the terrible Mjöllnir, Thor then prepared to deliver the death blow.

The Swiss-born artist Henry Fuseli must have been proud of his striking piece, for it was this that he chose to present to the Royal Academy of Fine Arts on his election to that august British body in 1790. The painting is significant in that it heralds a broadening view of what was considered suitable mythological subject matter for artistic representation, which was now about to move beyond the Classical, Greco–Roman canon to encompass Norse, Teutonic and Celtic themes.

See also **Norse & Germanic Symbols & Deities** (page 35).

Although the Norse tales do not recount that Odin watched this battle, Fuseli has included the "Allfather" in his painting, perhaps to emphasize the significance of the encounter between Thor and Jörmungand. For at the apocalyptic battle of Ragnarök ("twilight of the gods"), which, it was foretold, is yet to come, they are destined to kill one another. Odin is typically portrayed as an old, one-eyed man wearing a large hat.

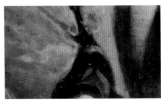

The wounded creature spits bright-red blood, as well as the deadly venom that will poison the skies and seas and spell Thor's doom at Ragnarök.

Thor's weapon of choice was Mjöllnir, the magical hammer that always returned to him. In symbolic terms, Mjöllnir signifies the thunderbolt, an unnervingly unpredictable force of nature that can strike any living creature dead with a terrible "crack." It was said that when Thor urged on the goats that pulled his chariot across the skies, the sound generated by the vehicle's wheels was the rumble of thunder.

The contrast between the sky-deity's light-hued body and sea-monster Jörmungand's dark, glistening coils underlines the age-old symbolic antipathy between sky beings—those that belong to the realm of light, or the heavens and chthonic creatures, or those that live in darkness, or the underworld.

The petrified Hymir, who thought that he had set out to sea simply to catch whales, shrinks back and covers his head protectively. One version of this myth tells that seconds later, he lurches across the boat and cuts the line (which Fuseli has chosen to depict as an iron chain so as to leave us in no doubt of the serpent's strength), thereby causing Mjöllnir to miss its mark and releasing Jörmungand, who sinks to the bottom of the ocean to live another day. A second relates that Thor's first blow fails to despatch Jörmungand, and that the line snaps before he can deliver another. Hymir is sometimes described as having a dog's head and a long white beard.

SACRED FIGURES & SYMBOLS

Above: *The Hindu goddess Durga, called "the unapproachable one," destroys the buffalo demon in this nineteenth-century painting. Hinduism spread from India to Polynesia: thus Durga is venerated in Bali and Java as the terrible goddess of death and disease, as well as of black magic. Indonesian folk art often displays a blend of indigenous and Hindu symbolism.* **Opposite:** *Da Vinci's* The Last Supper, 1495–97 *(see pages 110–13).*

Many of the world's enduring systems of sacred belief date back for millennia, or for centuries, at least. During that time, most have developed a rich and profound symbolic language, and, alongside it, a distinctive artistic style, with which to express mystical, supernatural, religious and philosophical concepts that are not easily conveyed by words alone, particularly within societies in which literacy was far from widespread. How better to give viewers an idea of a Hindu deity's overwhelming omnipotence or ferocity, for example, than by portraying him or her with a multitude of arms and hands, each clutching a different weapon? Or to communicate that which is almost incommunicable by other means, such as the higher level of awareness attained through meditation than by symbolizing its effects in the serene faces of meditative Buddhas and boddhisattvas?

Rather than being figurative, some of the most powerful sacred symbols are aniconic, however. Take Christianity's crucifix, for example: while artistic depictions of the crucifixion may inadvertently detract from the central message of suffering and sacrifice—perhaps because the scene appears clumsily executed or so outdated as to seem irrelevant to the observer—the crucifix is a timeless icon that evokes countless emotional associations with Christ's Passion in believers who behold it. Taoism's t'ai chi, or yin–yang, symbol is another ancient, unforgettable design that perfectly portrays both the coexistence of two diametrically opposed universal forces and the ideal, dynamic state of harmony that they may achieve. Still further sacred symbols gain resonance from their secret significance: the tetragrammaton of Judaism, or the four-letter name of God, the correct pronunciation of which is now lost in the mists of time, but is said to confer supernatural abilities on the speaker, for instance, or the fish that once identified practicing Christians to others at a time when they were being brutally persecuted for their faith. And because some religions, notably Islam, discourage depictions of living beings, geometric or vegetal designs that followers of other faiths may regard as being simply decorative assume divine importance as abstract expressions of Allah's universal, creative powers.

HINDUISM

Some of the world's most abstract faiths originated in the Indian Subcontinent and Asia, signaling a significant shift of belief from the sanctity inherent in the realm of nature to that of human spirituality. These religions emphasize the importance of the internalization of sacred beliefs—especially of striving for spiritual enlightenment—over the religious traditions in which humans passively accept their peripheral role as lowly subordinates of the omnipotent deities. Yet Hinduism retained an extensive pantheon of deities, its similarity to those of many European pagan sacred beliefs testifying to their common Aryan ancestry.

When the conquering Aryans arrived in the Indus Valley, before they reached the Ganges Plain, they found a widespread popular religion that focused on fertility, the objects of worship being the earth goddess Mahadevi, or "Great Goddess" (*see The Gods Worship Devi*, pages 86–87), and the components of the natural world. Although elements of this fertility cult were incorporated into the invaders' faith, and can be seen to this day in the worship of the Goddess (Devi), of serpents, or of other spirits of nature, the Aryan religion came to dominate the sacred beliefs of the inhabitants of the Indian Subcontinent, and, indeed, their very way of life.

Above: The Sanskrit letters of the sacred syllable Om, which Hindus believe is the sound of divine potency. Both the Sanskrit alphabet and this mystical sound were said to have been the gift of the Vedic Vāc, goddess of speech.

THE VEDIC DEVAS

The thirty-three deities (devas) of the Vedic period, who ruled the earth, atmosphere and sky, are described in the Veda, the three Vedic scriptures. Among the gods of the heavens were the father god, **Dyaus**; **Varuna**, the deity of order and the waters, who rode on a makara, a hybrid fish/crocodile (*see* page 64); **Surya**, the sun god; and **Vishnu**. The chief god, **Indra**, bringer of thunder and lightning, and the wind god, **Vayu,** dominated the atmosphere. The earth gods included **Agni**, the god of fire, messenger of the gods and a bringer of enlightenment, whose vehicle was a ram, a symbol of solar fertility; **Yama**, the god of the underworld; and **Soma**, the hallucinogenic-plant deity. From these Aryan gods developed the Hindu deities that still hold sway today.

Left: Varuna riding a makara.

THE HINDU TRIMURTI

According to Hindu belief, the various conflicting elements of cosmic power are reconciled and unified in the trimurti, or trinity—the divine trio of Brahma, Vishnu and Shiva. While Vishnu is the preserver, Shiva represents the destructive power; Brahma's role is that of the harmonizer of the two, as well as of the creator.

Brahma   Although he is the creator god, Brahma is not generally worshipped, being regarded as a more abstract divine entity. Nevertheless, Brahma is personified in sacred representations: he has four heads (the fifth was destroyed by Shiva and was used to keep track of his nervously agile consort, Sarasvati), and may hold a spoon (signifying sustenance), a necklace and mace (attributes of divine knowledge), a bowl of water (representing fertility) and a lotus flower (a cosmic symbol and also one of fertility); Brahma rides a swan or goose, representing wisdom. *See The Gods Worship Devi*, pages 86–87.

Vishnu   The preserver, the benevolent deity who maintains cosmic order, Vishnu may be associated with the Vedic Indra. He is usually depicted as having four arms, which hold respectively the conch shell (representing the primal sound, *Om*); the discus, a solar symbol; the bow and lotus; and the mace, also called *dorje* or *vajra*, the symbol of divine knowledge and authority that can be equated with Indra's thunderbolt. His mount is Garuda, an eaglelike bird (*see* page 64), which grasps a serpent in its claws to symbolize Vishnu's mastery of both the heavens and water. Another representational type shows Vishnu sleeping on the coils of the cosmic serpent, Ananta, the symbol of infinity; when he awakes, another universal age is initiated, the new cosmos being symbolized as a lotus that flowers from his navel. Vishnu may also be symbolized in the form of one of his avatars (*see Matsya*, pages 88–89). His most popular incarnation, however, is that of Krishna, the god of love who narrated the great moral discourse called the Bhagavad Gita, to the warrior Arjuna. *See also The Gods Worship Devi*, pages 86–87.

Shiva If Vishnu is clearly a "good god," Shiva's powers are far more ambiguous, comprising elements of the Indus Valley's fertility cult in one of his primary symbols, the phallic lingam, and also the bull-like characteristics of the Vedic god Rudra, with whom he is associated. Although he is known as "the destroyer" and lord of time (Mahakala), he is also a god of creation. His complex personality is composed of opposing principles, and the fact that he can reconcile all of these conflicting concepts testifies to his power. Shiva is represented as having a third eye, a dual symbol of enlightenment and destruction, and as having the matted hair of an ascetic. The goddess Ganga, the divine personification of the river most sacred to Hindus, the Ganges, may be depicted nestling in his hair; the Puranas tells how she fell to earth, but was caught in the matted hair of Shiva, whereupon the seven holy rivers were formed. In his hands, he may wield a drum, fire, a trident, a bow and a skull—symbols of destruction and death—while serpents may entwine his body. His mount is Nandi, the white bull that represents masculine sexual energy and is associated with the crescent moon. As the lord of the dance, Nataraja, Shiva is depicted performing the dance of creation and destruction within a ring of fire, stamping firmly on the body of the dwarf Apasmara, a symbol of ignorance. *See The Gods Worship Devi*, pages 86–87.

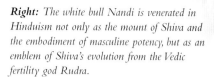

Above: Kali, "the black one."

phallic lingam, the rounded yoni represents shakti. Shakti is central to Tantric belief, but ordinary Hindus may also worship individual goddesses, particularly Durga, Kali and Pavarti, as the separate manifestations of the various powers of shakti.

Durga The ferocious, yet beautiful, Durga is celebrated as the killer of the buffalo demon, and is depicted riding a lion while brandishing such weapons as Shiva's trident.

Kali "The black one," Kali is the terrible goddess of the cremation grounds, whose tongue drips with the blood of her victims, such as the demon Raktavijra, who wears a belt made of severed arms and who is draped with a necklace of skulls; in Tantric belief, she has ten incarnations.

Pavarti Pavarti, the daughter of the mountain god Himalaya, is a benevolent goddess who, after being rejected by Shiva on account of her dark skin, caused her body to glow by means of concentrated asceticism, thus winning the attention of the god. Pavarti is usually depicted in the company of her husband, along with their children Ganesha (*see* page 64) and Skanda (or Kartikeyya), who battles evil and whose attributes are the spear and the peacock.

MAJOR HINDU GODDESSES

Although Hindu goddesses are generally regarded as inferior to their male consorts, they are the subjects of fervent devotional cults. This is partly a reflection of the worship of the earth mother by the original residents of the Indus Valley, but also because the goddess—collectively and individually—signifies the active cosmic female energy, shakti, the creative counterpart of Shiva's masculine power. While Shiva's sexual power is symbolized aniconically as the

Left: Hindu representations of goddesses entwined with trees, as illustrated in this bas-relief, derive from the worship of female fertility deities, a feature of the pre-Aryan culture of the Indus Valley.

Lakshmi Although not as powerful as Shiva's consorts, the lovely, gentle and chaste Lakshmi assumes importance as the loyal consort of Vishnu and as the embodiment of all wifely virtue. Even when Vishnu assumes the different forms of his various avatars, she accompanies him in such incarnations as that of Sita, the wife of Rama. Divali, the festival of lights, is sacred to Lakshmi as the goddess of good fortune, and she is welcomed by the lighting of lamps and by the drawing of rangolis—patterns featuring the lotus, which is her favored symbol, for besides representing the cosmos, it also symbolizes fertility and purity (*see also* page 130).

OTHER GODS & FANTASTIC CREATURES

Ganesha   The son of Shiva and Pavarti, Ganesha (or Ganesh) was given his elephant's head after having been decapitated by Shiva, whereupon his contrite father conferred the leadership of the ganas, Shiva's army of dwarves, upon him. Ganesha's elephantine head symbolizes wisdom, a concept emphasized by his single tusk, for he broke off the other in order to write down the Mahabharata, the sacred text that contains the Bhagavad Gita. Because he removes obstacles, and is plump, Ganesha is regarded as the patron of prosperity (also represented by his consort, Riddhi, or Siddhi) and of beginnings, who is invoked before journeys or business ventures are undertaken.

Hanuman   Hanuman is a hybrid god, having the head of a monkey. He is worshipped in recognition of his brave and decisive actions in helping Vishnu's avatar of Rama achieve victory over the demon king.

Nagas   Nagas—a legendary race of snakes—are generally represented as serpents in Hindu tradition, although they can also be depicted as human-headed snakes. Ananta is the thousand-headed king of the nagas, and represents infinity. The great god Vishnu sleeps upon the coiled Ananta, symbolizing wisdom and eternity; the two intertwined nagas sacred to him represent the fertilized water from which the earth goddess rises. As snakelike beings, nagas can also represent the guardians of material and spiritual treasure.

Makara   The makara is a mythical Hindu beast, generally portrayed as part fish and part crocodile, sometimes with an elephant head. It can also be represented as a shark, a naga, a dolphin or an antelope/fish. The makara is the vehicle of Varuna, the Vedic lord of the deep. It is associated with life-giving water and thus fertility. *See also* page 62.

Garuda   Half-man and half-eagle (and sometimes a wild goose), the "golden sunbird" Garuda is of crucial importance in Hindu and Buddhist mythology as the bird of life. Garuda is the king of the birds and the vehicle of the sky god, Vishnu—the preserver (*see* page 62)—and can be equated with the sun, the sky and victory.

Above: The temple façade reflects the Hindu concept of worship as both darshan *(viewing the sacred image) and* puja *(ritual), which is conducted here (and in the home as well) to bring the divine presence into communion with the seeker. Each band of symbols directs the eye upward, to the apex of the shrine, which is considered the pivot of the world.*

According to tradition, Garuda was fully formed when it emerged from the (cosmic) egg and lives in the wish-fulfilling tree of life. As a solar power, Garuda is the bitter enemy of the chthonic naga serpents (particularly Kaliya). For Tibetan Buddhists, Garuda is the mount of Buddha and a manifestation of the bodhisattva Vajrapani.

SYMBOLS & SYMBOLIC PRACTICES

Mandala   Spiritual communion with the deities may be achieved by meditating on a symbol like the mandala, or on the more abstract yantra, which employs geometric symbols rather than representations of deities. The circular mandala may have Mount Meru, the cosmic mountain, as its central feature, around which the sun, moon and stars revolve. Four continents are depicted on its periphery, along with the protectors of the cardinal directions, the Vedic deities Yama, Varuna, Indra and Kubera. (Hindu temples, or *murti*, may also be constructed according to the cosmic representation of Mount Meru.) Through meditation, the worshipper may penetrate the three levels of such sacred symbols as the mandala to unite ultimately with brahman. *See also* page 67 and pages 92–93.

Yoga   Yoga is an important tool in the achievement of enlightenment, of which there are four major forms: *karma* (ritual), *bhakti* (devotional), *jnana* (intellectual) and *dhyana* (meditational) yoga. In Tantric kundalini yoga, the female energy, shakti, is envisaged as lying in the form of a coiled snake at the base of the spine. Through meditation, the energy can be raised through the seven chakras, symbolized as wheels or lotuses, of the spine until it unites with Shiva, the embodiment of male power, in the head.

BUDDHISM

The primary symbols of Buddhism—the religion founded in India by the Buddha, Siddhartha Gautama, between the fifth and sixth centuries BC—are those representing the Buddha himself, as well as the principles that he taught to the world.

MAJOR FIGURES

Buddha Legend tells of Siddhartha Gautama's miraculous birth from the side of his mother, Queen Maya: he had been conceived when she dreamed that a white elephant, carrying a lotus, entered her side. Her husband, King Suddhodna, of the Shakya dynasty, cosseted his son, who enjoyed a life of protection and luxury. However, when he was twenty-nine, Gautama left the palace, whereupon he had four encounters that would change his life: with a bent old man, with a disease-ravaged man, with a dead body being carried to the cremation grounds and, finally, with a saddhu, or ascetic holy man. Profoundly shocked by "the three marks of impermanence" (old age, disease and death) that he had witnessed, Gautama resolved to abandon his life of luxury and follow the life of the saddhu, hoping that he would thus attain enlightenment (nirvana). The harshness of Gautama's new life was in marked contrast to his previously indolent existence, yet after years of fasting to the point of starvation, and traveling through India to sit at the feet of famous teachers, he felt himself no wiser in the quest for spiritual truth. In despair, he finally reached Bodh Gaya, where, sitting under a fig (*bodhi*) tree, he vowed to stay until he had achieved enlightenment. This he attained after forty-nine days, during which he battled with the evil embodiment of temptation, Mara. Known henceforth as the Buddha ("the Enlightened One"), Gautama spent the rest of his life disseminating his spiritual knowledge.

The dharma-chakra is perhaps the most profound aniconic symbol of Buddhism, but others also represent Buddha himself, as well as aspects of his credo. Many of these were originally Hindu symbols, for just as Hindus recognize Buddha as Vishnu's ninth avatar, Buddha's disciples found little difficulty in reconciling some tenets of Buddhism with those of Hinduism, whose deities were regarded as Buddha's benevolent patrons (illustrated by the fact that Indra is often shown holding the parasol or canopy of sovereignty over his head). Thus the primary aniconic symbols of Buddhism include footprints (*buddhapada*), which may be decorated with various representations of the 108 auspicious objects associated with Buddha, such as the lotus (signifying perfect enlightenment, for although it

Above: *One of the twelve scenes from the life of Siddhartha Gautama traditionally depicted in Buddhist art is the death of Buddha at the age of eighty, when he was released from the round of existence.*

is rooted in mud, it opens into a beautiful flower), whose form may also be equated with the dharma-chakra; Shiva's three-pronged trident (symbolizing the "three jewels," or *ortriratna,* of Buddhism; Buddha himself, dharma and the *sangha*—the enlightened community); the royal parasol or flywhisk; and Vishnu's solar disk and conch shell (whose sound represents the voice of Buddha).

Initially, Buddha was symbolized in such aniconic forms, but from the second century AD, his physical body began to be depicted, usually engaged in meditation, perhaps seated on a lotus throne in the shade of the bodhi tree, or surrounded

Above: The benevolent Chinese folk goddess Kwan-yin (Kuan Yin)—known in Japanese Shintoism as Kwannon (Kannon)—was transformed over time into a bodhisattva of compassion whose symbols include the jewel of sovereignty, indicated by her left hand; the cosmic mountain; and a flowering branch.

Bodhisattvas There are a number of Buddhist traditions, but it was Mahayana Buddhism that spread to China and Japan, among other countries, following Buddhism's decline in India. One of the most notable ways in which Mahayana Buddhism differs from other schools, such as that of the Theravada Buddhism prevailing in Sri Lanka, Indochina and Thailand, is in its emphasis on the bodhisattvas—"enlightened beings" who have achieved nirvana, but who have chosen to delay their Buddhahood in order to remain with humankind to help end its suffering. *See Padmasambhava (pages 90–91).*

The concept of the celestial bodhisattvas undoubtedly helped Buddhism's assimilation, not only into the sacred traditions of India, but also into those of the Far East, where many indigenous deities became equated with individual bodhisattvas. The characteristics of the benevolent goddesses **Kwan-yin** and **Kwannon** of China and Japan respectively, for example, were merged with the bodhisattva of compassion. **Jizo**, as the patron of children and journeys, is depicted in the garb of a monk, while **Vairocana**, the Buddha of the sun, may be equated with the Japanese sun goddess, **Amaterasu**. Further adaptations can be illustrated in China by the transformation of the future **Buddha Maitreya** into the pot-bellied "laughing Buddha."

SYMBOLS & SYSTEMS

Dharma Central to Buddha's teaching of "the middle way" is the importance of following the Buddhist *dharma* ("the law"), at whose heart lie the "four noble truths": those of suffering (*dukkha*), the cause of suffering (*tanha*), the end of suffering (*nirvana*) and the eightfold path that, if followed, will result in nirvana. In symbolic terms, dharma is represented by the wheel (chakra) that Buddha is said to have set in motion with his discourse at Sarnath, each of its eight spokes signifying one of the eight "right" (*summa*) concepts contained in the eightfold path: right understanding and thought, which together result in wisdom; right speech, conduct and livelihood, representing morality; and right endeavor, awareness and meditation, the components of joy.

Stupa Stupas are moundlike temples, which, in ancient times, were the burial sites of royalty, and among eight of which Buddha's remains were said to have been distributed after his death. An architectural representation of the steps of the path

by the deer of Sarnath, where he preached his first sermon. There are believed to be thirty-two physical attributes (*lakshana*) that identify "a great man" (*mahapurusha*) in Buddhist belief, including the monastic robes that represent the ascetic way of life; long, even toes; a halo and bodily aura of spirituality; the *urna* mark, or tuft of hair in the center of the forehead, signifying a third eye of spiritual vision; elongated earlobes, commemorating the heavy earrings that Gautama wore as a prince; and the *ushnisha*, a cranial protuberance or topknot symbolizing knowledge. Images of Buddha generally display all of these *lakshana*. Another important aspect of the Buddha image is its hand gestures, or mudras. Hinduism recognizes over five hundred mudras, but Buddha is generally depicted as making one of five: both hands joined upward in prayer; making the shape of the dharma-chakra; one hand lifted, signifying the dispelling of fear; pointing downward, representing Buddha calling the earth to witness (*bhumi sparsha*) following his victory over Mara; or with his palms facing upward, symbolizing the bestowing of blessings. *See Padmasamhava (pages 90–91).* The figurative image of Buddha may display these characteristics in sculpture and art, in which scenes from his life may be recreated.

leading to nirvana, the stupa is also a cosmic symbol, for it has a square base (representing the earth) and four doors (signifying the cardinal directions). Concentric circles leading to the dome (which symbolizes fire) represent the ascending stages to nirvana, while the spike that surmounts the dome may represent either Buddha himself, nirvana or the axis mundi/bodhi tree. In Tibet, the stupa takes the form of the chörten, and in Asian countries, that of the pagoda. *See Padmasambhava (pages 90–91).*

Mandala The Buddhist mandala, also a macrocosmic symbol, echoes the form of the stupa. In common with the oral chants of the mantra, the mandala is a meditational tool intended to facilitate the attainment of spiritual enlightenment. Typical subjects include the forms of Buddha, of which there are many, thus the mandala may contain symbolic images portraying the characteristics of the various Buddhas. It may also represent such Buddhist concepts as the round of existence, which illustrates the six cosmic worlds: those of the gods, dissenting gods, hungry spirits, hell, animals and humans. At its center may be shown the creatures that represent humanity's faults—the snake (hatred), the pig (greed) and the cock (ignorance). *See Tibetan Anuttara-yoga Mandala, pages 92–93,* and the Hindu mandala, page 64.

Prayer Flags and Wheels The mystical communion attained by chanting mantras (embodied in the sixty-four goddesses of speech) is accorded particular significance in Tibetan Buddhism, whose followers also believe that their supplications are borne to the heavens with the help of the wind. This belief is manifested either by means of fluttering prayer flags, which are inscribed with invocations, or by prayer wheels—cylindrical drums containing printed mantras—which are spun.

Left: Spiritual energy is believed to flow from the stupa's base through its dome and spire to the heavens.

Above: Buddhist prayer wheels, commonly seen in Tibet, are usually inscribed with the words Om Mani-padme hum, *referring to the mystical Jewel in the Lotus, or Buddha.*

The *Vajra* In Tibet, Buddhism became known as Vajrayana, "the Way of the Thunderbolt," and this tradition represents a dramatic fusion of Tantric Buddhism with Tibet's indigenous, shamanistic religion, Bon-Po. The primary and eponymous symbol of Vajrayana is the vajra, the staff that represents the thunderbolt that brings enlightenment through skill and compassion, and that was symbolically derived from Vishnu's mace (*see* page 62). The vajra has a masculine connotation, particularly when contrasted with the bell, which represents feminine power, wisdom, but also a vacuum; when the two are combined, perfection is attained.

Zen Japan evolved its own version of Buddhism, called Zen, from the Chinese school of Ch'an that had been founded by the ascetic teacher Bodhidharma. Both traditions emphasize the spiritual truth contained in the natural world, which may be expressed in the minimalist Zen garden, which unites the power of meditation with that inherent in nature. Further features of Zen, which rejects the worship of an image in favor of spiritual actions and meditation, include calligraphy, which not only records the words of dharma, but also unites the calligrapher with Buddha; the tea ceremony, for "Zen and tea are said to have the same taste"; and meditating on the wording of the paradoxical *koan* riddles.

Many examples of Buddhist art also include such hybrid animal guardians as fearsome lions, dragons, serpents or Vishnu's mount, the eaglelike Garuda (*see* page 64).

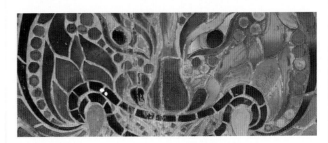

OTHER EASTERN FAITHS

Foremost among the important Chinese religions are those said to comprise the "three ways" (*san-chiao*): Confucianism, Taoism ("the way") and Buddhism.

CONFUCIANISM, TAOISM & SHINTOISM

Both Confucianism and Taoism place their primary emphasis on the dual nature inherent in all things and the corresponding need to achieve a harmonious balance of the conflicting forces of this duality—yin (the feminine, passive power associated with darkness and water) and yang (yin's masculine, active, solar and atmospheric counterpart).

Yin & Yang The most powerful symbolic expression of the Taoist concept of duality is that of the t'ai chi, whose circle of unity encloses the equal, sigmoid halves of yin (dark) and yang (light), each of which contains a small circle of the opposite color, representing the fact that each is present in the other and thus demonstrating both their independence and their interdependence. The t'ai chi may often be depicted surrounded by the eight pa kua trigrams, whose broken or continuous lines represent yin and yang respectively.

Confucianism and Taoism were also integrated into Japan, whose indigenous sacred tradition is that of **Shintoism** (a word either amalgamated from the Chinese *shen*, "divine entity," and *tao*, "the way," or from the Japanese words *shin*, "belief," and *to*, or "the community." Worship is conducted at shrines, *jinja*, in which the gods are believed to live, and whose sacred boundary is marked by the *torii* gateway, traditionally made of three pieces of wood, which symbolizes the right entrance to the sacred way of the gods. The benevolence of the gods may be entreated by means of "horse pictures" (the horse is traditionally believed to be the messenger of the gods) called *emas*—wooden boards on which a symbol of the blessing required is drawn.

Amaterasu The foremost Shinto deity is Amaterasu, the sun goddess and daughter of Izanami and Izanagi, the cre-

ator gods of Japan. She is represented with a halo of sun-rays, holding the necklace presented to her by her father when he made her the ruler of the heavens.

Above: *The Japanese Shinto deity Amaterasu is portrayed emanating solar rays, wearing the necklace symbolizing her rulership of the heavens and carrying the imperial sword.*

JAINISM & SIKHISM

In common with Buddhism, Jainism (or Jaina) and Sikhism are each associated with a historical figure from India: Vardhamana, or Mahavira ("Great Hero"), in the sixth century BC, and Guru Nanak (AD 1469–1539) respectively. Both sacred traditions arose in reaction to the prevailing beliefs, practices and rituals of Hinduism.

The *Siddhachakra* The five Jainist supreme beings may be collectively symbolized in the form of a mandalalike circle, the *siddhachakra*, in which the central figure of an *arhat* ("worthy one") is surrounded by representations of the other beings (siddhas, spiritual leaders, Jainist teachers and monks).

The Human Hand The primary symbol of Jainism is a hand, represented with its palm facing forward, a sign of peace.

Gurus Guru Nanak, the founder of Sikhism, believed that the path to the Sikh *sachkand* (release from the cycle of reincarnation) lay in meditation, devotion and service rather than in ritual. He was the first in a line of ten gurus, who may be depicted in figurative form: Guru Nanak, for example, is often shown holding a meditational *mala* (rosary) and displaying the solar star on the sole of his foot, representing his elevated status.

The *Khanda* One of the most revered symbols of Sikhism is the khanda, or sword, which represents armed protection and belief in God, and its blade is encircled by the *chakkar*, or steel quoit, which represents variously God, unity and humanity. Two *kirpans* flank the *khanda* and *chakkar*, representing spiritual and temporal power respectively.

Michelangelo's The Creation of Adam *captures the Judeo–Christian creation story from Genesis and illustrates the symbolic power of "the right hand of God."*

JUDAISM & THE BIBLE: THE OLD TESTAMENT

Representational art has traditionally been discouraged in Judaism, which is why it was typically the artists of another "religion of the book"—Christianity—who depicted Old Testament scenes. Judaism is nevertheless rich in profoundly significant sacred symbols.

MAJOR FIGURES

Adam and Eve The Book of Genesis tells how God created the world in seven days. Initially, God was pleased with his creation, but after the serpent tempted the first woman, Eve, to taste the apple growing on the tree of knowledge in the Garden of Eden, she and Adam were cast out of paradise, thus initiating a chain of increasingly disastrous human actions that would culminate in the wrathful God sending a flood to drown the world. *See Paradise*, pages 94–97, and page 71.

Cain and Abel The sons of Adam and Eve. After Cain murdered Abel, in a fury that God had accepted Abel's animal sacrifice and not his vegetable one, he fled to the land of Nod.

Noah Only Noah and his family were regarded as being worthy of surviving the flood, and the dove that returned to Noah's ark bearing an olive branch and the rainbow that God caused to shine in the sky are important symbols of both Judaism and Christianity, representing respectively peace and God's covenant with humanity that he would never again destroy the world with such a deluge. (*See The Animals Enter Noah's Ark,* pages 156–57.)

Abraham and Isaac *See* overleaf.

Rebecca The wife of Isaac and mother of Esau and Jacob, who tricked Isaac into giving Jacob, her favorite, his blessing rather than Esau, the first-born twin.

Jacob and Esau The symbol most often associated with Jacob, who stole his brother Esau's birthright, is the ladder whose rungs angels ascended—a sign from God that Jacob was the heir to God's promise to Abraham. Subsequently, God named him "Israel"; he founded the twelve tribes of Judaism.

Joseph The favorite son of Jacob, whose doting father's gift of a coat of many colors caused his jealous brothers to sell him into slavery. Joseph eventually gained high office in Egypt.

Below: Gauguin's Vision After the Sermon *(1880) depicts Jacob wrestling with the angel (Genesis 32:24–29), after which he received the name "Israel."*

Abraham and Isaac

Abraham and Isaac Clues

white-bearded old man,
    knife held at son's throat
ram
shofar (ram's horn)
angel

As Featured In:

Rembrandt van Rijn,
    Abraham and Isaac, 1635

God's covenant with Abraham, a descendant of Noah, promised Abraham and his heirs the land of Canaan (Israel). As a symbol of this covenant, God commanded that every male be circumcised (as are eight-day-old Jewish baby boys to this day). Yet Abraham and his wife, Sarah, remained childless until, when Abraham was a hundred years old, the apparently miraculous birth of Isaac was granted them. Among the primary symbolic images associated with Abraham and his son, Isaac, are Isaac's near-sacrifice by Abraham (known as the *akedah*, or "binding"), and, following his reprieve, that of a ram. The sacrifice of "pure" animals and birds was an important component of ancient Jewish ritual, and, as a test of his unquestioning obedience, God commanded Abraham to sacrifice the much-cherished son of his extreme old age. The sorrowing Abraham was on the verge of complying when God demonstrated his mercy by sending the Archangel Michael to stay his hand. In gratitude, Abraham sacrificed a ram instead. The *akedah* is narrated on the New Year's festival of Rosh Hashanah (which commemorates Adam's birthday and may also be equated with an annual—and, by extension, final—day of judgment) as a symbolic reminder of Abraham's demonstration of his devotion to God, and of God's compassion. During this festival, too, the shofar, a hollow ram's horn symbolizing Abraham's sacrifice of the pure ram, is blown to alert transgressors to the need to repent. Isaac himself became a symbol of martyrdom to those medieval Jews who experienced persecution.

Below: Caravaggio's Sacrifice of Isaac *(1603) portrays the moment when the archangel immobilized Abraham's hand, thus saving the life of young Isaac.*

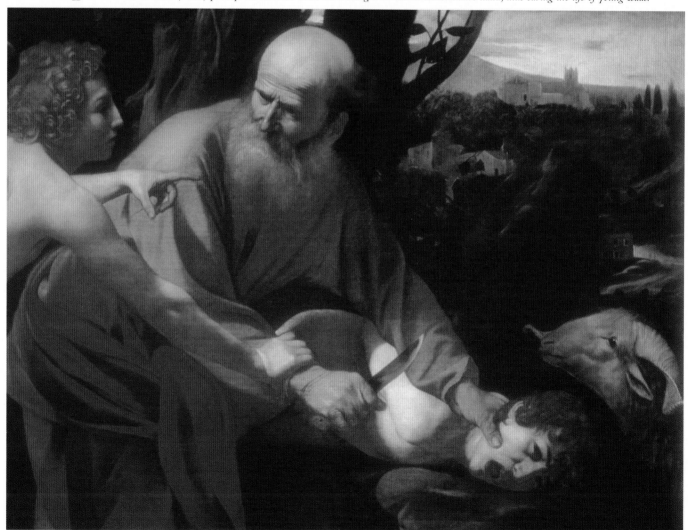

Angels

A ccording to Jewish and Christian lore, the triple hierarchy of angels consists of nine orders: seraphim, cherubim, thrones, dominions, virtues, powers, principalities, archangels and angels. Angels, usually depicted in beautiful human forms, have wings representing both their spiritual nature and their role as God's messengers (*see* page 102). They are often shown making music or singing, representing the divine music that brings harmony, as, for example, on pages 116–18.

Each of the four archangels who play prominent roles in the Bible has his own symbolic attribute. The Archangel Michael's is a sword, representing divine judgment (*see Altar of the Last Judgment from St. Mary's Church, Gdansk*, pages 116–18, *and Paradise*, pages 94–97). The Archangel Raphael's is a pilgrim's staff, representing divine protection. The Archangel Uriel's is a book, signifying divine wisdom. The Archangel Gabriel's is a lily, signifying purity, or a messenger's staff (*see The Annunciation to Mary and St. Luke the Evangelist*, pages 102–03).

Above: Botticelli's Madonna of the Pomegranate *(1487).*

Right: Adam and Eve's shame and grief are portrayed vividly in Masaccio's fresco The Expulsion from the Garden of Eden *(c. 1426), in Brancacci Chapel, Florence, Italy. The Archangel Michael brandishes his sword of justice.* **Far right:** *In Giotto's masterpiece* The Lamentation, *the angels and humans alike grieve for their beloved Jesus after He is deposed from the cross.*

Angel Clues

wings
halo
musical instruments

As Featured In:

Raphael, *The Sistine Madonna*, 1513-14
Various artists' depictions of the Annunciation

Moses From Moses, whom God commanded to lead his people from slavery in Egypt, derive some of the most significant sacred Jewish symbols, including that which represents God's name. Because it is regarded as too holy to enunciate (Jewish people speak of it as "the name," *hashem*), the written name of God, as revealed to Moses, is one of the most profound Jewish symbols, consisting of the Hebrew letters YHWH (in non-Hebrew interpretations, "Yahweh"). The tetragrammaton, as it is known, is often inscribed on amulets or is a central feature of the *shivviti* plaques that hang on walls in the synagogue and in Jewish homes. It was Moses, too, to whom God gave the Law, the Decalogue (Ten Commandments), on two stone tablets on Mount Sinai, symbolizing the renewal of his covenant with the Jewish people. On descending the mountain, however, Moses found his people engaged in the idolatrous worship of the golden calf, which caused the text to disappear from the tablets. Moses dropped them in horror, and they smashed. Then he returned to Mount Sinai and engraved two new tablets with the Decalogue himself. It was said that not only could the text be read from both sides, but the letters appeared to hover above the stone. It was these duplicate tablets that were placed in the Ark of the Covenant, along with the fragments of the first set. *See The Destruction of the Golden Calf, pages 98–99, and detail, page 121.*

David and Solomon The most prominent symbol of King David, who, it was said, carried a shield in the form of a hexagram against the giant Goliath, is the six-pointed Star of David, or *magen david*. Each point of the star may represent a day of the week—or of Creation—with the center representing the Sabbat (Sabbath). Its interlocking equilateral triangles signify the reconciliation of fire and water, masculinity and femininity and of the flesh and the soul. David and Bathsheba were the parents of Solomon, who built the First Temple in Jerusalem to house the Ark of the Covenant that David had recovered from the Philistines. The First Temple was destroyed by the Babylonians in 586 BC.

Daniel A Jewish seer and prophet in Babylon who interpreted King Nebuchadnezzar's dreams. Later thrown into the lion's den by King Darius, God prevented him from being devoured.

Above: *Caravaggio's* David and Goliath *(1599) emphasizes that David was a mere boy when he defeated and decapitated the giant Goliath, the champion of the Philistine army.*

Elijah A Jewish prophet during the time of King Ahab who held, and won, a prayer contest with the prophets of Baal. He later ascended to heaven in a whirlwind.

Job A Jewish patriarch who remained devoted to God throughout the various afflictions that God inflicted on him in order to test his faith.

Samson and Delilah *See Samson and Delilah, pages 100–01.*

Saul and Samuel Saul was the flawed first king of Israel, and Samuel, the judge, prophet and priest who anointed him as such. Saul died in battle against the Philistines.

Judith and Holofernes Judith was a beautiful Jewish widow who deliberately attracted the attention of Holofernes, the general of the Assyrian army that had besieged her city of Bethulia, in order to save her people. Pretending to welcome his advances, Judith first rendered Holofernes insensible with alcohol, then beheaded him with his own sword and, finally, departed the Assyrian camp with her maid. When the Assyrians discovered their leader's headless corpse the next morning, they fled in disarray.

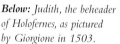

Below: *Judith, the beheader of Holofernes, as pictured by Giorgione in 1503.*

JEWISH & OLD TESTAMENT SYMBOLS

The Ark of the Covenant The Ark of the Covenant housed the tablets of the Decalogue in the sacred area of the Tabernacle—and later of the First Temple—known as the Holy of Holies, and was believed to have miraculous powers. It is recorded as consisting of a gilded wooden box surmounted by a pair of golden cherubim, symbols of God's love, which were said to embrace or to turn away from each other depending on the prevailing level of Israel's devotion to God. After the destruction of the First Temple, the Ark was hidden away, to reveal itself only in the age of the future messiah.

Although Jewish people honor God in their homes, particularly on the Sabbat, communal worship occurs in the synagogue. Here, within the Holy of Holies, facing Jerusalem, is kept a holy ark

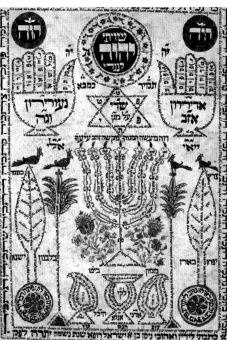

Above: Calligraphy and sacred symbols form the basis for Jewish illustrative art. A design from southern Germany (left) features the Star of David and the Hebrew word eleh ("these"), which is the first word of the Book of Deuteronomy. Mystical symbols, including the Star of David and menorah, adorn this page (right) of a Kabbalistic manuscript.

(often decorated with depictions of lions, symbolizing the tribe of Judah), a cupboard that contains the sefer torah, or Torah scrolls. A *ner tamid*, or "eternal lamp," burns constantly above the ark, both as a symbol of God's perpetual presence and as a reminder of the original menorah, one of whose lights always burned.

The Menorah Moses is credited with having created the first menorah, the seven-branched candelabrum that is now a primary symbol of Judaism. Its prototype was said to have been formed miraculously when Moses cast gold into fire; it was fueled by olive oil, and even if all of the other flames were extinguished, one always burned. A symbol of God's wisdom, the menorah's seven branches may represent, among other concepts, the sun, moon and planets, as well as the seven days of Creation.

The Sefer Torah In a synagogue, the sefer torah (two scrolls containing the word of God as set down in the Pentateuch—the first five books of the Old Testament) is hidden behind a curtain (*parokhet*), symbolizing the division of the sacred from the profane, and is draped with a mantle or enclosed in a wooden case, covered with a silver breastplate and topped with two crowns surmounted by bells. The text of the sefer torah must be handwritten according to prescribed rules, and may not be touched except with a *yad* ("hand"), a pointer culminating in a carved hand with a pointing index finger.

Jewish Festivals The major Jewish festivals commemorating various aspects of Jewish sacred history are filled with symbolic resonance. Pesach (Passover) celebrates the Exodus from Egypt, during which unleavened bread (matzah)—"the bread of affliction"—is eaten (*see also* page 113), along with bitter herbs signifying the Israelites' enslavement; a nut, apple, wine and cinnamon mixture in memory of the mortar that they mixed, and salt water symbolizing their tears; green herbs represent spring; while an egg symbolizes sacrifice, as does the roasted bone of a lamb, for the smearing of the blood of the paschal lamb on their doorposts identified the Israelites and saved them during the tenth plague of Egypt. All of these symbols are seen in depictions of Exodus scenes. Shavuot ("the Festival of Weeks") commemorates Moses's receipt of the tablets of the Decalogue, and the blooms that decorate the synagogue recall the flowering of Mount Sinai, while Yom Kippur ("the Day of Atonement"), which involves the confession of sins and requests for forgiveness, is marked by the wearing of white clothes, symbolizing purity. Chanukkah, "the Festival of Lights," celebrates the victory of the Maccabees over the Selucids and the subsequent rededication of the desecrated Temple in 165 BC, when the menorah burned miraculously for eight days on a single day's supply of oil. A candle is lit each night on an eight-branched candlestick until the eighth evening.

Fra Angelico's depiction of mothers-to-be Mary and Elisabeth (by then six months' pregnant) following the Annunciation, as related by Luke (1:39–41).

CHRISTIANITY & THE BIBLE: THE NEW TESTAMENT

Christianity shares part of its heritage with Judaism, for both traditions regard the Biblical texts collectively known as the Old Testament as sacred. Yet Judaism and Christianity disagree on a fundamental point: while Jewish people are still awaiting their messiah, Christians believe that he has already manifested himself as Jesus Christ, whose life story and teaching are related in the second part of the Bible, the New Testament. Therefore, the symbolism of Christianity is drawn primarily from the inspirational life of its savior, who led by example and died an agonizing death to redeem humanity.

PRINCIPAL FIGURES

Jesus Christ   *See* opposite.

The Virgin Mary   *See* page 76.

Joseph   A carpenter of Nazareth who married the Virgin Mary and acted as a foster father to the infant Jesus. Joseph is usually portrayed as an older man carrying a staff. *See Adoration of the Kings* (pages 104–05).

Zacharias and Elisabeth   The parents of John the Baptist were so elderly when he was conceived that their evident old age is the clue to their identity in paintings; the Archangel Gabriel is also sometimes shown delivering the news of John's amazing conception.

John the Baptist   John the Baptist was Jesus's cousin, the son of Elisabeth and Zacharias and an ascetic Nazarene who preached the coming of the messiah and is therefore known as the "Precursor." He baptised Jesus, among others, in the River Jordan. John the Baptist was eventually beheaded on the orders of Herod Antipas. He is usually portrayed as a thin, scruffy figure wearing a camel-hair or sheepskin shirt and carrying a cross-shaped staff, sometimes adorned with a lamb (representing Christ), or with a lamb in the vicinity.

Below: John the Baptist carries the cruciform staff that is one of his symbolic attributes in del Verrochio and da Vinci's The Baptism of Christ *(c. 1472–75).*

Jesus Christ

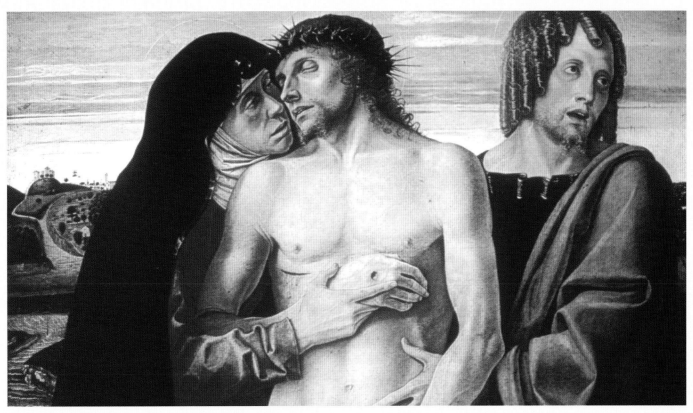

Above: *Bellini's* Pietà with the Virgin and Saint John *(1470) depicts Jesus's body being supported by his mother and John the Evangelist following his crucifixion.*

Christ's incarnation as a human being is celebrated on Christmas Day, December 25, and his birth in a stable in Bethlehem is commemorated in sacred art as the Nativity. Watched over by his mother, the infant Jesus lies in a straw-lined manger, closely regarded by an ox (a creature of service and self-sacrifice, which, like the bull, is an ancient symbol of strength), who "knoweth his owner," and who warms the child with his breath, and an ass (which is said to know its master's crib). The three Magi ("wise men" or "kings") are usually depicted kneeling before the child. The shepherds, too, whom an angel apprised of the divine birth, are present as a reference to Christ's future role as the Good Shepherd who gathers his lost sheep into a single flock. *See Adoration of the Kings*, pages 104–05.

Many other scenes from Christ's life have been depicted artistically, including his baptism in the River Jordan by John the Baptist, his miraculous feats of healing, his entry into Jerusalem (commemorated with palm leaves on Palm Sunday) or the Last Supper that Christ shared with his disciples (*see* pages 110–13). However, along with the Nativity, the image of the Crucifixion is paramount both in religious and symbolic terms. In such images, Christ is depicted in his agony, nailed to the cross, wearing the crown of thorns and bleeding from his five wounds. The letters INRI (the Latin abbreviation for "Jesus of Nazareth, king of the Jews") may be inscribed on a scroll above his head. At his feet, the three Marys—the Virgin Mary; Mary, the mother of James; and Mary Magdalene—may be shown in deep mourning with Saint John, called "the beloved disciple." In many Christian traditions, the events of Christ's Passion and death, collectively termed the Stations of the Cross, are depicted in fourteen pictorial images that hang on church walls.

After his Crucifixion (which is mourned by Christians on Good Friday; *see* pages 114–15), Christ rose miraculously from the dead and joined God, the Father, in heaven (his Resurrection being celebrated on Easter Sunday).

Jesus Christ Clues

babe in arms

cross

crown of thorns

five wounds

halo

lamb

blessing gesture

simple clothing

As Featured In:

Bartholomäus Bruyn the Elder, *The Temptations of Christ* (pages 106–07)

Giotto di Bondoni, *The Raising of Lazarus from the Dead* (pages 108–09)

The Virgin Mary

Above: *Da Vinci's* Madonna of the Rocks *(c. 1491–1508) depicts a scene that does not occur in the New Testament: the meeting of (from left to right) John the Baptist, the Virgin Mary, Jesus and the Archangel Uriel during the Flight into Egypt.*

The New Testament tells how God chose the Virgin Mary to bear his child by immaculate conception, sending the Archangel Gabriel to inform her of her divine mission. In artistic representations of this Annunciation, Mary usually wears a blue cloak (*see* page 102), which symbolizes compassion, fidelity and the waters of baptism, as well as a veil symbolizing her modesty. As the white dove that represents the Holy Spirit hovers above, signifying the divine presence, Gabriel holds his messenger's staff, which often takes the form of a lily—a symbol of purity.

Mary has a unique status: the mother of God's son was herself immaculately conceived and therefore free of original sin, and after her death, her body ascended to heaven (known as the Assumption). She is deeply revered by many Christians, and her symbols include the halo, veil and the blue cloak under which she provides shelter for the faithful (as the Lady of Mercy, *Maria Misericord*). As the Lady of Sorrows (*Maria Dolorosa*), her breast is pierced by seven swords. Other potent images of Mary include those known generically as the Virgin and Child, and *La Pietà* (Lady of Pity), who sorrows over the crucified body of Christ, which lies in her lap.

As Christianity spread throughout the world, the attributes of various pagan goddesses came to be identified with Mary in her status as the primary female figure of Christianity. Thus the crescent moon, the lunar symbol of mother goddesses, and also of chaste goddesses like the Greek Artemis (the Roman Diana), as well as such symbolically associated creatures as the pure-white unicorn and swan, became her attributes. A scallop shell similar to that on which the sea-born Greek goddess Aphrodite (the Roman Venus) floated ashore, which contains the "sacred pearl" (Christ) may also represent Mary. As queen of heaven, she may be crowned with the stars (*see* page 126) that symbolized the Mesopotamian mother goddess Ishtar and the West Semitic Astarte, an association extended to the starfish (for Mary is also called *Stella Maris*—"Star of the Sea"). The thornless white rose, which was a Greco–Roman symbol of love sacred to Aphrodite and Venus, is another symbol of Mary, who is called "the Mystical Rose of Heaven." One of the leading instruments of devotional meditation—the rosary, or *rosarium*—is thus a Marian symbol of Christianity (although it is also a feature of many other religions). Traditionally, the rosary consists of fifty or 150 small beads strung together into a circle and divided by larger beads into five or fifteen "decades," each of which represents a major event that marked Mary's life. When at prayer, each small bead indicates the recitation of the *Ave Maria* ("Hail Mary"), and the larger beads, the *Gloria* and *Pater Noster* ("Our Father") prayers.

Right: *The Virgin and Child: detail from an icon of the Orthodox Church.*

The Virgin Mary Clues

blue mantle

veil

white lily

white rose

halo

rosary

stars

As Featured In:

Benedetto Bonfigli, *The Annunciation to Mary and St. Luke the Evangelist* (pages 102–03)

Filippino Lippi, *The Adoration of the Kings* (pages 104–05)

Andrea Mantegna, *Crucifixion of Christ* (pages 114-15)

Hans Memling, *Altar of the Last Judgment from St. Mary's Church, Gdansk* (pages 116-18)

Albrecht Dürer, *The All Saints' Picture* (pages 119-21)

Above: An ointment-containing vessel (seen here at left in Titian's The Penitent Saint Mary Magdalene, 1565) *is a traditional symbol of the saint who anointed Jesus's feet.*

Mary Magdalene Mary Magdalene was a devoted follower of Jesus, whose identity is linked with that of Mary of Madgala, whose devils Jesus exorcised; Mary of Bethany, the sister of Martha and Lazarus; and a repentant prostitute. Because the latter two figures both washed and anointed Jesus's feet, Mary is depicted in art with a jar containing ointment and with her hair flowing loose. She is often portrayed in the presence of the newly risen Christ in so-called *noli me tangere* (Latin for "don't touch me") scenes, sometimes wearing red, as a "scarlet woman." *See* The Raising of Lazarus from the Dead *(pages 108–09) and* The Crucifixion of Christ *(pages 114–15).*

The Magi The three Magi ("wise men," also called "kings"), Caspar, Melchior and Balthazar, who had been alerted to Christ's impending birth by a moving star and traveled from their Eastern lands to worship the newborn king, are often pictured kneeling in adoration before the child, bearing their costly gifts. Their coming is celebrated at Epiphany (twelfth night), on January 6. *See Adoration of the Kings, pages 104-05.*

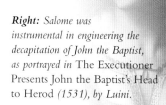

Right: Salome was instrumental in engineering the decapitation of John the Baptist, as portrayed in The Executioner Presents John the Baptist's Head to Herod *(1531), by Luini.*

Salome The daughter of Herodias and Herod Philip I, Salome gained Herod Antipas, her great-uncle and the son of Herod the Great, as a stepfather when her mother remarried. Encouraged by her mother, who objected to John the Baptist's denunciation of her second marriage as adulterous, Salome asked for the saint's head as a reward for pleasing Herod Antipas with her dancing.

St. Paul As the rabbi Saul of Tarsus, Paul persecuted Christians until converted to Christianity by a vision on the road to Damascus. Thereafter, he worked as a missionary and theologian of the early Christian Church. He may be depicted with a scroll or with the sword of his martyrdom.

Below: Caravaggio painted more than one scene depicting the conversion of St. Paul. In this 1600 painting the saint is stunned and prostrate, blinded by divine light.

THE EVANGELISTS & APOSTLES

The authors of the Gospels, the evangelists Matthew, Mark, Luke and John (of whom Matthew and John were also apostles) may be represented by (usually winged) tetramorphs ("four signs"), whose images are drawn from descriptions in the Biblical books of Ezekiel and Revelations: Matthew's is a man; Mark's, a lion; Luke's, an ox; and John's, an eagle. Christ's twelve apostles, the foremost disciples, also have their own symbols. *See also The Last Supper*, pages 110–13.

Mark   A disciple of St. Peter and the author of the Gospel of St. Mark, Mark's primary symbol is the winged lion, one of the four tetramorphs.

Luke   A Gentile Christian and physician who composed the Gospel of St. Luke, and whose symbol is a winged ox. *See The Annunciation to Mary and Saint Luke the Evangelist*, pages 102–03.

Peter   Once a fisherman, Peter was the leader of the apostles who denied Christ three times. He may be represented by the crossed gold and silver keys to the gates of the kingdom of heaven (since he was the first bishop of Rome, this is also, by extension, the symbol of the papacy). Further of Peter's symbols include fish and fishing accouterments, a cock, chains and an inverted cross (because he was crucified upside down).

Matthew   As an erstwhile collector of taxes, Matthew (also called Levi) may be represented by a purse. As an evangelist, he is symbolized by a man, usually winged, as well as by a scroll or book. And because he was martyred, another of his attributes is a sword.

Below: St. Thomas is also known as "Doubting Thomas" because it was only when he touched Christ's wounds, illustrated here by Caravaggio in 1597, that he believed in the Resurrection.

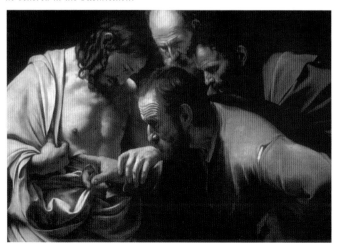

Above: *Judas is identified in Caravaggio's* The Capture of Christ *(c. 1600) by his yellow robe and his symbolic gesture of betrayal, the kiss that sealed Jesus's fate.*

John the Evangelist   John, the son of Zebedee and younger brother of James the Greater, was a fisherman by occupation. As the author of a gospel (and the Book of Revelation), John's symbol is an eagle. He may also be represented by a chalice containing snakes, for he was said to have drunk poison and to have survived unscathed.

Andrew   As a fisherman, the brother of Peter may be identified by a fishing net. He is said to have been crucified on an "X"-shaped cross, which is why Andrew may alternatively be symbolized by a saltire cross.

Bartholomew   Bartholomew was skinned alive and crucified, which is why his primary symbol is a flaying knife.

James the Greater   A son of Zebedee, a fisherman and the older brother of John, James the Greater may be symbolized by the sword with which he was martyred, or else by a pilgrim's staff and clothing and scallop shells.

James the Less   James the Less led the Christians in Jerusalem and was stoned and bludgeoned to death with a fuller's club, which has become his attribute.

Simon the Zealot   Simon the Zealot is said to have suffered martyrdom in Persia either by being sawn in half, which is why he is typically represented by a saw, or by having his throat cut.

Thomas   Also called Didymus, Thomas was nicknamed "Doubting Thomas" because he initially doubted Christ's Resurrection. Because he is said to have been invited to construct a palace for King Gondophorus of India, Thomas may be represented by a set square or T-square.

Jude/Thaddeus Jude, who is also known as Thaddeus or as Judas Thaddaeus, is said to have been martyred alongside Simon the Zealot in Persia, and his symbolic attribute is consequently the weapon that caused his death, which may be depicted as a lance, spear or club.

Philip Philip was present when Jesus fed the five thousand, which is why he may be symbolized by loaves of bread. Because he was crucified, he may also be represented by a cross.

Judas Iscariot The apostle who betrayed Jesus in the Garden of Gethsemene, Judas may be symbolized by his kiss; by coins or the moneybag containing the "blood money" that he accepted in return for identifying Jesus; by his yellow cloak; by the presence of a demon on his shoulder; or by the rope with which he later hanged himself.

Matthias As a result of Judas Iscariot's treachery, Matthias is often named as the twelfth apostle instead. Matthias is symbolized by the instrument of his martyrdom, which may be a lance, ax or halberd.

POPULAR SAINTS

Those who have been canonized as saints by the Roman Catholic Church may be symbolized by those attributes that made them holy: St. Francis, for example, by his stigmata (the bloody marks of Christ's Passion). Martyrs (those who died for their faith) may be represented by the instruments of their torture or death, such as the wheel on which the body of St. Catherine of Alexandria was broken. *See also The All Saints' Picture*, pages 119–21.

Right: *Titian's fresco of 1523 shows St. Christopher carrying the infant Jesus across a river.*

Christopher
According to legend, Christopher was a huge Canaanite who carried the Christ child across a river. Amazed by the infant's increasing weight, he nevertheless struggled on in order to convey his "passenger" safely to the opposite bank. Christopher was finally martyred in Lycia, but is typically depicted in art as the "bearer of Christ" (which is what the Greek name, Christopher, means).

Francis of Assisi An Italian monk who founded the Franciscan order in Assisi. Having become a hermit, the crucified Christ appeared to him and he developed stigmata. He is typically depicted in the robes of a monk, with a cord around his waist, whose three knots represent poverty, chastity and obedience, and with visible stigmata, often accompanied by birds.

Below, left: The Mystic Marriage of St. Catherine *(c. 1526–27), by Correggio, portrays St. Catherine dedicating herself exclusively to Jesus.*
Below: *The Italian artist Sassetta (1394–1450) painted this image of St. Francis as part of an altarpiece (c. 1437–44).*

For **George** see St. George, pages 178–79. For **Catherine of Alexandria**, **Agnes** and **Dorothy** see The All Saints' Picture, pages 119–21.

Nicholas   St. Nicholas was an Anatolian bishop of Myra, in Lycia, who has become associated with Santa Claus. As well as being depicted as a bearded, crosier-carrying bishop, Nicholas may be symbolized by the three money-bags that he gave to a trio of young women as dowries to save them from prostitution, as well as by an anchor, for he is said to have carried out miracles at sea.

Cecilia   Three blows to her neck failed to decapitate this Roman virgin martyr, and it was three days before she died in defense of her faith. Cecilia may be depicted with a musical instrument—usually an organ—for she is said to have made music on the way to her death.

Jerome   One of the four Latin doctors of the Church, Jerome was born in Dalmatia, converted in Rome and spent three years as a hermit in the Syrian desert. Back in Rome, he translated the Bible from Greek into Latin. He is often portrayed in the desert; removing a thorn from a lion's paw; or composing his Vulgate version of the Bible.

Below: Da Vinci has depicted St. Jerome as a hermit, performing his three-year penance in the Syrian desert.

Above: Titian's exquisite rendering of St. Margaret of Antioch shows her taming a dragon with the crucifix she clasps.

Margaret (or Marina) of Antioch   Born in Antioch, Margaret was a shepherdess who converted to Christianity. Imprisoned for refusing to break her vow of chastity, she was devoured by a dragon while praying, but cut her way out of its stomach with her crucifix. She was later tortured and decapitated. Margaret is generally depicted holding a crucifix and in control of a dragon. *See also Portrait of Giovanni Arnolfini and his Wife*, detail, page 188.

Agatha   A virgin who rejected the advances of Quintian, the prefect of Sicily, who ordered that her breasts be ripped off with a pair of pincers. She died after being dragged across red-hot coals. Agatha is generally portrayed holding pincers or a platter bearing her severed breasts.

Barbara   Barbara was imprisoned in a tower by her pagan father, Discorus, and converted to Christianity. A virgin martyr, she was tortured on the orders of her father; when she was finally beheaded, a bolt of lightning struck him dead. Barbara is usually symbolized by a tower with three windows (denoting the Holy Trinity).

Sebastian   The Italian commander of the Praetorian Guard under Diocletian, Sebastian was a Christian convert who was condemned to death by being pierced by arrows (which is how he is most often portrayed). Having survived this onslaught, he subsequently had the life beaten out of him and was thrown into a drain.

Lucy   A Sicilian virgin martyr who was executed by being stabbed in the throat with a sword. She may be depicted with this weapon, but is more often portrayed holding her eyes on a plate, for it is said that either her torturer or she herself gouged out her eyeballs.

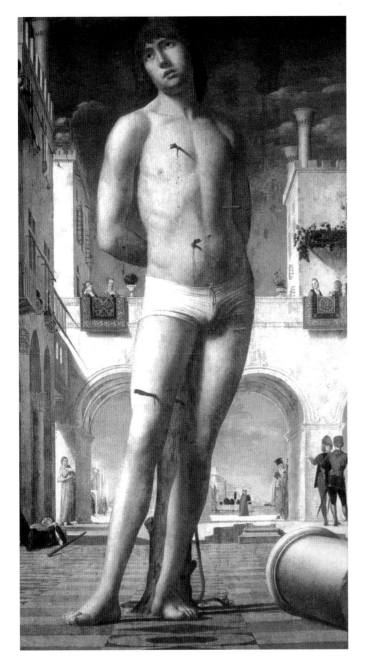

Above: The Emperor Diocletian punished St. Sebastian for his Christianity by ordering that arrows be fired into his body, as illustrated here by da Messina (c. 1475–76). *Below:* The Burial of St. Lucy, by Caravaggio (1608), shows the virgin martyr being laid to rest after having been set alight and stabbed in the throat.

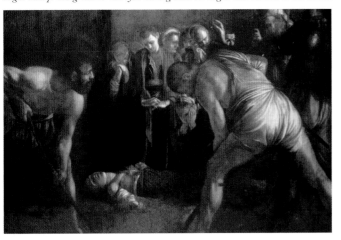

CHRISTIAN SYMBOLS

Cross   Although all of the instruments associated with Christ's suffering and death, such as the lance with which his side was pierced, the nails that attached his feet and hands to the cross or the crown of thorns (which, when depicted crowning a skull, signifies eternal damnation) are symbolic of Christ's Passion, it is the cross on which he hung that has become the leading symbol of Christianity. The Latin cross, which can also be equated with the tree of life, may either bear an image of Christ, symbolizing his self-sacrifice for humanity, or may be "empty," representing his Resurrection. Many other variants of the cross have also evolved, including the shepherd's cross—whose apex takes the form of a shepherd's crook—which symbolizes Christ as the Good Shepherd (and has associations with Osiris's scepter) and the cross fitchy, which terminates in a sword, representing willingness to fight for the Christian faith. Jesus's halo is sometimes depicted enclosing a cross (*see* page 108).

Fish and Labarum   The cross was not adopted as an emblem of Christianity until the Council of Constantinople in AD 692; until then, it was considered too graphic to be used as a symbol; additionally, this sign would instantly identify Christians for persecution by their Roman enemies. Thus the two earliest symbols of Christ and Christianity were the fish, which identified the secret meeting places of Christians in the Roman catacombs, and the labarum.

The use of the fish as a Christian symbol has many interpretations: not only did Christ call his disciples "fishers of men," but the Christian fathers termed the faithful *pisculi* ("fish"). Furthermore, besides representing baptism with blessed water, the Greek word for fish, *ichthus*, is an acrostic of the Greek term "Jesus Christ, Son of God, Savior" (*Iesous Christos, Theou Huios, Soter*).

The use of the labarum (also known as the monogram of Christ, the Chrismon, the Christogram, the *chi-rho* and Constantine's Cross) traditionally dates from AD 312, when, on the eve of the Battle of Milvean Bridge, the Roman emperor Constantine saw a vision of a cross in the sky accompanied by the Latin words *in hoc signo vinces* ("with this sign comes victory"). Having placed the symbol on his army's shields, Constantine was victorious, whereupon he became a Christian and adopted the *chi-rho* (so called because the letters from which it is composed, *chi* (X) and *rho* (P) are the first letters of the Greek spelling of Jesus Christ) as his emblem.

Above: *Jesus' earthly role was to protect and heal his "flock," and He is often portrayed with a symbolic lamb, as in this detail of a painting by Leonardo da Vinci.* **Left:** *Raphael's beautiful painting* The Miraculous Draught of Fishes *(1515) depicts the disciples pulling in their nets, burdened with a multitude of fishes where earlier they had found none. The painting was a cartoon for a tapestry created early in the sisxteenth century.*

Agnus Dei Other important symbols of Christ include the *agnus dei*, the Latin for "lamb of god," as John the Baptist (whose emblem is also the lamb) called Christ. As well as being a symbol of innocence, the lamb was sacrificed in Jewish rituals as a symbolic washing-away of sin, and can thus be identified clearly with Christ. The lamb is frequently depicted in association with the banner of the Resurrection, a red cross on a white background.

Further creatures with which Christ may be symbolically equated are the **pelican** (*see also* page 140), which, it was said, selflessly tore open its breast in order to feed its young, and the **dolphin** (*see also* page 142), which was believed to guide the drowning to safety.

Halo All holy figures, including angels and saints, are depicted in sacred Christian art with haloes (aureoles, or nimbi) above their heads. Originally the attributes of pagan solar gods symbolizing sun rays, in the Christian context, haloes represent sanctity or enlightenment. Although the generic halo is a golden disk or rayed corona, God's halo sometimes has a triangular or diamond shape; Christ's may assume that of a cross; and those of living people, such as the pope, may be square (symbolizing the earth). Holiness may also be indicated symbolically by the almond-shaped mandorla (or *vesica pisces*) that surrounds the whole body, representing both the cloud upon which Christ ascended into heaven and the fish that is his symbol. *See also The Raising of Lazarus from the Dead, pages 108–09.*

The Holy Trinity Although God may sometimes be depicted in human form as a wise elder, iconography has traditionally shrunk from attempting to personify the Creator. While Christ is depicted in his humanity, and the Holy Spirit as a dove, God, the Father, is regarded as being intangible. Although he may be represented by a ray of light (signifying enlightenment), or as the divine eye that sees all, the most important aniconic symbol of God is that of the Holy Trinity (the Father, Son and Holy Ghost), which may take the form of an equilateral triangle, three interlocked circles or the trefoil. *See also The All Saints Picture (pages 119–121).*

Satan and his Demons If Christ is the embodiment of good, evil is personified in the form of Satan (his devilish adversary), who tempted Christ three times, and with whom Christ continues to wage war for the salvation of human souls. In this battle, Christ may be represented as the solar eagle, and Satan, as the chthonic serpent. Damned souls will be consigned to the fiery realms of hell, where they will endure eternally the torture of the Devil's demonic minions, which, like their master, are depicted as hideous, hybrid creatures, with the goatlike nether regions, including cloven hooves and tails, that symbolize God's enemies. *See also The Temptations of Christ, pages 106–07, Altar of the Last Judgment from St. Mary's Church, Gdansk, pages 116–18, and The Witches' Sabbath, pages 174–75.*

ISLAM

Although Islamic tradition accepts such Judeo–Christian prophets as Moses (Musa) and Jesus Christ ('Isa) as messengers (*nabi*, or *rasul*) of God's word, Muslims believe that they were merely the precursors of Muhammad, the only true prophet, for it was he who was the mouthpiece of Allah ("He who is God") in giving humanity the sacred words of the Qur'an, and he who established the Islamic *din* ("way of life," or "religion"). In obedience to his ban on idolatry, Allah is never represented in any form in Islamic art. Islam shares the Jewish and Christian hierarchies of angels (including the fallen angel Lucifer, whom Christians call Satan and Muslims Iblis, or Shaytan), and these are also represented with haloes and wings (*see page 71*).

After Muhammad's death, Islam split into two: the Sunnis chose Muhammad's companion, Abu Bakr, as their spiritual leader, or caliph, and today they follow those of Muhammad's customs (*sunna*) contained in six texts called the Hadith. The Shi'as (Shi'ites) instead elected Ali, Muhammad's cousin and son-in-law, as their imam. A further tradition, known as Sufism, evolved later. Sufism is characterized by the desire for mystical communion with Allah through such techniques as fasting, or the ecstatic dancing of the "whirling dervishes."

MUHAMMAD

Muhammad (*c.* 570–*c.* 632) was born in Mecca, Arabia, into the family of Quaraysh, the hereditary guardians of the Ka'bah shrine of Mecca. He was orphaned at the age of six and was subsequently trained as a merchant by his uncle before entering the service of the wealthy widow Khadijah, whom he subsequently married. In a society in which Jewish, Christian and other, polytheistic, religious traditions were practiced, Muhammad felt himself compelled to discover the true nature of Allah, and frequently retired to a cave in Mount Hira (Jabal al-Nur, "the Mountain of Light") to contemplate this question. Here, in about AD 610, he received his first instructions from Allah—now enshrined in the Qur'an—which the illiterate Muhammad continued to receive until his death, dictating the sacred words via his companions to scribes. Among Allah's instructions were that idols should not be worshipped and that the wealthy should share their riches with their poorer brethren.

Following this, the first revelation, Muhammad spread the word of Allah, but by 622 (by which time Khadijah and his uncle had died), the preaching of the now impecunious Muhammad that there was no god but Allah had become unpopular among the polytheistic Meccans. Thus he was

Above: The Hejira, Muhammad's epic spiritual journey, is central to Islamic belief.

forced to migrate to Yathrib (later renamed Medina, "the City of the Prophet"), whose sympathetic inhabitants (*ansar*—"the helpers") had invited him to mediate in their feuds. (Muhammad's migration to Yathrib is called the hejira and marks the beginning of the Muslim lunar calendar.) From 623, Muhammad and his followers waged a holy war (jihad) against those hostile to Islam, notably the citizens of Mecca. After six years of warfare, during which Muhammad was himself wounded, he captured Mecca in 629, promptly rededicating the Ka'bah to Allah. Having subsequently spread Islam throughout most of Arabia, the prophet made his final pilgrimage to Mecca and Mount Arafat in 632, whereafter he died and was buried at his mosque in Medina.

Muhammad is not now depicted in figurative art, but because he was a historical personage, his human form was once shown in manuscripts only, with his face hidden behind a veil. The scenes of Muhammad's life that were illustrated in this way include the descent of the Archangel Gabriel (Jibr'il) to the cave in Mount Hira and his exhortation to Muhammad to "recite [*iqra*] in the name of Allah." Muhammad is generally depicted wearing a green mantle and encompassed by a fiery halo in artistic representations of such momentous events as his night journey from Mecca to Temple Mount (Haram) in Jerusalem, from which he ascended through the seven heavens into the presence of Allah. Thus the Dome of the Rock that was erected later on Temple Mount is one of the most sacred sites of Islam, and the rock is said to bear the imprint of Muhammad's footstep. Nearby is the Masjid al-Aqsa mosque, where it is believed that humans will be judged on the Day of Judgment.

MECCA

The most sacred city in Islam is Mecca, where the cube-shaped Ka'bah, toward which Muslims must turn when praying, stands within the al-Masjid al-Haram mosque. *See The Ka'bah in Mecca* (pages 122–23).

THE FIVE PILLARS OF ISLAM

The five pillars of Islam regulate Muslim life. The first pillar is the affirmation of faith contained in the text of the Shahada: "There is no god but Allah and Muhammad is his messenger" (the words embroidered on the *kiswa*, the cloth that covers the Ka'bah, which also introduce the daily call to prayer, the *adhan*). The second is Salat—the five daily prayers (at dawn, midday, afternoon, sunset and evening). Fasting during the month of Ramadan—Sawm—is the third pillar, and a reminder of those who live in poverty, while giving alms to the poor forms the fourth pillar, Zakat. The fifth pillar is the Hajj (*see* below). The five pillars may be symbolized in the form of a human hand, known as the Hand of Fatima (Muhammad's daughter by Khadijah), which may also represent the hand of Allah—itself a Shi'ite symbol.

The Hajj Making a pilgrimage—Hajj—to Mecca during Dhu al-Hijja, the twelfth month of the Islamic calendar, at least once during one's lifetime is the fifth of the five pillars of Islam that regulate Muslim life. On entering the al-Masjid al-Haram mosque through the Gate of Peace, pilgrims (who must wear a white cloth, the *ihram*, indicating their purity) enter the sacred area around the Ka'bah, the al-Mataf. There they perform the *tawaf*, circling the Ka'bah and the Multazam—the wall adjoining it—seven times (the number of perfection) in a counterclockwise direction. Leaving by the Gate of al-Safa, they run back and forth between the hillocks of al-Safa and al-Marwa (Mounts Cana and Marnia) seven times, recalling Hagar's quest for water. On the eighth day of their pilgrimage, they must travel to the Mount of Mercy (Arafat) to present themselves before Allah.

Below: The Mosque of Mecca *is a detail from the* Dehail oul Khairat, *an eighteenth-century miniature, showing the sacred Ka'bah at the center.*

SIGNIFICANT SYMBOLS

The Mosque Ideally, Muslims should perform their five daily prayers at the mosque (*masjid*, "place of prostration"), to which they are called from the minaret, the tower that flanks it, by the muezzin. Before entering, worshippers must purify themselves by washing in a fountain within the courtyard that encloses the mosque. The architecture of the mosque reflects a symbolic cosmic pattern: its square base represents the earth, its dome (if built in domical form), the celestial realm, and its minaret (which may be regarded as an axis mundi) and internal columns (if it is a hypostyle mosque), the soaring desire for unity with Allah. After cleansing themselves, Muslims enter the mosque to perform their prayers. They must face Mecca as they worship Allah, and the direction (*qibla*) is indicated by the *mihrab* (the empty niche that focuses the mind on Allah, which may also symbolize the cave at Mount Hira). The *mihrab*, the *minbar* (the pulpit from which the preacher, the *khatib*, delivers his sermon on Friday, the day of assembly) and the *kursi*, the stand on which the Qur'an is placed, usually comprise the mosque's only furnishings. Worshippers prostrate themselves on the carpeted floor, or on the individual prayer mats (*sajjada*) that symbolize a clean space, which may be decorated with vegetative or geometric designs in a style similar to that of the walls.

Decorative Art In accordance with the proscription on representing human figures (thus competing with Allah as Creator), the usual forms of sacred Islamic decorative art include the beautiful, flowing Arabic calligraphy (of which there are many styles) that spells out the sacred texts from the Qur'an. Abstract geometric patterns and floral and vegetal arabesques may also decorate the fretwork, tiles, mosaics and textiles of the mosque, symbolizing the sacred laws of nature and the Garden of Paradise respectively. *See also The Ka'bah in Mecca*, pages 122–23.

Above: An Islamic miniature showing ritual ablutions before prayer against a background of floral and geometric designs typical of mosque ornamentation.

Above: The many calligraphic traditions in Islam include the naskhi *and* rukah *styles; reproduced here is an example of Kufic script, which is characterized by both its elaborate decorative beauty and its formal composition. Through such exquisite calligraphy, the writer is praising and amplifying the beauty of Allah's message to Muslims.* **Below:** *The* hilal, *or star and crescent, is today the universal symbol of the Islamic religious community.*

The Hilal Although not directly linked with Muhammad, the symbol most closely associated with Islam today is the *hilal*, or star and crescent, which represents sovereignty and divinity, as well as concentration, openness and victory. The adoption of this symbol is traditionally believed to derive from the waxing moon whose brilliant light saved Byzantium from the attack of Philip of Macedon in 339 BC. Thereupon, the grateful citizens of Constantinople (Istanbul) adopted the crescent moon of Diana as their civic symbol (when the city became Christian in 30 BC, the symbol became associated with the Virgin Mary). Sultan Osman had a vision of a crescent moon before his conquest of the lands now known as Turkey in 1299, and it became the emblem of his Ottoman dynasty, to whose scion, Mehmed II, Constantinople fell in 1453. The star was added to the crescent moon in 1793 by Sultan Selim III (possibly because the Ka'bah is said to lie directly beneath the Pole Star), its points being set at five in 1844. From its origins as a dual symbol of the city of Constantinople and of the Ottoman sultans—the secular leaders of the Islamic world who made it their capital—the hilal evolved into a universal symbol of Islam.

The Gods Worship Devi

c.1860, gouache on paper, Sri Partap Singh Museum, Srinagar, Kashmir, India

Painted in the vibrant, jewel-like colors that are characteristic of the Basohli manner, a Pahari-school style that developed in the Indian foothills of the Himalayas from the late seventeenth century, this miniature painting depicts four of Hinduism's most important deities: Brahma, Vishnu, Shiva, and Devi ("Goddess" in Sanskrit, or Mahadevi, "Great Goddess").

The three male gods—Brahma ("the Creator"), Vishnu ("the Preserver"), and Shiva ("the Destroyer")—portrayed here gratefully paying homage to Devi are collectively called the trimurti (Sanskrit for "having three forms"), a trinity that is believed to represent the three main aspects of brahman, the divine reality of the universe, namely creation, preservation, and destruction. Yet it was local fertility goddesses who were worshipped before Aryan invaders introduced these male Vedic gods to the Indus Valley, and the celebration of Devi's supreme triumph reflects the hold that female divinity retained on the Indian psyche—one so powerful that it could not be suppressed. Add the influence of Tantrism to this melting pot of sacred beliefs, and goddesses are considered the shaktis ("powers"), or incarnated female creative energies, of the gods. In Tantrism, Devi is regarded as the shakti of Shiva, but it is also told that all of the gods had a hand in bringing her into being, for when only a female force could defeat the buffalo demon Mahisha, the waves of aggressive energy that radiated from the minds of the gods combined and took shape to form the goddess Durga, who, armed with their weapons (symbols of their special powers), leapt onto a lion, charged at the demon, and mercilessly beheaded him. Durga is just one of the wrathful (*krodha*), as opposed to the benevolent (*shanta*), aspects of the Great Goddess; another is Kali, the bloodthirsty black goddess and a shakti of Shiva whose characteristic attributes match many of those detailed in this image.

See also **The Vedic Devas** (pages 62–63), **Major Hindu Goddesses** (page 63).

That Devi is a goddess of both life and death is evident. Her dark skin may represent her terrible, destructive powers, but, like Vishnu's, can signify infinity, while the lotuses that she, along with Brahma and Vishnu, wears in her hair, symbolize cosmic creation.

The corpses of the monstrous demons dispatched by Devi lie in a bloody heap.

Brahma is identifiable by his four heads, with each face pointing in a different cardinal direction. Among other quartets, they can denote the four Vedas, the most sacred of the ancient Hindu scriptures. (Before Shiva destroyed it, Brahma once had a fifth head with which he kept track of the movements of Sarasvati, his skittish shakti.)

Shiva's animal-skin loincloth signals his status as "lord of the beasts," as does the snake that coils around his neck, although it is also present because its venom is an antidote to the poison that Shiva swallowed during the churning of the ocean of milk, which stuck in his throat and turned it blue. His third eye (which signifies transcendental knowledge and can express the god's displeasure by shooting out flames), and the crescent moon (a symbol of both creation and destruction) that adorns his hair, are replicated in the image of Devi.

The trident, Shiva's *trishula*, that Devi grips in her hand, points at his head, indicating that the goddess is the god's feminine energy incarnated.

Vishnu is recognizable by his blue skin (being the color of the endless sky, blue signifies infinity) and crown, which represents authority.

Devi also holds
a bowl (an
attribute of
Shiva, which is
often depicted
as an upturned
human skull) of her victims' blood
in one of her hands; she is literally
bloodthirsty, for she relies on
blood—a symbol of life, as well
as death—for sustenance.

Her sword is also
borrowed from Shiva. As a
weapon, its symbolism is
straightforward: it denotes
the willingness to mount
an aggressive attack in
order to wound or kill.

In her fourth hand,
Devi holds Shiva's
drum, the instrument
with which, as the "lord
of the dance," he marks
the rhythm of life, or else
warns of imminent
destruction.

Matsya

artist unknown

c.1650, materials and location unknown

Of all of the Hindu gods, it is Vishnu, the "Preserver," who has historically been the focus of the artists working in the Central Plains region of India, and the Rajasthani, or Rajput, style that they developed is notably replete with symbolism, partly as an expression of both metaphorical and metaphysical concepts, and partly because the ten different forms of Vishnu's avatars ("descents" in Sanskrit) provide such rich symbolic subject matter. The ten incarnations that Vishnu assumed when he descended to earth to save the cosmos from various evil threats are: the fish, Matsya (1), the tortoise, Kurma (2), the boar, Vahara (3), the man-lion, Narasimha (4), and the dwarf, Vamana (5); the following four were the human heroes Parasurama (6), Rama or Ramachandra (7), Krishna (8), and Buddha (9); while the last, which is yet to come, is the white horse Kalki or Kalkin (10). Scholars believe that this series of avatars partly symbolizes the evolution of life on earth, and partly reflects the types of gods that were worshipped locally before being subsumed within the cult of Vishnu.

This exquisite miniature depicts Vishnu in his first avatar as Matsya, the fish, in which form he descended from the heavens to save humankind (represented by Manu Vaivasvata) from a great flood in a story that has striking parallels with that of Noah in the Old Testament. He also retrieved the Vedas, Hinduism's sacred texts, that the demon Hayagriva had stolen from Brahma as the creator god slept. It is the latter strand of the tale that an unknown artist has focused on here in illustrating the moment when Matsya, having tracked Hayagriva down to the depths of the ocean, prepares to kill the demon and recover the Vedas.

See also **The Vedic Devas** (pages 62–63), **Fish** (page 142).

Vishnu grasps one of his traditional attributes in each of his four hands.

The lotus signifies creation, for, encouraged by the light of the sun, it bursts into beautiful life and flowers within apparently lifeless, muddy waters.

Vishnu's gold-colored robe symbolizes the Vedas.

As Matsya, Vishnu is depicted emerging from the mouth of a fish, perhaps to make it clear that his piscine avatar serves merely as a convenient vehicle for his mission. Indeed, his blue skin, denoting endlessness, and his magnificent crown, signifying supreme authority, make this figure's true self unambiguously clear.

The conch shell (*shankha*) represents the waters and sound (*Om*) of creation, and particularly the feminine creative principle, as well as having a practical purpose as a war trumpet.

The disk, or chakra (which can serve as a weapon), represents the sun, and thus identifies Vishnu as the sustainer of life.

The *gada*, a mace or club, has multiple symbolism, denoting both Vishnu's authority as the maintainer of universal stability and his knowledge (while it can be equated with a thunderbolt, its form is alternatively thought to have been derived from a human skull mounted atop a thigh bone). It is also a phallic symbol, symbolizing his masculine energy.

Although Hayagriva has attempted to disguise his true identity by hiding in a shell, his horns make him instantly recognizable as a demon. The Sanskrit name Hayagriva can be translated as "Horseneck," and he is therefore sometimes depicted as a horse, or else with a tiny horse nestling in his hair.

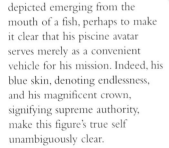

In his incarnation as a fish, Vishnu tows Manu Vaivasvata's vessel to the safety of a Himalayan peak to wait until the flood has subsided before hunting down Hayagriva. The dry land illustrated here signifies that the floodwaters are falling, and that for humankind, the crisis is over.

श्रीगंणिसाय १
रघुनेद घरै

श्रीगंणिसाय २
स्यांम्बेद छै

श्रीगंणिसाय ३
जुरुजबेद६

श्रीगंणिसाय ४
अर्थबरावे

Padmasambhava

unknown date, wall painting, Bodnath Stupa, near Kathmandu, Nepal

This colorful painting by an unknown artist can be seen at the Bodnath Stupa, a fourteenth-century Buddhist temple in the vicinity of the Nepalese capital of Kathmandu that is the base of the Chini Lama, and that has become a vital focal point for exiled Tibetan Buddhists as both a sacred site and a communal gathering place.

Although it clearly conforms to the Buddhist artistic canon, with the figures depicted being, for instance, portrayed sitting in some of the many asanas (Sanskrit for "mystic positions of the lower limbs"), and making the traditional, stylized hand gestures that are termed mudras ("signs"), the central figure is not Shakyamuni, the Buddha himself, as is so often the case, but a bodhisattva whose distinctive clothing and attributes identify him as Padmasambhava. Bodhisattva means "enlightened essence" in Sanskrit, and is used to describe Buddhist beings who have attained enlightenment, but have chosen to remain on the mortal plane—rather than passing irreversibly beyond it, into the state of nirvana ("extinction")—in order to guide and assist humans, much as certain bodhisattvas did when they were alive. Padmasambhava, for example, was an Indian missionary monk who traveled to Tibet in around AD 750 intent on ensuring that Buddhism, which had been introduced to the remote Himalayan kingdom in AD 640, took root and flourished there. And so it did, largely thanks to his success in incorporating the region's indigenous shamanic deities into the ranks of Buddhism's divinities. It is consequently he who is credited with being largely responsible for creating Lamaism, the form of Mahayana ("Great Vehicle") Buddhism that became, and remains, peculiar to Tibet and Mongolia. Indeed, so revered is Padmasambhava among Tibetans that members of the Nyingma sect venerate their Guru Rinpoche ("Precious Master") as the second Buddha and speak in awe of his eight manifestations, of which Guru Padmasambhava is one.

See also **Buddha** (pages 65–66), **Stupa** (pages 66–67).

In the abhaya mudra, the raised hand signals protection and the dispersal of fear.

Padmasambhava wears the distinctive red headdress that identifies him as the founder of the Nyingma (Red Hat) denomination.

It is common for the Buddha and bodhisattvas to be depicted seated on lotus thrones symbolizing their enlightenment and divinity. In addition, this flower has special significance in relation to Padmasambhava (which means "Lotus Born" in Sanskrit), for in his fourth manifestation the bodhisattva was incarnated as an eight-year-old boy, emerging from a lotus blossom floating on Lake Dhanakosha. In this image, Padmasambhava's lotus throne is supported by the stem of a vigorous lotus plant that has thrust itself upward, above the waters of illusion.

Bodhisattvas are often depicted in "relaxed" pose, as is Padmasambhava here, as well as wearing fine clothes and ostentatious jewelry, all of which serves to highlight their more worldly qualities and sympathies, thereby emphasizing that they are still, in a sense, of this world.

The bodies of Buddhist deities are often surrounded by an aureole, while their heads may be encircled by a halo, or nimbus. The former signifies the flaming light of divinity, while the latter can represent the Buddhist wheel of the law, or dharma chakra.

The bhumiparshsa mudra is called "touching the earth" because Shakyamuni made this gesture with his right hand when he called upon the earth to bear witness to his enlightenment.

The bodhisattva's trident-tipped staff (which Buddhism borrowed from the Hindu god Shiva) is called the *khatvanga*. Its three points signify the "three jewels" of Buddhism, which are the Buddha, dharma (the Buddhist law) and the *sangha* (the enlightened ones). Beneath the trident can be seen a skull and two human heads, a reminder that the khatvanga was probably once a ritualistic shamanic object or weapon that consisted of a human long bone surmounted by a skull.

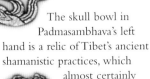

The skull bowl in Padmasambhava's left hand is a relic of Tibet's ancient shamanistic practices, which almost certainly involved human sacrifice and cannibalism.

The *vajra* that Padmasambhava holds in his right hand was originally an attribute of Indra, the Vedic sky god (*see* page 62), and represents a double-ended thunderbolt, which in Buddhist iconography symbolizes the all-conquering, diamond-hard truth that is nirvana.

Tibetan Anuttara-yoga Mandala

artist unknown

date unknown, thangka (fabric painting)

This Tibetan mandala is packed with symbols, many so esoteric that only those who have been initiated into anuttara yoga, or "the unexcelled yoga," may understand their meanings.

Anuttara yoga is the highest of the four levels of Vajrayana ("the Vehicle of the Thunderbolt," or "the Diamond Path"), a tantric branch of Buddhism that dates back to the eighth century and is thought to have been introduced to Tibet from India during the eleventh century, where it assumed some of the characteristics and iconography of both the native Bon system of spiritual belief and the Hindu cult of Shiva. In Tibetan anuttara art, Buddhist bodhisattvas (beings that are roughly equivalent to Christian saints) may consequently be portrayed in wrathful or benevolent form. The tutelary and protective deities known as yidams have particular significance in the teachings of anuttara-yoga tantra, which has three divisions: mother (or wisdom) tantra, which is linked with the deity Chakrasamvara; father (or compassion) tantra, which is associated with Guhyasamaja; and nondual tantra, whose patron deity is Kalachakra; other notable yidams include Hevajra and Vajrayogini. All such male Tibetan Buddhist deities (which denote active energy and compassion) are typically depicted embracing their shaktis (female figures that represent passivity and wisdom) in the *yab-yum* ("father–mother") position.

Visualizing and meditating on the yidams is an important aspect of anuttara yoga, for its practitioners believe that this will help them to achieve nirvana, or enlightenment, which is why they are often represented in mandalas. Diagrammatic aids to meditation, mandalas (also known as yantras in Hinduism) can take many forms, including permanent structures like Buddhist stupas, or temples, and impermanent creations made of sand. This example conforms to the Tibetan thangka (Tibetan for "flat painting") tradition, in that it has been painted on fabric and can be rolled up to facilitate its transport or storage when not in use.

See also **Buddhist Symbols and Systems** (pages 66–67).

Mandala means "circle" in Sanskrit, and the enclosing circle denotes the universe and consciousness.

The petal forms fringing the mandala's inner circle together represent the lotus, as does the eight-petaled floral shape surrounding the mandala's central circle. This flower, one of Buddhism's Eight Symbols of Good Augury, symbolizes purity and perfect enlightenment, as well as being a yoni, or female, symbol in tantric Buddhism.

Certain birds and animals have symbolic significance in Buddhism, and may act as the vehicles of specific gods. The deities portrayed within the yidam's mandala–palace are all associated with him in some way, and may even represent his many different aspects.

The four gates or doorways represent the four entrances to the central deity's "palace" and the four cardinal directions (in Tibetan art, the north is to the right and the south, to the left, the west is at the top, while the east is at the bottom). Each is protected by a guardian deity, which is often depicted in aggressive pose wielding a *vajra*, or the thunderbolt that gives Vajrayana its name, which, in tantric Buddhism, can also be a lingam, or masculine, symbol. The steps to each gate represent the steps that lead to knowledge or nirvana. Each "stairway" resembles the structure of a stupa, which has a spike at its apex (similar to that surmounting the mandala's outer circle) that may symbolize the axis mundi (axis of the world).

The canopies flanking each "stairway" number eight in total. Eight is a significant number in Buddhism, which teaches that there is an "Eightfold Path" to nirvana; the canopy is also one of the Eight Symbols of Good Augury, denoting both protection and sovereign status.

Squares symbolize the earth, as well as the walls of the mandala–palace. The conch shell shown at bottom, right, signifies the sound of Buddha preaching the dharma, or law, and is one of the Eight Symbols of Good Augury.

Although details are not discernible, the yidam at the center of this mandala, and its focal point, is recognizable as such on account of his blue skin. His ferocious demeanor signifies his determination to overcome ignorance and illusion, both obstacles to nirvana. Yidams are usually depicted with multiple heads and arms, each clutching a weapon or accouterment of death, with their shakti clinging to them within a fiery aureole.

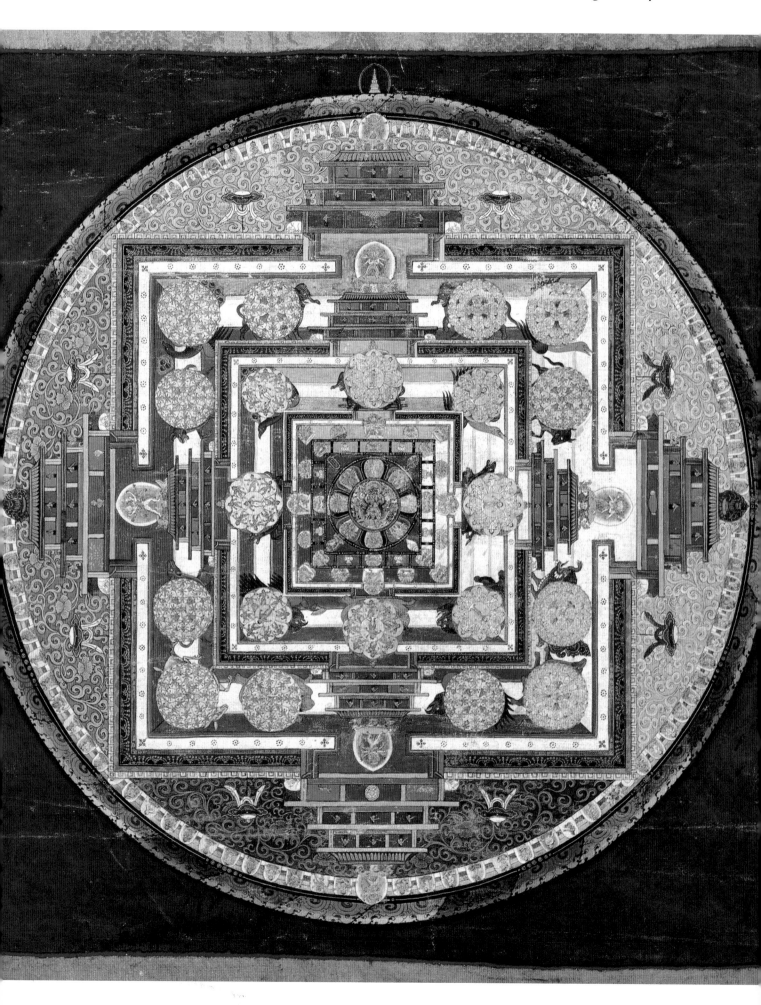

Paradise

Lucas Cranach the Elder

1530, oil on poplar, Gemäldegalerie, Alte Meister, Dresden, Germany

Cranach's interpretation of Adam and Eve's short-lived stay in Paradise is unusual in two respects. Firstly, the German artist has broken with early Christian tradition in disregarding the Judeo–Christian convention that God should not be represented except in symbolic form (as a hand emerging from a cloud, for instance). And, secondly, he has incorporated seven Old Testament scenes into one image, thereby continuing a medieval artistic tradition that enabled a largely illiterate congregation to follow the unfolding details of Biblical stories for themselves. This may initially appear strange to us, but may not seem so alien when you consider that comic strips and graphic novels are its twenty-first-century equivalents.

The story that Cranach has portrayed in paint can be read in the Old Testament Book of Genesis (2:7–3:24) and starts with God's fashioning of Adam from "the dust of the ground," after which he animated the first man and "planted a garden eastward in Eden" for Adam to tend before giving form to every animal and bird, and, finally, creating a woman, whom Adam later named Eve, from Adam's rib to be his companion. The parents of humankind were naked in the Garden of Eden, but because they were innocent beings, this was not a source of shame to them. But Eve, tempted by the serpent, ate the fruit of the tree of the knowledge of good and evil, and then prompted Adam to do the same, whereupon they became aware of their nakedness and, in shame, covered their genitals with fig-leaf aprons. The wily serpent had persuaded Eve to do the one thing that God had expressly forbidden, and although she and Adam did not die as a result, as their creator had threatened, they and their descendants paid a terrible price for their disobedience and original sin: expulsion from Paradise and mortality, pain in childbirth and subordination to her husband for woman, and terrible toil in order to live off the land for man. As for the serpent, it was condemned to crawl on its belly, eating dust, forever after.

See also **Animals** (pages 133–38), **Tree of Knowledge** (page 131), **Snake** (page 141).

God, who is portrayed as a venerable old man with long, gray hair and a flowing beard, forms Adam from clay and breathes life into him.

In addition, although some of the creatures illustrated here are associated with God, Christ or the Christian community (the noble lion, the king of the beasts, for example, as well as sheep, the faithful "flock") and others, with Satan (such as the lustful goat and the deceitful fox), they are nevertheless interacting peacefully with one another here.

Having rendered Adam comatose, God brings Eve into being by removing the rib that will serve as the raw material for her body.

Genesis tells us that while God created "every beast of the field and every fowl of the air," he left it up to Adam to name them. Cranach has emphasized that an ideal state of affairs exists in Paradise by representing fantastic creatures like a unicorn, as well as wild animals—merciless predators elsewhere—coexisting in harmony with creatures that are otherwise their prey.

Yet look hard, and you can see that Cranach has introduced a discordant note by depicting two snarling, black animals engaged in a vicious fight, suggesting that there is trouble brewing in Paradise. If they are bears, they may represent Satan (and they certainly look devilish), as well as anger, evil and cruelty.

Pointing to the tree of the knowledge of good and evil, God prohibits Adam and Eve from tasting its fruit.

The serpent smirks as Eve hands Adam the forbidden fruit that symbolizes temptation, sensual desire and humankind's Fall. That the apple (which is not named in Genesis as the fruit that grew on the tree of knowledge of good and evil) was enduringly tainted by its association with the Fall is reflected in its genus name, *Malus*, which is derived from the Latin word *malum*, which means both "apple" and "evil." That said, the apple also denoted divine wisdom.

Mortified by their nudity, Adam and Eve try to conceal themselves from God, but there is no hiding from the all-seeing creator.

As is traditional, the serpent is depicted with female characteristics, for it and the woman were in cahoots in leading the man astray. Previously a symbol of wisdom, healing and regeneration, its role in the Fall (from God's grace) led the serpent, or snake, to be equated with Satan, evil and temptation.

Brandishing his sword, which represents both power and justice, the Archangel Michael enforces God's will by chasing the sinners from Paradise.

The Destruction of the Golden Calf

Andrea Celesti

1690, oil on canvas, Sala della Quarantia Civil Vecchia, Doge's Palace, Venice, Italy

Whether or not the Italian artist Celesti intentionally included it, there is a subliminal symbol in *The Destruction of the Golden Calf* that strongly alludes to the background to, and significance of, this dramatic scene: the compositional triangle at the center of the painting that has the golden calf at its apex. For the triangle is equated with the pyramid, and the pyramid is a symbol of Pharaonic Egypt, from which the Israelites, led by Moses, had fled in search of the Promised Land prior to the event (described in the Old Testament Book of Exodus 32:19–20) that Celesti has depicted here.

Three months after leaving Egypt, the Israelites arrived in the wilderness of Sinai, where they pitched camp, and Moses ascended Mount Sinai to receive God's instructions. The result was a covenant between God and the Israelites that required the latter to keep Ten Commandments, and, crucially, not to worship any other gods or graven images (Exodus 20:3–5), God additionally specifying, "neither shall ye make unto you gods of gold" (Exodus 20:24). Having secured the Israelites' agreement that they would abide by this covenant, Moses went back up Mount Sinai to receive the "tables [tablets] of stone," where he remained, communing with God, for forty days and forty nights. So prolonged was his absence that the Israelites eventually believed that he was not coming back, prompting them to ask Aaron, Moses's brother, to provide them with an alternative god, and a tangible one. Aaron complied, melting down the Israelites' golden earrings and molding the molten gold into the figure of a calf. Having "offered burnt offerings" to the golden calf, the Israelites then feasted and "rose up to play" (Exodus 32:6). It was this debauched scene that greeted Moses when, alerted by God, he hurried down from Mount Sinai. So furious was he that he smashed the tablets of stone, destroyed the golden calf and ordered the Levites to punish the idolaters, as a result of which three thousand people died.

See also **The Ark of the Covenant** (page 73), **The Old Testament, Major Figures** (pages 69–71).

Aaron probably modeled the golden calf on the Apis bull, which was worshipped in Memphis in ancient Egyptian times as a manifestation of the creator god Ptah. Although archeologists have discovered statuettes depicting it, the Apis bull was very much alive—that is, until death by natural causes claimed it, whereupon all of Egypt was scoured for its reincarnation, the next Apis bull being identified by the three-cornered blaze on its forehead and the patterning on its body that resembled either a vulture, a winged sun disk or a scarab. The golden calf's floral coronet is slipping slightly as the Levites begin to destroy it in accordance with God's injunction to "quite break down" the images of "foreign" gods (Exodus 23:24).

Celesti has depicted Aaron in the headdress that will subsequently mark him out as a priest of God, the miter that God had just decreed that he, and subsequently his descendants, should wear. Looking more like an Eastern turban than the miters worn by Christian bishops, Aaron's headdress is described as comprising a golden plaque inscribed with the words "Holiness to the Lord," fixed to a piece of blue lace that was in turn attached to a miter of fine linen (Exodus 28:36–39).

It is thanks to St. Jerome, who translated the Septuagint from the Greek and Hebrew into Latin to create the Vulgate version of the Bible, that Moses is often portrayed as having horns (or else a beard that has two points), for when translating Exodus 34:29, he misinterpreted a Hebrew word describing the skin of Moses's face, so that "shining" (or radiant) became "horned' (*cornutam* in Latin).

A flaming torch hints at what will happen to the golden calf next, and, indeed, Exodus 32:20 states that Moses "burnt it in the fire," after which he "ground it to a powder and strawed [strewed] it upon the water, and made the children of Israel drink of it."

The smashed tablets of stone symbolize the idolatrous Israelites' broken covenant with God. Using his finger, God himself had engraved the Decalogue, or the Ten Commandments, on both sides of the heavy stone slabs. It was Moses, however, who inscribed a replacement set of stones after climbing Mount Sinai again, which he later placed in the Ark of the Covenant that he installed in the Tabernacle.

Samson and Delilah

Michelangelo Merisi da Caravaggio

1610, oil on canvas, Hospital Tavera, Toledo, Spain

Such is the expressiveness of Caravaggio's rendering of the Old Testament story, told in Judges 16:4–20, of mighty Samson's lust and misplaced trust, and of unscrupulous Delilah's greed and betrayal, that even those unfamiliar with this sorry tale would look from the confident young woman to the vulnerable, sleeping man, and then to the edgily alert soldiers, and rapidly deduce the gist of what was happening. They might misinterpret one detail, however, for neither Delilah nor the razor that the traitorous beauty is wielding will bring about Samson's death—or not directly, at least.

Samson was a miracle baby, for his mother, the wife of Manoah, had been barren until informed by an angel that she would bear a son who would liberate Israel from Philistine domination. It was made clear, however, that Samson must be a Nazarite from the moment of his conception, which meant that neither she nor he, after his birth, should drink alcohol or eat "unclean" food and, crucially, "no rasor shall come on his head" (Judges 13:5). His mother complied, as did Samson, who grew up to demonstrate awesome strength when "the Spirit of the Lord came upon him," but also a predilection for teasing and womanizing. Samson having aroused their enmity by burning their cornfields, vineyards and olive groves, the Philistines approached his mistress, Delilah, "a woman in the valley of Sorek" (Judges 16:4–5), and offered her eleven hundred pieces of silver in return for the secret of his strength. It took much wheedling, pouting and foot-stamping on Delilah's part, as well as three failed attempts to ensnare him, but in the end Samson, "his soul vexed unto death" by her pestering, revealed that his superhuman strength lay in his hair, so that if it were shaved off, he would "become weak, and be like any other man" (Judges 16:16–17). And so it was that Delilah, having first demanded, and received, payment from the Philistines, lulled Samson to sleep in her lap, whereupon her oblivious lover was shaved. Now as weak as a kitten, Samson was powerless to resist, let alone overcome, the vengeful waiting Philistines.

See also **Colors** (page 146).

Delilah's clothing signals her wantonness, as well as her seductiveness. The bright-red colour of her dress symbolizes life, energy and passion, but also the spilling of blood, and therefore death.

Her black sleeves may denote death, too, but may also subtly allude to Samson's impending blinding at the hands of the Philistines, who will gouge out his eyes when they get their hands on him.

Her exposed breasts suggest the sexual nature of her hold over Samson, but also her shamelessness, for she clearly feels no need to display modesty by lacing up her bodice when the Philistine soldiers intrude on this intimate scene.

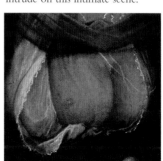

The "shushing" gesture that Delilah is making sends a nonverbal message expressing the need for silence, but also denotes secrecy, for Samson must remain unaware of the honey trap that has been set for him until he has been completely shorn.

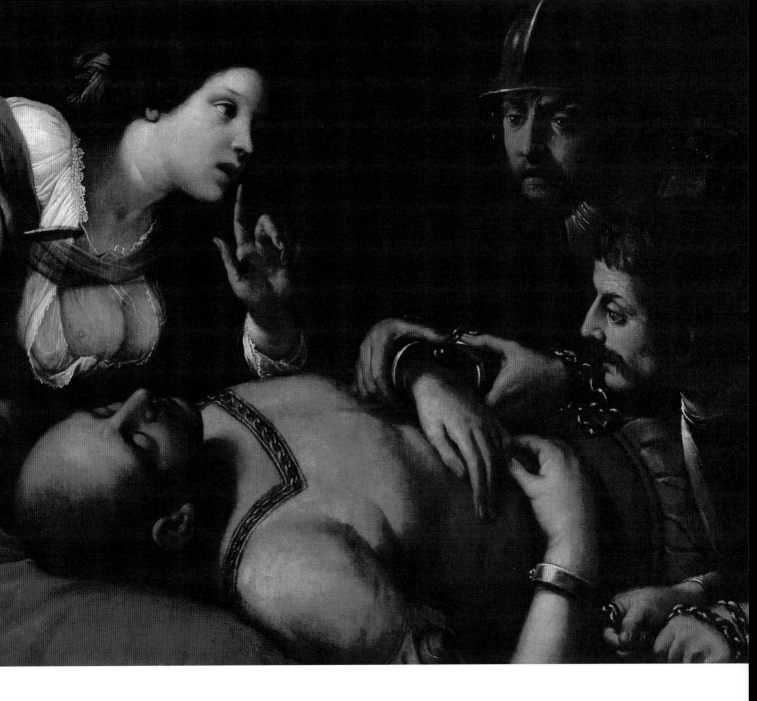

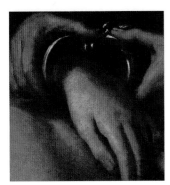

Samson has already been fettered with chains by the Philistines, Caravaggio perhaps thus anticipating his chaining to the prison millstone. Handcuffs and chains denote imprisonment and bondage, which may have an erotic connotation in this sexually charged context.

Hair is associated with the life force and vitality, for the healthier we are, the thicker and faster it grows. Men's hair in particular can be associated with the rays of the sun (a symbol of masculinity) and hence virility, while according to many superstitious beliefs, to possess someone's hair is to have power over the essence of that person.

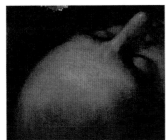

These considerations, along with the phallic shape of the razor, may point toward the helpless Samson being in the process of being emasculated (metaphorically, if not literally) by a powerful, hostile woman (in fact, the Old Testament states that Delilah called for a man to shave off Samson's locks), the implication perhaps being that moral weakness in the face of a fascinating femme fatale can lead to physical impotence and humiliation, and ultimately to total ruin.

The Annunciation to Mary and St. Luke the Evangelist

Benedetto Bonfigli

1445, tempera on wood, Galleria Nazionale dell'Umbria, Perugia, Italy

There are at least two reasons why the Italian artist Benedetto Bonfigli has placed St. Luke in such a prominent position in his rendition of the Annunciation. Firstly, it is in this evangelist's gospel—Luke 1:26–38—that the story underpinning the scene is described, and, secondly, Luke is a patron saint of lawyers and notaries, and this painting was commissioned by Perugia's College of Notaries. Luke is said to have known the Virgin Mary—and, indeed, to have painted her from life—so his central placement between the Archangel Gabriel and Mary as the momentous news of Jesus's miraculous conception is imparted and received additionally conveys the sense that the crux of Luke's account came directly from Mary herself.

In the gospel according to Luke, the angel Gabriel appeared to Mary alone, the virgin fiancée of Joseph, in the Galilean city of Nazareth. Having puzzled Mary with his greeting—"Hail, thou that art highly favoured, the Lord is with thee: blessed art thou among women" (Luke 1:28)—Gabriel went on to announce that she would conceive a son, whom she should call Jesus. And when the bemused Mary asked how this could possibly happen, given her chastity, Gabriel replied, "The Holy Ghost shall come upon thee, and the power of the Highest shall overshadow thee: therefore also that holy thing which shall be born of thee shall be called the Son of God" (Luke 1:35). Then, before departing, Gabriel informed the awed, accepting Mary that her elderly, previously infertile, cousin Elisabeth had also conceived a son.

Luke's simple tale has been added to and embroidered over the millennia, so that, for example, Roman Catholics now believe that Mary's mother, Anna, similarly conceived her child by immaculate conception, so that the mother of Jesus was free of the original sin with which the rest of humankind had been cursed following the Fall. And when, in 336, Christ's date of birth was decided to be December 25, it followed that the Annunciation took place nine months earlier, which is why Roman Catholics celebrate the Annunciation on March 25, or Lady Day.

See also **The Evangelists and Apostles** (pages 78–79), **Angels** (page 71).

God the Father is portrayed as a graying, paternal figure holding an orb, or globe, signifying his sovereignty over the entire universe. The angels that cluster around him are seraphim, in the celestial hierarchy, a first-order class of fiery-red angels that attend and glorify God, each of which is said to have three pairs of wings.

God directs the Holy Ghost's descent on a ray of light from heaven toward the Virgin Mary's womb. As an attribute of Aphrodite (Venus) in Greco–Roman mythology, the dove was a symbol of fertility, but represents the Holy Ghost, or Holy Spirit, in Christian belief because after Jesus was baptised, "the Holy Ghost descended in a bodily shape like a dove upon him" (Luke 3:22).

Gabriel acts as a messenger in revealing God's will to humans. Usually portrayed as androgynous-looking with wings and a halo, he may carry a messenger's scroll or staff. In Annunciation scenes, his staff may be replaced with a white lily, a symbol of purity that has become the attribute of Mary, Jesus and virgin saints.

St. Luke sits on the ground scribbling down his account of the conversation being conducted above his head, almost as though he were taking down dictation. His scroll winds over and curls around the winged ox that is his attribute. One of the four tetramorphs— a winged man, a winged lion, a winged ox and an eagle—described in Ezekiel 1:5–12 and Revelations 4:6–8 as representing the evangelists, the ox was thought to symbolize Luke because it was a sacrificial beast, and his gospel emphasizes Christ's sacrifice.

The tome that is propped up between the ox's forelegs is Luke's gospel, while the open book on the evangelist's left leg denotes his scholarship.

Mary's garment is the color of life (but also of bloodshed, and may therefore symbolically anticipate Christ's passion), while her blue mantle is the hue of heaven and the waters of baptism, as well as the shade associated with constancy, compassion, peace and protection. Her veil signifies her modest and submissive nature, and the book that she holds, her piety. In Christian tradition, the text that she is reading is in the Old Testament: "Behold, a virgin shall conceive, and bear a son" (Isaiah 7:14).

There is a parallel to be drawn between the basket and Mary's womb, but by filling it with spools of red and purple threads, Bonfigli is alluding to an apocryphal story that the Temple priests had allocated these colors to Mary as one of a weaving team comprising seven virgins chosen to create a new veil for the Temple.

The Annunciation is traditionally depicted as occurring in Mary's house, which, over the centuries, became increasingly grandiose and followed architectural fashions. The frieze that runs along this wall features baskets and swags of fruit, scallop shells and cherubic children, all Classical symbols of female fertility.

Adoration of the Kings

Filippino Lippi

1496, tempera on wood, Galleria degli Uffizi, Florence, Italy

The adoration of the kings was a popular theme in the art of Catholic Italy during the fifteenth century, partly because it expressed the piety of the person, or body, that had commissioned the work (in this instance, the monastery at San Donato, Scopeti), and partly because it provided the artist with the opportunity to juxtapose sumptuousness and simplicity, as well as to introduce exotic touches. Art historians also believe that Lippi sought to ingratiate himself with some powerful local personalities—potential patrons and their families—by portraying them worshipping the newborn Jesus.

Two versions of the Nativity are described in the New Testament. From St. Luke (2:1–20) we learn that Joseph and the pregnant Mary traveled to Joseph's hometown of Bethlehem to be taxed. There, Mary gave birth to Jesus "and laid him in a manger; because there was no room for them in the inn" (Luke: 2:8), and it was in this humble setting that the divine infant was "adored" by local shepherds, who had been alerted to his birth by an angel. St. Matthew's gospel (Matthew 2:1–11), by contrast, makes no mention of the manger or shepherds, and instead tells us that following Jesus's birth in Bethlehem, an unspecified number of wise men (*magi* in Latin) from the East arrived in Jerusalem and asked King Herod where they could find "he that is born King of the Jews? for we have seen his star in the east, and are come to worship him" (Matthew 2:2). Herod eventually instructed them to go to Bethlehem, which they did, guided by the star, which "stood over where the young child was" (Matthew 2:9). Following a later convention in depicting the Magi as three kings, and giving the scene a contemporary look by portraying many of the peripheral characters in the latest Florentine fashions, Lippi has reproduced the scene described in Matthew 2:11: "And when they were come into the house, they saw the young child with Mary his mother, and fell down, and worshipped him: and when they had opened their treasures, they presented unto him gifts; gold, and frankincense, and myrrh."

See also **Jesus Christ** (page 75), **The Virgin Mary** (page 76).

This venerable-looking old man (whose features are believed to have been modeled on those of Pier Francesco de' Medici) is clutching an astrolabe. By including this astronomical instrument, Lippi is suggesting that it was used to track the movement of the Star of Bethlehem, thereby underlining the Eastern visitors' profound knowledge of matters astrological and astronomical.

An attendant removes the young king's crown as he prepares to pay homage to the Christ Child. In life, this face belonged to another Medici, Lorenzo, while his brother, Giovanni, is portrayed in the process of handing him the chalice that contains his gift. If Lorenzo represents Caspar, the youngest king, he also stands for youth and Europe, and his gift is frankincense, an aromatic resin burned in religious rituals that consequently denotes Jesus's divinity.

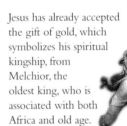

Jesus has already accepted the gift of gold, which symbolizes his spiritual kingship, from Melchior, the oldest king, who is associated with both Africa and old age.

Lippi has painted Mary's girdle, or belt, so that it forms a cross shape, reminding us that the baby squirming against it will die by crucifixion. A star embroidered on her softly draped veil glints on Mary's arm, a reference to her future role as "queen of heaven."

According to non-Biblical tradition, the third king is Balthazar, who corresponds to middle age and the continent of Asia. His gift is myrrh, a spicy resin that was once applied to corpses before burial, and that therefore symbolizes death, and specifically the ultimate act of self-sacrifice that the baby will make as a man. By kneeling before Jesus, and paying tribute to him in the form of expensive gifts, the kings are acknowledging Christ's supreme and universal superiority and authority as the son of God, before whom everyone, no matter how foreign, wise or royal, cannot help but bow down.

Lippi has depicted the Christ Child's birthplace as the most rudimentary of shelters. The Classical ruins from which it arises represent the destruction and decay of the old order that the fledgling religion of Christianity will one day replace.

Joseph leans on his traditional attribute, a staff or rod, as he gazes intently at his divine foster-child.

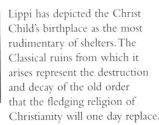

Some scholars believe that both the Star of Bethlehem and Jesus were referred to in the Old Testament Book of Numbers (24:17), where the coming of a "Star out of Jacob" is prophesied, representing Jesus, "the bright and morning star."

The inclusion of an ox and ass in Nativity scenes is believed to have been inspired by an Old Testament observation, "The ox knoweth his owner, and the ass his master's crib" (Isaiah 1:3): these domesticated animals instinctively recognize Christ's divinity. The ox, a creature of service and sacrifice, may denote Christians, while the ass, which is often perceived as being obstinate, may signify Judaism. Less negatively, the donkey is equated with both Mary and Jesus's gentleness and humility.

This figure is thought to be Piero del Pugliese, a notable Florentine patron of the arts.

The Temptations of Christ

Bartholomäus Bruyn the Elder and workshop

1547, oil on canvas, Rheinisches Landesmuseum, Bonn, Germany

Those familiar with the New Testament will recognize the scenes depicted in this narrative painting by the German artist Bartholomäus Bruyn and members of his workshop as the three temptations with which Satan attempted to corrupt Christ, as described, with slight variations, in the gospels of St. Matthew (4:1–11), Mark (1:13) and Luke (4:1–13). That a subtext is also evident in this image may not be so easily discernible, however.

Between them, the three evangelists relate that after his baptism, Christ retired to the wilderness for forty days of fasting and contemplation. At the end of this period, the Devil materialized by his side and attempted to take advantage of Christ's hunger: "If thou be the Son of God," the wily tempter said, "command this stone that it be made bread." Christ, however, rebuffed Satan with the words, "It is written, That man shall not live by bread alone, but by every word of God" (Luke 4:3–4). Next, according to St. Matthew, the Devil transported Christ to the summit of the Temple in Jerusalem, where he dared Christ to throw himself to the ground far below, saying that no harm would come to the Son of God, for it was written that the angels would "bear thee up, lest at any time thou dash thy foot against a stone," an invitation that Christ countered with, "It is written again, Thou shalt not tempt the Lord thy God" (Matthew: 4:6–7). Finally, Satan took Christ to the top of an extremely high mountain. There, he offered him power over all of the kingdoms of the world, if only Christ would worship him. But Christ again emphatically rejected him, saying, "Get the hence, Satan: for it is written, Thou shalt worship the Lord thy God, and him only shalt thou serve" (Matthew 4:10), at which point Satan admitted defeat by departing.

As for that subtext, read on . . .

See also **Angels** (page 71), **Satan and his Demons** (page 82).

Christ's drab-brown, coarse-textured hermit's robe conveys his spirituality, asceticism and complete lack of worldly vanity.

His miter, crosier, episcopal ring and cope identify the kneeling figure—who has aligned himself unequivocally on Christ's "side" and appears to be praying fervently—as a bishop. This is likely to be Adolf III von Schaumburg, a Counter-Reformationist who became archbishop of Cologne (where Bruyn worked) in 1547.

Thanks to his goatish horns, there is no mistaking Satan's identity as he exhorts Christ to throw himself off the Temple.

Having been abandoned at the top of the mountain by the thwarted Satan, Christ is ministered to by angels, as described in Matthew 4:11.

Satan has many disguises, but because he is frequently referred to as a "serpent" in the Bible, the agent of humankind's Fall, the Devil is often depicted in the form of a snake, or else of a dragon (the Latin word *draco* means both "snake" and "dragon"). Although he has assumed a man's face, and has donned a black hat and robe, in order to tempt Christ to turn the stone that he holds into a loaf of bread, his serpentine tail, along with his bird of prey's claws and talons, reveal that he is anything but a harmless human. Those who viewed this painting on its completion in Germany's devoutly Roman Catholic Rhineland region in 1547 would also have noticed that he is the spitting image of the recently deceased Martin Luther (1483–1546), the divisive initiator of the Reformation, whom many Catholics considered to be the Devil incarnate.

St. Mark tells us that Jesus was "with the wild beasts" in the wilderness, which are represented here by an elephant and camels, just visible behind Satan. These creatures symbolized Eastern lands in sixteenth-century northern Europe, and were furthermore associated with specific Christian virtues (*see* page 137).

The Raising of Lazarus from the Dead

Giotto di Bondone

1303, fresco, Cappella degli Scrovegni, Padua, Italy

Giotto's dramatic rendition of Christ's restoration of life to the dead Lazarus would be arresting in any circumstances, but has particular poignancy as part of a cycle of frescoes of New Testament scenes that decorate the Paduan chapel (which is sometimes called the Arena Chapel) that Enrico Scrovegni commissioned in 1300 in an attempt to atone for the sins of his father, Reginaldo. For although Reginaldo was an unscrupulous usurer, and, as such, destined for eternal damnation at the Last Judgment, Enrico hoped that this pious—and expensive—gesture would help to obtain redemption for his father, and perhaps also for himself. Indeed, the central message in the story of the raising of Lazarus, which is told in the gospel according to St. John (11:1–46), is that those who believe in Christ will triumph over death. "I am the resurrection, and the life," said Jesus to Martha, "he that believeth in me, though he were dead, yet shall he live: And whosoever liveth and believeth in me shall never die" (John 11:25–26).

This, perhaps the most awe-inspiring of Christ's miracles, took place shortly before his own death and resurrection. While in the wilderness, Jesus and his disciples received word from his friends, the sisters Martha and Mary of Bethany, that their brother, Lazarus, was sick. Two days later, Jesus and his disciples set off for Bethany, but by the time that they arrived, Lazarus had been dead for four days. Having met, and wept with, the grieving sisters, Jesus approached Lazarus's grave. He ordered that the stone that covered it be removed and called to Lazarus to "come forth." Then, "he that was dead came forth, bound hand and foot with grave-clothes: and his face was bound about with a napkin. Jesus said unto them, Loose him and let him go" (John 11:44). And so Jesus provided visual proof of God's power over life and death, as well as promising a spiritual "rebirth" to believers. In so doing, he won many converts, but also convinced his enemies that he had to die.

See also **Christian Symbols** (pages 81–82), **Shapes** (page 145).

The round, golden halo is derived from the nimbi that, in sacred art, emanated from the heads of such sun deities as the Persian Mithras and the Roman Sol like solar rays. In Christian iconography, the halo symbolizes sanctity and spiritual enlightenment, and can thus be interpreted as a radiant aura of goodness and glory or a blaze of divine energy. Haloes may, however, take different forms, depending on the identity or nature of the personages whose heads they embellish. Jesus is the only individual whose halo encloses a cross, or is cruciform, for example, as seen here.

The round haloes that "glorify" the heads of some of those who surround Jesus denote that they are saintly people who, at the time of their portrayal, were no longer living, but in heaven. A square halo signifies that its "owner" is still alive, or of this earth, while a triangular halo denotes the Trinity and God, and hexagonal haloes identify various virtues personified.

Lazarus's sisters have prostrated themselves before Jesus. While Martha's New Testament character sketch tells us that she was a busy housekeeper, the biblical clues suggest that her sister, Mary, and Mary Magdalene, the repentant prostitute, were one and the same, not least because both anointed Jesus's feet. Mary (Magdalene) is consequently often portrayed wearing a red dress, with her hair flowing loose—both indicative of an erstwhile immodest harlot—with an ointment-containing vessel to hand. When the sisters are depicted together, Martha can represent the active life, and Mary, a contemplative existence.

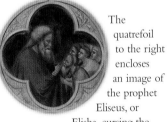

The quatrefoil to the right encloses an image of the prophet Eliseus, or Elisha, cursing the disrespectful young men of Bethel.

God's creation of Adam is portrayed within the quatrefoil to the left.

His deathly pallor, sunken cheeks and lipless mouth all give Lazarus the appearance of a corpse. Yet his eyes appear to be opening as one of Jesus's disciples starts to unwind the strips of linen that secure his shroud.

John informs us that Lazarus's grave was "a cave, and a stone lay upon it" (John 11:38), and in Giotto's representation, this stone is still being carried away as Lazarus rises from the dead. In Biblical times, such gravestones were whitewashed each year so that they, and the burial places that they marked, remained visible.

The nose-covering gesture made by an onlooker echoes the ever-practical Martha's apprehensive words to Jesus, "Lord, by this time he stinketh: for he hath been dead four days" (John 11:39).

The Last Supper

Leonardo da Vinci

1495–97, fresco, the Convent of Santa Maria delle Grazie, Milan, Italy

Despite its disastrous disintegration (the result of the combination of sealants that the artist used on the dry refectory wall that acts as its "canvas"), Leonardo da Vinci's *The Last Supper* was, for centuries, one of the most famous paintings in the world before becoming the subject of intense global interest following the publication of Dan Brown's *The Da Vinci Code* in 2003. In his thriller, the U.S. author suggested that the disciple traditionally identified as John was actually Mary Magdalene, an intriguing theory that relies on the artist having deliberately subverted the evangelists' accounts that tell us that Jesus sat down to eat the Passover meal with his twelve disciples (Matthew 26:20), all of whom are named elsewhere in the New Testament, and who do not include Mary Magdalene.

Accounts of the Last Supper vary slightly: John (13:4–12) was the only evangelist who stated that Jesus washed and dried the disciples' feet, for example, while Matthew, Mark and Luke, like many artists, chose to focus on the institution of the Eucharist, when Jesus blessed and broke the bread on the table before distributing it among the disciples saying, "Take, eat: this is my body" (Mark 14:22), and then passed around a cup of wine, stating, "This is my blood of the new testament, which is shed for many" (Mark 14:24). Da Vinci, by contrast, has envisaged the immediate aftermath of Jesus's announcement to his fellow diners that "one of you shall betray me" (John 13:21). The disaffected Judas Iscariot had indeed done a deal with the chief priests that he would identify Jesus to their men in return for thirty pieces of silver, an act of treachery of which the other eleven disciples were unaware, thinking that the bag of booty that Judas was clutching contained their communal funds. Da Vinci's capturing of Jesus's serenity, Judas's shock and the remaining disciples' confusion and consternation, is incredibly lifelike, almost cinematographic, and must have seemed disconcertingly so to the monks dining alongside it when the image was still pristine.

See also **The Evangelists and Apostles** (pages 78–79).

Old records have helped scholars to put names to faces, even though da Vinci included few of the disciples' symbolic attributes (indicated here in parentheses) in his masterpiece. Looking from left to right, the first three men are thought to be Bartholomew (whose attribute is a flaying knife), James the Less (a fuller's club) and Andrew (a saltire cross).

The coats of arms in the lunettes above *The Last Supper* are those of the Sforza family, the artist's tribute to Duke Ludovico Sforza, who commissioned the work.

James the Less is sometimes referred to as "the Lord's brother" in the New Testament, hence his striking resemblance to Jesus.

Judas seems smaller and darker than the other disciples, while his goatish beard is reminiscent of portrayals of the Devil, an effect that emphasizes Luke's description of him approaching the chief priests: "Then entered Satan into Judas" (Luke 22:3). Later replaced as an apostle by Matthias, it is due to Judas's presence at the Last Supper that thirteen has become an unlucky number in both Christian and Western belief. Here, Judas keeps a tight grip on the moneybag that is one of his traditional attributes.

An older man with white hair and a short, dense beard, in this image, the volatile Peter wields a knife—perhaps a reference to the blade with which he will soon cut off the ear of Malchus when Jesus is arrested— but may otherwise hold keys.

St. John the Evangelist has been depicted as a beardless young man with wavy, brown hair. He speaks of himself in the third person as follows: "Now there was leaning on Jesus' bosom one of his disciples, whom Jesus loved. Simon Peter therefore beckoned to him, that he should ask who it should be of whom he spake" (John 13:23–24). (Communal meals like this would have been partaken of Roman-style, with the diners reclining on couches, so the leaning position was not uncommon.) Da Vinci has remained faithful to John's account in portraying Peter consulting him. John's symbol is either an eagle or a chalice from which snakes emerge.

None of the people in this painting has a halo, but da Vinci has not only made Jesus the focal point of this rectangular image, but has highlighted his head by framing it within a distant window, so that it is illuminated by light. In addition, the semicircle that can be discerned above that central window suggests a golden aura surrounding Jesus.

In his positioning of Jesus and Judas's hands, da Vinci has rendered in paint Christ's words, "But behold, the hand of him that betrayeth me is with me on the table" (Luke 22:21).

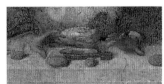

The bread that Jesus blessed and broke was unleavened, as is traditional at Passover, for this Jewish feast recalls the Hebrews' exodus from Egypt, from which they fled in such haste that the bread that they had prepared did not have time to rise.

Thomas (whose symbol is a set square), James the Greater (a pilgrim's staff or scallop shell) and Philip (a cross) entreat Jesus to reveal the traitor's identity.

Matthew (whose attribute is usually a winged man), Jude (a lance) and Simon the Zealot (a saw) conduct a heated debate among themselves.

Crucifixion of Christ

Andrea Mantegna

c. 1457–60, oil on wood, Musée du Louvre, Paris, France

The central image in a predella, or series of paintings along the lower edge of an altarpiece, Italian Andrea Mantegna's *Crucifixion of Christ* was once positioned below a large portrait of the Virgin Mary in Verona's San Zeno Church, where it was flanked by scenes depicting Christ's Agony in the Garden of Gethsemane and his Ascension. Following the French emperor Napoleon I's plundering of the predella from Italy, the latter two pieces ended up in Tours, while the centerpiece can today be viewed in the French capital. Although it retains a powerful presence in its splendid isolation, the paintings that once preceded and succeeded it put this distressing scene into context, illustrating as they do Christ's betrayal and arrest following the Last Supper on the one hand, and his glorious Ascension into heaven following his excruciating self-sacrifice on the other.

In the New Testament, all four evangelists describe the traumatic events of Christ's Passion (a term derived from the Latin word *passio*, "suffering") and Crucifixion, their accounts differing only in small details. Having been found guilty of blasphemy by the high priest Caiaphas for admitting to being "king of the Jews"—a claim that was punishable by death under Jewish law—Christ was dragged before Pontius Pilate, the Roman governor, who reluctantly sanctioned his death by crucifixion, an agonizing form of execution that was reserved for lowly criminals. Roman soldiers beat him brutally before stripping Christ of his clothes, jamming a crown of thorns on his head, draping scarlet fabric around him and thrusting a reed into his hands (Matthew 27:28–29) in a vicious parody of the Roman emperor's royal regalia of a wreath of roses, purple mantle and golden scepter. Then he was hustled from Jerusalem to Golgotha, where he was nailed to a cross and mocked by a mob of gleeful spectators until, six hours later, he finally sighed, "it is finished: and he bowed his head, and gave up the ghost," in the words of St. John (19:30), who witnessed Christ's demise.

See also **Jesus Christ** (page 75), **Christian Symbols** (pages 81–82).

Two thieves were crucified on either side of Christ. Luke (23:39–42) relates that one, traditionally hanging to Christ's left, ranted and raved at him, saying, "If thou be Christ, save thyself and us," but that this "bad thief" was rebuked by the other, who implored Jesus, "Lord remember me when thou comest into thy kingdom," whereupon Christ promised the "good thief" that they would soon be together in paradise.

The skulls and bones piled to the side partly indicate that this has long been a place of execution, and partly refer to its name, Golgotha, or Calvary, whose respective Hebrew and Latin roots mean "a skull," perhaps because it was a hill that was cranial in shape.

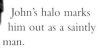

John's halo marks him out as a saintly man.

Although the evangelists list different women as being present, Mary Magdalene is specified by all four. John also names the Virgin Mary (portrayed here wearing a black cloak, in a state of collapse) and Mary, the wife of Cleophas.

That the spectacle is over is suggested by the stream of people wending their way back up the road (the Via Dolorosa, or "sorrowful road" in Latin) toward Jerusalem.

The soldier who has just thrust his spear, or lance, into Christ's side (John 19:34) to check that he is indeed dead is traditionally said to be Longinus, the centurion who, Luke tells us (23:47), proclaimed, "Certainly this was a righteous man," and consequently converted to Christianity.

Blood drips from Christ's pierced hands, feet and chest; the nails and lance that inflicted these, the "five wounds," are among the "instruments of the Passion."

 Soldiers have just broken the legs of the "bad thief"— an action called the "crucifragium" —in order to hasten his death.

The cross on which Christ was crucified has been the primary symbol of Christianity since its designation as such at the Council of Constantinople in 692. The sign above Christ's head bears the letters "INRI," the abbreviation for the Latin phrase *Iesu Nazarenus Rex Iudaeorum*, which means "Jesus of Nazareth, King of the Jews." Luke (23:38) tells us that these words were inscribed by Pontius Pilate in Greek, Latin and Hebrew.

The skull at its foot refers to the belief that Christ's cross was made from the wood of the tree of knowledge of good and evil, a branch of which was planted on Adam's grave. The skull is therefore Adam's, and together the skull and cross symbolize the redemption of the first man's original sin and the eternal life promised to Christian believers, both of which were achieved by Christ's death. Christ's cross may therefore also be equated with the tree of life that grows in the center of paradise (Genesis 2:9).

Having already divided most of his clothes among themselves, four Roman soldiers cast lots to ascertain who should have Christ's coat. The standing centurion is holding a standard whose pennant is emblazoned with the letters "SPQR," which stand for *Senatus Populusque Romanus*, the Latin for "the Senate and the People of Rome," which was the motto of the Roman legions.

Altar of the Last Judgment from St. Mary's Church, Gdansk

Hans Memling

1471–73, oil on wood, Pomorskie Museum, Gdansk, Poland

Maybe it was the sight of the petrified, screaming faces of the damned that persuaded the pirate captain Pawel Beneke that, for the sake of his soul, it would be prudent to donate the triptych found beneath decks on the Burgundian ship that his men had stormed and looted off the English coast to St. Mary's Church, in his hometown of Danzig (now Gdansk, Poland). Before its violent interception in 1473, the wooden altarpiece had been on its way from Bruges, Burgundy's richest port, to the chapel of St. Michael, in the Medici-funded Badia Fiesolana Church in Florence, Italy. Having been commissioned from the Netherlandish artist Hans Memling by the Italian banker and Medici agent Angelo di Jacapo Tani in 1465, it was finally completed in 1471, by which time Tani had been succeeded in his post by Tomaso Portinari. Both men are portrayed in the triptych (whose side panels, one depicting the welcoming of the blessed into heaven, the other, the casting of the damned into hell, are not reproduced here), Tani and his wife on the reverse of the wings, and Portinari in a far more prominent position.

The apocalyptic scene that Memling has depicted is the Last Judgment, an event foretold in both the Old Testament and the New Testament, when, according to Christian belief, Christ will make himself gloriously manifest in his "Second Coming," whereupon everyone who has ever lived will rise up from their graves to be judged (2 Corinthians 5:10). Those who are deemed worthy, those on Christ's right hand (which is why, in art, the blessed are always depicted on the left from the viewer's perspective), will enter paradise (Matthew 26:34), and will then live forever with Christ and the saints in eternal happiness. Those who are found wanting (those on Christ's left, or on the right-hand side of a painting), however, will spend eternity suffering the torments of hell administered by the Devil and his demonic minions (Matthew 26:41).

See also **Jesus Christ** (page 75), **Angels** (page 71), **The Virgin Mary** (page 76).

St. Michael, the armed and armored archangel who leads the angelic host in the fight against Satan, holds aloft the scales with which he weighs the worthiness of the resurrected and points his cross-surmounted crosier toward the soul being judged.

Being light spells eternal damnation, but Memling has pictured Portinari as weighing down the scales on the side of the saved.

The four angels on either side of Christ carry some of the instruments of the Passion: the scourge and the pillar of flagellation; the cross; the crown of thorns (which the angel is gingerly carrying in a cloth, perhaps to avoid being pricked); and the lance, the sponge mounted on a stick and the hammer and nails.

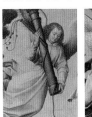

Angels trumpet the news all over the earth that the Day of Judgment has arrived, thereby waking the dead and summoning them to rise from their graves and report for judgment. This, according to Joel 3:12, will take place in the Valley of Jehoshaphat (today, the Valley of Kedron or Kidron, a ravine under the eastern wall of Jerusalem).

The pure-white lily and red-hot sword are often depicted together in Last Judgment scenes, when the lily on Christ's right represents the innocent and mercy, as well as spiritual power, and the sword on his left denotes the guilty, punishment and temporal might.

continued overleaf

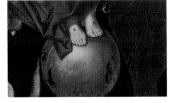

Christ, whose five wounds are painfully visible, is portrayed as Pantocrator (derived from the Greek for "All-ruling" or "Sovereign"). With his right hand, he makes the sign of absolution, or blessing (his extended thumb and two fingers represent the Trinity), and raises the righteous to heaven, while his left hand points downward, condemning the wicked to hell.

The rainbow on which he is enthroned symbolizes his exaltation, his bridging of heaven and earth and God's Old Testament covenant with humankind. The globe upon which his feet rest represents the universe, and his mastery over it.

An angel rescues one of the blessed from a demonic abduction attempt.

As fallen angels, Satan's demons are typically depicted as horrible, hybrid, winged creatures, often with horns, beaks and claws. While angels are beings of light and beauty, dark and hideous demons are their reverse, or angels in negative.

The twelve apostles flank Christ, one group of six ranged behind the Virgin Mary,

and the other, behind Saint John the Baptist, who can be identified by his desert-dweller's camel-hair tunic.

Memling has portrayed Mary and John in the Deësis (from the Greek for "humble petition") position as intercessors for humanity, that is, on their knees and with outstretched hands as they implore Christ to show mercy to the souls below (*see left*).

The All Saints' Picture

Albrecht Dürer

1511, oil on poplar, Kunsthistorisches Museum, Vienna, Austria

An alternative title for *The All Saints' Picture* is *The Adoration of the Trinity*, from which we can deduce that those ranged around the periphery of this image are the saintly congregation of heaven, and that the subject of their intent gaze is the Holy Trinity. In fact, while unmistakably conveying the identities of these two collectives, the German artist Albrecht Dürer also painted a far more complicated picture of paradise when he picked up his brush at the behest of Matthäus Landauer, a wealthy metal merchant and fellow citizen of Nuremberg (Nürnberg), who commissioned this image for the chapel of an almshouse that he had just endowed (which is why it is sometimes also called the Landauer Altarpiece).

Dürer has portrayed the *Civitas Dei*, the Latin for "City of God," a Christian concept that was introduced by Saint Augustine of Hippo (354–430) in his twenty-two-book *The City of God* (412–27). In his work, Saint Augustine describes the battle between the spiritual and temporal that has raged on earth since the time of Adam, the eventual future victory of the City of God and the eternal happiness that will prevail there following the Last Judgment. The City of God is envisaged as being more of an ageless community than a place, which is why Dürer's paradise of saints and the saved is populated by all manner of people—some not even Christian, but Old Testament Jews—from all walks of life and from all eras of history. While there are many individuals to be identified among the faithful, the depiction of the Trinity is an interesting variant on the portrayal of a sacred triplicity that is usually symbolized in aniconic form (for instance, as a triangle or triqueta), a representation that is variously called the "Throne of Grace," the "Seat of Mercy" or the "Mercy Seat." In the Old Testament, the Mercy Seat was the golden lid of the Ark of the Covenant that was also regarded as God's throne, over which the Jewish high priest sprinkled blood in an annual ritual of atonement. If a parallel is drawn, this Christian Mercy Seat, with its central image of the bleeding Christ, consequently emphasizes the Son of God's supreme self-sacrifice (Hebrews 9).

See also **The Holy Trinity** (page 82), **Popular Saints** (pages 79–81).

The Throne of Grace comprises a portrayal of the Holy Ghost as a dove hovering above the head of God the Father (a formidable figure whose crown signifies his sovereignty over the City of God), who supports the crucified body of the Son.

Some of the angels flanking the cross hold the instruments of the Passion (*see* page 115), reminders of the terrible suffering that Christ endured before his sacrificial death by crucifixion.

The Virgin Mary, who has been crowned queen of heaven, kneels at the forefront of a host of martyrs, their status as such being signified by the palm branches that they hold. A symbol of military triumph in Roman times, in Christian symbolism, the palm branch denotes victory over death, glory and immortality.

Saint Catherine of Alexandria, a fourth-century virgin, can be seen to the left of the Virgin Mary. She is identifiable by her spiked wheel, the means by which the Emperor Maxentius intended to break and kill her, had an angel not destroyed the wheel with a thunderbolt (an event that is commemorated by the Catherine-wheel firework). Many martyrs' attributes are the instruments with which they were tortured or murdered, which is why Saint Catherine may be symbolized by the sword with which she was beheaded, too, which can also be discerned here.

Two further virgin martyrs stand alongside the Virgin Mary, namely Saint Dorothea (or Dorothy), with the basket over her arm that she sent back to earth filled with apples and roses after her execution. Next to her is Saint Agnes, whose name means "pure" in Greek, who clutches the lamb whose Latin name, *agnus*, sounds much like hers, and that can also represent her innocence.

The tablets of the Decalogue, or Ten Commandments, identify Moses, the dominant figure of the Old Testament.

In front of him is David, a direct ancestor of Christ. He was a musician king, and is therefore depicted playing a harp and wearing a glittering crown.

A richly attired emperor is prominent among the secular members of the City of God.

Dürer has portrayed Matthäus Landauer, his patron, being welcomed to the City of God by a red-robed cardinal.

John the Baptist, garbed in his ascetic's robes, kneels opposite the Virgin Mary. Because, in Christian belief, he was the last of the prophets to foretell the coming of the Messiah, he heads a contingent of Old Testament personages that include fellow prophets, as well as the patriarchs and kings who were considered the forerunners of Christ.

The distinctive tiaras, or conical headdresses decorated with three crowns (symbolizing the Trinity), of two popes are visible among the nuns' wimples and bishops' miters amid the crowd of ecclesiastics.

Albrecht Dürer has included a portrait of himself, albeit with his feet still firmly on the ground, standing next to a plaque on which he has inscribed his name and the date, as well as his hallmark signature, an initial "A" sheltering the letter "D."

The Ka'bah in Mecca

c.1550, chromolithograph after a faïence, Palace of Kurshid Pasha, Cairo, Egypt

Hours of patient work must have gone into designing and painting the individual faïence tiles that make up this intricately decorated wall in the Palace of Kurshid Pasha in Cairo, the capital of Egypt. It would furthermore have been created with at least three purposes in mind: to help to create a cool interior in a frequently baking-hot climate through the use of ceramic; to serve as an aid to devotion in this Muslim establishment through the inclusion of a centerpiece depicting a sacred Islamic site; and to please the eye with an enchanting interplay of colors and shapes.

The site represented here is the most holy place in the Islamic world, namely the al-Masjid al-Haram mosque in Mecca, Saudi Arabia. And the reason for its sanctity is that it houses the Ka'bah ("cube" in Arabic), the shrine that incorporates the Hajr al-Aswad, the black stone (possibly a meteorite) that the Archangel Gabriel is said to have given Adam, the first man, according to Islamic, Jewish and Christian belief. Muslims also believe that Allah commanded Ibrahim (or Abraham, the first of the Old Testament patriarchs), to construct a shrine at the spot—once Adam's sanctuary, or *haram*—where the Ka'bah now stands, and that it was he who built the black stone into its southeastern corner. Over the centuries that followed, however, the purity of the Ka'bah was sullied when the people of Mecca became polytheistic and venerated a number of local deities, ultimately prompting the Prophet Muhammad (whose family, the Quaraysh, acted as the hereditary guardians of the Ka'bah) to flee to Medina. From there, he launched a jihad, or holy war, against Mecca, which he captured in 623 AD, whereupon he rededicated the city—and the Ka'bah—to Allah.

Wherever they are in the world, Muslims now turn toward Mecca to pray, while making a Hajj akbar ("great pilgrimage") to the Ka'bah is one of the five pillars of Islam, the most important of the requirements made of Muslims.

See also **The Five Pillars of Islam** (page 84), **The Mosque** (page 85).

The circular area immediately surrounding the Ka'bah, the al-Mataf, is today paved with marble.

The semi-circular Hijr is venerated as the place where Isma'il (or Ishmael, Ibrahim's son) and Hajar (or Hagar, Isma'il's mother) are buried.

Some of the features within the al-Masjid al-Haram mosque's central courtyard have changed over the course of the five centuries or so since this artistic representation was created, but the position of the most sacred object, namely the Ka'bah, remains the same. The Ka'bah, a cube-shaped shrine, is covered in a black cloth, the *kiswa*, on which is embroidered in flowing Arabic calligraphy the words of the central tenet of the Islamic faith, "There is no god but Allah, and Muhammad is his messenger." The *kiswa* is replaced every year at the end of Hajj.

The modern al-Masjid al-Haram mosque's outer wall also encloses the well of Zamzam, from which pilgrims traditionally drink after circling the Ka'bah seven times. The spring that the well houses is said to have sprung up spontaneously when an angel led the distraught Hajar to the place where her thirsty baby Isma'il lay. Nearby, a stone (today encased within a protective glass structure) known as the Maqam Ibrahim marks the spot where Ibrahim is said to have stood to direct and supervise the builders of the Ka'bah, and this is believed to bear the imprint of his feet.

Because Islam prohibits the depiction of humans and animals in art, Muslim artists have focused on exploring the artistic possibilities inherent in geometric and organic shapes, as well as in calligraphy. And over the millennia, they have developed the portrayal of flowers and foliage into a breathtaking art form. Indeed, it is to such characteristically stylized interpretations of curving, intertwined stems (here punctuated by exquisitely described blooms) that we owe the word "arabesque," or "in the Arab style."

ALLEGORICAL FIGURES & SYMBOLS

Left: *Clowns are frequently depicted with sad or inscrutable expressions, emphasizing that their painted smiles are an artifice; they can also represent the archetypal tricksteer. This 1868 painting is by Pierre-Auguste Renoir; perhaps the butterflies on the clown's costume refer to the transience of the artiste's stage persona.* **Far left:** *Paul Cezanne's 1866 still life features a skull, a symbol of death.* **Opposite:** *Byss's* The Air, *c.1718 (see pages 158–61).*

"Every picture tells a story" may be a truism, yet doesn't always tell the whole truth, for there is always at least one additional, invisible, dimension to a story told in paint: the artist's intention, which was not always simply faithfully to record a person or place's appearance or to illustrate a scene from the annals of history, myth or legend. In some instances, artists have deliberately included a coded communication in a painting that speaks only to fellow initiates, for instance. More prosaically, in rendering his or her subject, the painter may, perhaps, have been motivated by the desire to please or impress a wealthy or influential patron in order to receive further commissions, in which case flattery or propaganda—sometimes overt, sometimes subtle—may have been brought into play. The subliminal message lying beneath the surface of an innocuous image may, on the other hand, be immensely profound and have nothing to do with personal profit or shameless glorification, instead reflecting the artist's preoccupation with the human condition, with all of its virtues and vices, joys and woes, trials and triumphs, rites of passage, significant milestones and, traditionally most significantly in art, its inevitable ending. Indeed, the terrifying enormity of the thought of dying, along with the ugly, undignified details of death, are generally issues and images that we prefer not to confront head-on, yet haunt our unconscious minds. This explains why this subject especially is often depicted allegorically, or through the use of such symbolic allusions as timepieces, skeletons and wintry landscapes.

With a history as ancient as art itself, the language of artistic allegory is a rich and varied one that encompasses a whole gamut of categories, ranging from the concepts conveyed by different creatures, plants and other components of the natural world through the symbolism of colors, shapes and numbers to archetypal human images and such entirely symbolic genres as the *vanitas* paintings that allude to the transience of life on earth. In addition, thousands of ordinary objects are used in art to convey hidden meanings, some of which are detailed in the featured plates. While ancient artifacts like the hourglass have acquired connotations as universal symbols—in this case, the passing of time and the inevitability of death—others must be interpreted in their particular context. So next time you find yourself in an art gallery or leafing through an art book, remember: every picture may tell a story, but in the case of some, nothing is what it seems.

Paul Cezanne's, Snow Thaw in L'Estaque *(1870). The transition from winter to spring represents renewal and rebirth.*

NATURE

THE COSMOS

Astronomy and astrology have always fascinated humans trying to make sense of their position in a microcosm of the great universal macrocosm. When set against the vastness of space—our own galaxy of sun, stars, moon and planets and the infinity beyond—humankind's significance seems tiny. Yet several philosophies note a cosmic parallel in the concept of universal man, and according to the Christian theologian Origen, "You are another world in miniature . . . in you are the sun, the moon and also the stars."

The Sun One of the most important symbols, the sun is the primary source of light and warmth, the crucial force for the creation and maintenance of life, and its cosmic, generative role was recognized by the earliest civilizations. Its active energy was regarded as being male and spiritual, and it was believed to be the eye of the all-seeing sun god, the universal father. The pharaoh of Egypt was said to be descended from the sun. Because it rises in the east and sets in the west, it is a symbol of both resurrection and death, and in some traditions, its passage across the sky during the day is likened to a chariot of the gods. The sun is associated with intelligence and enlightenment. The rising sun is a symbol of hope and new beginnings, while a rayed sun signifies illumination from the center. The sun's astronomical symbol is believed to be derived from Egyptian hieroglyphics, although it was prevalent in a number of ancient cultures. *See also* Halo, page 82, and *The Battle of Issus*, pages 194–95.

The Moon In most cultures, the moon was regarded as the regulator of natural cycles and time, the passive, feminine counterpart of the sun. Thus it became a symbol of the lunar consorts of male solar deities, and of mother and virgin goddesses. Moon goddesses, such as Astarte in Phoenicia, Isis in ancient Egypt, the Greco–Roman goddesses Hecate and Artemis (Diana)—also known as Phoebe,

Cynthia, Selene and Luna—and even Christianity's Virgin Mary, all have the crescent moon as their attribute. Its appearance at night makes it a symbol of the dark and mysterious, and it is widely believed to have power over humanity's fate. Because of its relationship with natural cycles—especially the tides and menstruation—it signifies water and female fertility, also representing the unconscious. Due to its phases of waxing, waning, disappearing for three days and then becoming "new," the moon is a symbol of the cycle of life, death and rebirth. The round, full moon signifies completeness and unity; the half-moon, death; the waning moon, demonic powers; and the crescent and waxing moons, resurrection from death, creation and fertility. In alchemy, the moon—*luna*—is linked with silver and purified emotions. The crescent moon is the most important symbol of Islam, representing sovereignty and divinity. *See also The Battle of Issus*, pages 194–95.

The Planets The planets Mercury, Venus, Mars, Jupiter, Saturn, Uranus, Neptune and Pluto are all named after Roman deities, and may therefore symbolize their divine namesakes when represented in art. (Note that as in astrology, the sun and the moon may be counted among the planets.)

Stars In general terms, stars signify the divine presence, but of less powerful deities than those of the "king" and "queen" of heaven, the sun and the moon. Female deities, such as the Babylonian goddess Ishtar (whose emblem was an eight-pointed star), the Phoenician Astarte and the Egyptian Isis, and Christianity's Virgin Mary (*Stella Maris,* or "Star of the Sea"), are often represented with a crown of stars as queens of heaven. Because they light up the dark night sky, stars signify spiritual enlightenment and wisdom, as well as human aspiration. Some cultures believe that stars are the souls of the dead. *See also Adoration of the Kings,* pages 104–05.

THE WEATHER

Weather conditions are often used to build up a background atmosphere in art, sunshine, for example, conveying on the one hand, happy, carefree days full of nature's blessings, or, on the other, the burning heat of an arid, desert landscape.

Rain   A universal symbol of the life-giving bounty of the gods and of fertility (the raindrops of the sky god were believed to fertilize the earth), rain thus represents life, but also purification, both because it falls from heaven and because it shares the cleansing properties of water. In a related concept, a deluge can be interpreted as the sky god's wrathful determination to purify a corrupt world. Because raindrops resemble teardrops, rain may also signify depressed spirits in art.

Below: The Ancient of Days, *from* William Blake's Europe: A Prophecy. *This engraving shows God parting the clouds with his hand.*

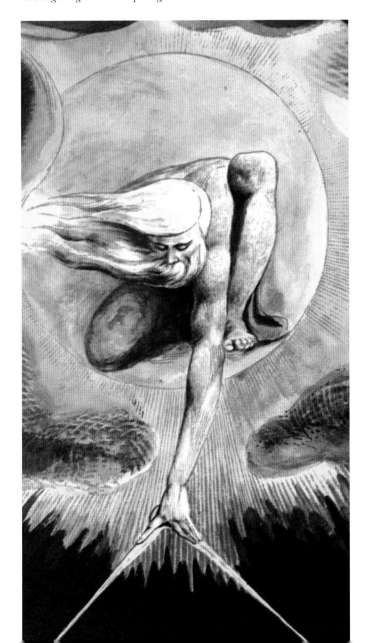

Above: A flash of lightning injects an electrifying sense of tension and impending doom into the otherwise tranquil scene depicted by Giorgione in The Tempest *(1506).*

Clouds   The symbolism of clouds is of nebulousness, mystery, obscured truth and hidden secrets. Because clouds can bring rain, they can also symbolize nature's bounty and human fertility. The gods of many religions were believed to live in clouds; they would sometimes emerge to reveal themselves to humans. Judeo–Christian scriptures say that God occasionally conceals himself from human view in the clouds (*see* page 178), and in Christian iconography, God is sometimes represented by a hand emerging from a cloud. It was said that Christ ascended to heaven through a cloud (in later artistic representations, this was transmuted into a mandorla).

Thunderstorms   In early civilizations, lightning and its accompanying rolls of thunder were universally considered manifestations of the wrath of the gods. Originally an instrument of divine punishment in the ancient religions of the Middle East, in the Greco–Roman pantheon, Zeus (Jupiter) wielded the thunderbolt, while in Norse mythology, Thor (the Germanic Donar) was the god of thunder (*see* page 35). The Vedic Indra brought rain with his *vajra* thunderbolt (a sign of truth), as did the storm god, Rudra. As the Buddhist *dorje*, or *vajra*, the thunderbolt assumes great importance as a symbol of enlightenment and knowledge, and is carried by buddhas and the bodhisattva Vajrapani. As well as signifying punishment, lightning can represent creative activity, revelation and spiritual enlightenment. Lightning can also be symbolized by means of an arrow, a trident, an ax, a hammer or a zigzag.

For **Rainbow** *see The Air* (pages 158–61), and pages 38–39 and 116–18.

THE SEASONS & ELEMENTS

The four seasons can be likened to any cycle of four components, including life, the phases of the moon and the positions of the sun. They can also be associated with the elements, of which there are four in the West (earth, air, fire and water). *See also Fruit Garlands with Cybele*, pages 152–53.

Spring and Air   Spring is a symbol of the renewal of life and of hope for the future. For Christians, it is associated with the resurrection of Christ. In Western tradition, spring is symbolized by a lamb or by the color green, or by daffodils and crocuses. In relation to humankind's life cycle, spring is likened to infancy. The element of air can be equated with spring, for this season implies freedom and possibilities. *See also The Air*, pages 158–61.

Summer and Water   Various symbols have been used to denote summer: in Greco–Roman tradition, it was Dice (or Demeter/Ceres, who was depicted as crowned with ears of corn and carrying a sheaf and sickle); in medieval Europe, the solar dragon or lion and the color yellow were emblems of this season. Summer is regarded as being the developmental period of humankind's life cycle, when approaching one's prime. Like the other seasons, summer can be compared to a specific element—in this case, water, which creates and sustains life.

Above: Vincent van Gogh's flowering orchard (1888) bursts with new life.
Below: Flora was the Roman goddess of flowers and the spring, a pleasure-loving deity who was celebrated during the riotous Floralia festival that heralded the reawakening of nature after its long winter sleep.

Fall and Fire   In Greco–Roman imagery, fall was personified by a Hora (or by the god Dionysus/Bacchus), who is laden with bunches of grapes and a cornucopia (*see page 25*). In Western cultures, this season is sometimes represented by a hare. Fall is associated with the third age of humankind's life cycle, when it represents maturity. In association with the four elements, fall can be likened to fire, as fire consumes the past in preparation for a rebirth.

Winter and Earth   In Greco–Roman art, winter was represented by the bareheaded Irene standing beside a leafless tree or by Boreas (god of the north wind) or Hephaestos (Vulcan, *see* page 22). In Western tradition, this season was once symbolized by the cold-blooded salamander, but could also be represented by a cloaked old man with frosted hair, as well as by a deer or a wild duck. Likened to the fourth and final phase of a person's life, winter symbolizes hopelessness, decrepitude, old age and the inevitability of death. Winter is linked with the element of earth.

FRUIT & FLOWERS

Collectively, fruit represents the bounty of nature. The juxtaposition of many different types of fruit is a wishful symbol of prosperity and of abundant fertility, because it signifies both rich, productive soil and clement weather. Ripe fruit symbolizes maturity. Because it contains the seeds of growth, fruit, like the egg, indicates potential, immortality and cosmic origins. The cornucopia—a horn overflowing with fruits and flowers—is one of the most resonant symbols of natural abundance (*see The Union of Water with Earth*, detail, page 40).

Below: The glowing colors of van Gogh's Autumn *(1888) illustrate why the season of fall is linked with the element of fire.*

Artists may include flowers in their works merely as embellishments, but even then, their choice of flower may reveal much about their state of mind or the overall message that they intended to convey by means of their creation. Color symbolism (*see* page 146) is an important aspect of floral symbolism, as are the myths and legends associated with particular blooms, some of which also have sacred connotations. Generally, however, flowers denote beauty and the transience of life.

See also Fruit Garlands with Cybele, pages 152–53.

Apple The symbolism of apples is complex, having particular significance in Judeo–Christian belief as the forbidden fruit (*see* pages 94–97) and in Greco-Roman mythology as an attribute of Aphrodite/Venus (*see* page 22). It is a universal symbol of both love and fertility.

Rose One of the most important floral symbols in the Western world, the rose is a beautiful, fragrant flower, protected by thorns, representing beauty, secrecy, love, life, blood, death and rebirth. In ancient Greece and Rome, the rose was sacred to Aphrodite (Venus), representing beauty and love. Dionysus (Bacchus) was garlanded with roses because they were thought to cool the brain during intoxication. A rose is often carved on confessionals or plastered on ceilings of meet-

Above: Irises (van Gogh, 1889) were named after the Greek messenger goddess; they signify a link between the mortal and divine worlds.

ing rooms as a warning that discussions are *sub rosa* ("under the rose"—i.e., secret). The Romans scattered roses at funerals as a sign of resurrection. In Christian tradition, it was said that the rose of paradise was thornless, and that the rose's thorns serve as a reminder of the Fall. The white rose is linked with the Virgin Mary (who is the "Mystical Rose of Heaven," the rose without thorns) and was a medieval symbol of virginity. The red rose was said to have grown from the blood of Christ, and is hence a sign of martyrdom, charity and resurrection.

Iris and Lily The iris and lily share much of their symbolism (they are rival contenders for the flower of the fleur-de-lys), both representing light and hope. Because of its pointed leaves, the iris can be called the "sword lily" and is an emblem of the sorrows of the Virgin Mary. The flower was named after the Greek goddess of the rainbow and can therefore represent the bridge between God and humans.

A symbol of purity, perfection, mercy and majesty, in most cultures, the lily once signified light and the male principle (due to the phallic shape of its pistil). In Greco–Roman mythology, the flower was sacred to Hera (Juno), for it was believed to have sprung from her milk, and to Artemis (Diana) as a sign of her virginity. According to Christian tradition, it grew from Eve's tears of repentance, shed as she left the Garden of Eden. In Christian iconography, the lily is most strongly associated with the Virgin Mary (and thus also with the Archangel Gabriel, *see The Annunciation to Mary and Saint Luke the Evangelist*, pages 102–03), signifying chastity, but Joseph is also sometimes shown with a staff blossoming with lilies. It has become an attribute of all virgin saints.

Below: Leonardo's Madonna with the Carnation *(c. 1478) shows the infant Jesus reaching to grasp a red bloom. Among its symbolic interpretations (see also pages 184–86), the carnation represents the nails that would be driven through the adult Jesus's flesh at His crucifixion—hence, perhaps, the Virgin's melancholy expression.*

Lotus   A variety of water lily, the lotus rises in the morning from muddy waters to flower and is therefore a symbol of purity, resurrection and perfect beauty in Asia. The lotus symbolizes the creation of life from the slime of the primordial waters (*see The Gods Worship Devi*, pages 86–87, and *Matsya*, pages 88–89. As well as having profound symbolism in ancient Egypt and Hinduism (*see* pages 15, 37 and 62–64), the lotus is sacred to buddhas and bodhisattvas (*see* page 65), who are often portrayed seated on a lotus or issuing as a flame from the lotus center (*see Padmasambhava*, pages 90–91). The closed lotus bud symbolizes potential. The open lotus represents a spiritual *chakra* and the round of existence. With eight petals, the flower signifies cardinal directions and cosmic harmony and is used in mandalas as a meditational symbol (*see Tibetan Anuttara-yoga Mandala*, pages 92–93). The union of bliss and emptiness that is the goal of tantric practice is termed *mani padme* ("Jewel in the Lotus")—the lotus with Buddha as its heart.

Poppy   The poppy has the dual symbolism of sleep and remembrance; both interpretations, however, can signify death. Because it produces the narcotic opium, in ancient Greece, it was sacred to both Hypnos and Morpheus, the gods of sleep and dreams. It was also an emblem of lunar mother goddesses. Signifying both fertility and oblivion, it was an attribute of Demeter (Ceres) and of Persephone, representing the annual death of nature (see pages 23 and 25). In Christian iconography, the poppy can represent Christ's Passion and death. Since 1920, the poppy has been a symbol of the remembrance of soldiers who died serving their country.

Below: Like most flowers, poppies (rendered in profusion below by van Gogh in 1886) symbolize the transience of life, while their scarlet hue recalls spilled blood.

Above: Just as plants denote nature's bounty, so harvesting—such as the haymaking depicted by Gauguin in 1889—signifies reaping the rewards of agricultural labor.

Daisy and Marguerite   The daisy's symbolism is intertwined with that of the marguerite: both are representative of tears and blood. In association with the Virgin Mary, the daisy additionally symbolizes innocence, salvation and immortality, sometimes also representing the innocence of the Christ child in Christian art. As the "day's eye," it is a solar symbol. The marguerite, like the daisy, is likened to a pearl, thus representing tears and the spilled blood of Christ and other Christian martyrs. See also Pour Fêter le Bébé, pages 192–93.

PLANTS

Plants that provide food, such as fruit and cereal crops, may be portrayed in art as symbols of natural abundance, of agriculture and generally of times of plenty. By contrast, certain nonedible plants may have symbolic resonance on account of their growing habit (which may be reminiscent of human qualities, for instance), color or shape.

Wheat and Maize   Wheat and maize, or corn, have the universal symbolism of agriculture, natural fertility and harvest. Because wheat is sown, grown and then harvested, it can signify the cycle of birth, life and death, as well as rebirth. Wheat signified the Egyptian mother goddess and the resurrection of Osiris, and Egyptians and Romans planted wheat on graves to bring life both in this world and the next. In ancient Greece and Rome, ears of corn were attributes of

Demeter (Ceres), Gaia and Virgo, and also symbolized the Eleusian mysteries. Wheat was sacred to the Phrygian mother goddess Cybele (*see* pages 152–53). In Christian tradition, along with the grape, wheat (the main ingredient of bread) is associated with the Eucharist and Christ and can represent the Virgin Mary as the mother of Christ.

Ivy   As an evergreen, the ivy represents immortality and, because it clings while climbing, friendship and faithfulness (*see La Pia dei Tolomei*, pages 190–91). This characteristic also led to its significance as representing the feminine need for protection, although the shape of its leaves identifies it as a male symbol. In ancient Egypt, it was the plant of Osiris, signifying immortality. Because it is prolific, ivy symbolizes the generative power of plants, sensuality and revelry. The Greco–Roman god Dionysus (Bacchus, *see* page 25) had an "ivy cup" and was crowned with the ivy leaves that also decorated the thyrsus (the staff carried by Maenads, itself a fertility symbol).

Mushrooms and Toadstools   Because of their phallic shape and speed of generation, both mushrooms and toadstools signify fertility. In popular Western tradition, small supernatural spirits, such as elves and pixies, live in toadstools.

Below: The fruit borne by the tree of knowledge of good and evil is usually portrayed as apples, but may sometimes take the form of grapes.

Above: The tree of life is universally difficult for the mortal to find and is frequently guarded by a pair of monsters or animals, or, as depicted here, angels.

TREES

Trees can have great symbolic significance when depicted in art. A tree can, for example, have cosmic resonance as the *imago mundi* (Latin for "world image"); as a "family tree," or representation of the founders and branches of a dynasty; or as a symbol of an individual person and his or her life (and if a single tree symbolizes one person, it follows that groves and forests can denote communities). Some trees evoke further symbolic associations, too.

Tree of Knowledge   In the Bible, the tree of knowledge of good and evil (sometimes depicted as a vine) grows in paradise and bears the enticing—but forbidden—fruit that the serpent tempted Eve to taste (*see Paradise*, pages 94–97). A dualistic symbol, it offers an intellectual awakening, albeit with perhaps ambiguous results, and was variously seen as symbolic of free will, sexual experience and self-indulgence. The alchemical tree of knowledge, called *arbor philosophica*, denotes creative evolution. In Judaism, it is believed that God will burn the tree of knowledge at the coming of the messiah, whereupon its true meaning will finally be revealed.

*For **Tree of Life** see The* Chasseur *in the Forest*, pages 154–55.

For **Evergreens** *see* pages 154–55.

Deciduous Trees Unlike evergreens, deciduous trees follow the cycle of nature and the seasons, shedding their foliage in fall and renewing it in spring. They therefore signify regeneration, rebirth and the irresistible power of life triumphant over apparent death.

Olive Just as the olive branch is a universal symbol of peace, so is the tree, but it also symbolizes knowledge, purification, fertility, longevity, abundance and victory. Because it produces a rich oil that can be burned in lamps, the olive tree was sacred in Greco–Roman times to Athena (Minerva), goddess of learning. The olive of the Acropolis also had power over the life and future of the Greek people. (*See also Minerva Competing with Neptune for the Possession of Attica,* pages 46–49.) The cleansing properties of its oil make the tree a symbol of purification. The olive tree can live for centuries, so it signifies long life. It is a fertility symbol, and the brides of antiquity carried olive garlands. The olive wreath of Zeus (Jupiter) was the highest prize of the ancient Olympic Games, representing victory. Christianity's Virgin Mary can sometimes be represented with an olive branch of harmony instead of a lily.

Oak King of the forest, the mighty oak tree represents strength, masculinity, military glory and immortality. The oak was widely believed to attract lightning, and was therefore sacred to the thunder gods of many cultures, including the Greco–Roman Zeus (Jupiter). The oak was especially revered by Druids (in conjunction with the "female" mistletoe) and the Germanic, Celtic and Norse peoples, who worshipped it in sacred oak groves. In all of these cultures, it was representative of divinity and masculinity. In antiquity, it was dedicated to Juno (Hera) and Cybele; the Dryads were oak nymphs. The hard wood of the oak was once equated with incorruptibility; combined with its potential to live to a great age, this belief caused it to signify both strength and eternal life. In Christian iconography, the oak symbolizes Christ's unshakeable faith and virtue, and is often believed to be the wood of the cross. An oak under the foot of the missionary saint Boniface represents his conversion of the Druids.

Palm Because of its height and radiating leaves, the palm tree was an early fertility and sun symbol. Later, it represented fame, victory, peace and righteousness. Because of its solar associations, the Babylonians considered it a divine tree, and it was also sacred to Re in Egypt and to Helios and Apollo in Greece. The palm was a tree of life

Below: Cypress trees, such as the towering exemplar depicted here by van Gogh in 1889, are evergreens, and consequently carry connotations of eternal life.

in many early Middle Eastern civilizations. In ancient Rome, victors were presented with palm branches—the origin of its victory symbolism—and from early Christian times, evergreen palm leaves were used as funerary emblems, signifying both martyrdom and victory over death. When Christ entered Jerusalem, palm branches were strewn in his path, an event commemorated by Palm Sunday.

Above: Goya's depiction of a bullfight (1812) refers to an Iberian spectator sport in which the bull symbolizes the animal aspect of human nature, which must be confronted and conquered.

ANIMALS

In the symbolic language of art, animals can sometimes represent the "bestial" aspect of human nature, that is, our potential to act unthinkingly, driven instead by our animal impulses, appetites and energies. Certain creatures may additionally symbolize particular human characteristics and qualities, be they good or bad, usually either on account of their behavior or the use to which human beings have traditionally put them.

Below: While pigs and the color black often carry negative symbolism, Paul Gauguin's Black Pigs (1891) depicts the lush fertility of Tahiti, where these creatures may be eaten on feast days.

Bull and Ox The bull, or steer, retains its age-old significance as a symbol of masculine strength and virility. Its symbolism can, however, be ambiguous: its vitality and masculine virility associate it with the sun and resurrection, but because it has crescent-shaped horns, it can also represent lunar deities and death. To the Hindus, Agni is the mighty bull and it is the breath of Aditi; Nandi is the mount of Shiva, while both Indra and Rudra can take this form. The ox, which shares the symbolic characteristic of strength with the bull, is imbued with less ambiguous symbolism: it represents agriculture, patience, chastity and (along with its yoke) self-sacrifice. To Christians, it can therefore signify Christ, and the winged ox is the emblem of St. Luke (*see* page 102).

Cow As the provider of milk, the cow is a universal symbol of motherhood, fertility, nourishment and abundance. Furthermore, because its curved horns are reminiscent of the crescent moon, it is a celestial symbol of all mother goddesses, as well as being a representative of Mother Earth (*see Landscape with House, Dog and Cow*, pages 162–63). In ancient Egypt, the cow was sacred to Isis and Hathor, mothers of the gods, as well as to Nut, the "Celestial Cow," whose legs are the four quarters of the earth. It is a sacred animal to the Hindus, and may not be killed; variously known as the "melodious cow" and "cow of abundance," its milk is believed to form the Milky Way, and, in association with the heavenly bull, it represents female cosmic power.

Pig and Boar The intelligent pig, or swine, has long been burdened with the negative symbolism of uncleanliness, ignorance and gluttony. In the world of antiquity, however, the sow was a fertility symbol and thus sacred to Isis in Egypt and to the agricultural goddess Demeter (Ceres) in ancient Greece and Rome, partly because it roots up earth.

Horse *See* overleaf.

The Horse

Considered a noble animal, the horse represents courage, grace and speed, as well as virility in Western tradition, and is solar in the East, signifying both fire and the heavens. It was once thought to be a chthonic creature, and can therefore also be associated with water and the moon, symbolizing death; it is known as a guide to the underworld, too. In many ancient cultures, the horse was regarded as an intelligent animal, combining strength and reason with the power of divination and magic, making it the most significant animal to sacrifice. Its color is an important factor in interpreting its symbolism: the white horse is solar, but can also signify the sea and moon; the black horse, however, is a sign of death and destruction. The Greco–Roman horse was an omen of war dedicated to Ares (Mars), Hades (Pluto) and Poseidon (Neptune), who was said to have created the first horse. Moreover, because Pegasus (*see* page 32) was a winged horse, it can additionally represent a messenger of the gods. To the Hindus, the horse can be equated with Varuna and thus the cosmos; Vishnu's last avatar will be as the white horse, Kalkin. In Islam, Muhammad was carried to heaven by the steed al-buraq, and thus the horse signifies happiness. Christians regard the horse as a symbol of courage, generosity and the swiftness of life. The four horses of the Apocalypse are white (signifying pestilence), red (war), black (famine) and pale (death).

Above: White horses, such as the magnificent equine portrayed by Gauguin in 1898, can symbolize solar power.

In Norse mythology, Sleipnir is Odin's magical eight-legged steed, and the greatest of all horses. A gift from Loki, the god of mischief and Odin's foster brother, his name means smooth or gliding. The offspring of Loki and the horse of the Giants, Svadilfari, he was the swiftest on earth, and could bear Odin over sea, through the air, and into the underworld.

Sleipnir having eight legs is considered to be symbolic of the four men who traditionally bear a coffin, but could also represent the directions of the compass.

See also *Odin*, page 35.

Symbolic Associations

Poseidon (Neptune)

Pegasus

Varuna

Kalkin

al-buraq (Borak)

the Apocalypse

virility

magic

As Featured In:

Edgar Degas, *Race Horses*, 1885–88, series

Franz Marc, *Blue Horse I*, 1911

Above: A docile donkey carries the Virgin Mary and the infant Jesus to safety in Giotto's rendition (created between 1303 and 1306) of the Flight into Egypt.

Donkey   The donkey and ass are creatures of contrasting symbolism, including danger, poverty, obstinacy, stupidity, foolishness and laziness, but also virility, patience, courage, meekness and gentleness. Christians sometimes portrayed the ass as a heathen symbol, but because Mary rode a donkey to Bethlehem, and Christ, into Jerusalem (from which it is said to derive the dark cross on its back), the animal signifies gentleness and humility. The talking ass of Balaam denotes communication with God. *See also* page 105, detail.

Goat   Goats have complex symbolism, both positive and negative. Still used in many societies as a sacrificial animal, it can represent vitality and sacrifice. In ancient Greece, it was sacred to Zeus, Pan and Artemis; in Hinduism, it represented the higher self; while in Norse mythology, Thor's chariot was drawn by goats. In the Bible, however, unbelievers are termed "goats," and the sins of the world were recorded to be laid on a goat's head (hence the "scapegoat"). As well as denoting lechery ("goatish") and lust, the goat has strong connections with Satan, who is often depicted in this form. *See* El Aquellare *(The Witches' Sabbath)*, pages 174–75, and *The Temptations of Christ*, pages 106–07.

Sheep   Because it is a docile and trusting creature, the sheep symbolizes blindness and stupidity; in a religious context, however, similar qualities are not negative as they can denote unquestioning faith. In its juvenile form, the lamb (an ancient sacrificial animal) signifies purity, innocence, meekness and martyrdom. In Christianity, it is thus the lamb of God (*agnus dei*)—Christ—who carries the sins of the world (*see* page 82). The lamb can be portrayed as both suffering and triumphant, or as heralding the Apocalypse. In a reversal of this role, however, Christ can also be portrayed as the Good Shepherd who tends to his flock (apostles and believers). Satan is powerless against the unblemished lamb, which is, in addition, an emblem of John the Baptist.

Ram   The brave, fierce, energetic ram embodies these aggressive qualities, as well as being a symbol of male strength and virility. Its unmistakeable masculinity and erect horns (reminiscent of both sun rays and thunderbolts) combine to make it a symbol of sun and sky gods in many cultures. In the Bible, the ram caught by its horns in a thorn bush was sacrificed by Abraham in place of his son, Isaac; in Judaism, the blowing of the shofar horn commemorates this event (*see* page 70).

Dog The symbolism of the dog is truly that of man's best friend, for dogs signify loyalty, vigilance and courage. The Celts believed that dogs had powers of healing, as did the Greeks, who linked them with Asclepius. Faithfulness is probably the dog's prime virtue, and ancient Egyptians and Greeks believed that it followed its master to the afterlife. The dog (Sirius) was sacred to the messenger god Hermes (Mercury) and to Artemis (Diana), goddess of the hunt (*see Diana and Endymion*, pages 42–43). *See also Giovanni Arnolfini and his Wife*, pages 187–89.

Cat Once sacred to Bast in ancient Egypt, since the Middle Ages (when it became known as a familiar of witches), the cat has attracted mainly negative symbolism—although today a black cat can be a bringer of good luck. Because of its perceived Satanic associations within Western tradition, the cat was regarded a cruel, deceitful, malevolent creature. Female cats were considered promiscuous and epitomized lustful women; their "nine lives" were regarded as suspiciously supernatural. *See also* page 155.

Above: The ancient Mesopotamian poem The Epic of Gilgamesh *tells how the king of Uruk rescued a lion cub, a symbol of nascent solar and regal power.*

Lion The magnificent lion is traditionally king of the beasts and the leading emblem of royalty. It is endowed with the various virtues of life, strength, conquest, valor, wisdom, pride, authority, courage and protection. Because of its strength, regal bearing, mane and golden fur, the lion is an ancient symbol of the sun and embodies earthly power—making it the enemy of the eagle. The lioness, however, represents the moon, femininity and fierce motherhood. In Egyptian art, two lions sitting back to back signify the rising and setting sun, the past and future; the pharaoh was frequently depicted in the form of a lion. As a fertility symbol, the virile Greco–Roman lion drew the chariots of Cybele (*see* page 40) and Hera (Juno) and was sacred to Dionysus (Bacchus) and Aphrodite (Venus).

Bear The bear's primary symbolism is that of bravery and strength, and it is therefore a popular heraldic symbol in Europe. Because it hibernates, the bear

Below: The dogs in Titian's Venus and Adonis *(c. 1555) identify Adonis (see page 30) as a hunter; dogs were sacred to Diana, goddess of hunting.*

Below: The richly adorned elephant in this Indian painting carries a royal throne and riders.

can signify resurrection. It is also linked with the moon and was sacred to the Greek lunar goddess Artemis (Diana), whose acolytes were called bears. The nymph Callisto and her son were transformed by Hera (Juno) into the bear constellations Ursa Major and Minor. In Christian tradition, the bear is a negative creature signifying bad temper, evil, cruelty, crudeness, greed and even Satan. However, because it was believed that the bear was born formless and was licked into shape by its mother, the bear can symbolize both the conversion of the pagan and the virgin birth.

Elephant Indigenous to Africa and Asia, the elephant's symbolic resonance is greatest in these continents and, indeed, it can symbolize both India and Africa. There it represents the various qualities of strength, royalty, dignity, patience, wisdom, longevity and happiness and is a symbol of good luck. Some cultures believe that the elephant is a cosmic, caryatid animal bearing the world upon its back; this image has been carried over into architectural devices. Because it has often been the preferred mount of royalty, the elephant represents status and power. Through its long lifespan, it symbolizes longevity and memory ("an elephant never forgets"). The Hindu god Ganesha has the head of an elephant, thus signifying his sagacity (*see* page 64). In Christian tradition, the elephant personifies the virtues of chastity and temperance and is also a symbol of Christ trampling a serpent (Satan) underfoot.

Above: The primary symbolism of the stag, depicted here by Velázquez in 1626, is derived from its antlers, which, because they resemble branches, link it with the tree of life.

Camel In most cultures, the camel is a symbol of arrogance, wilfulness, laziness and bad temper, yet in the countries where it is used as a beast of burden, it is endowed with more positive symbolism. In North Africa, for example, because it stores water in its hump and draws on its supply sparingly, it can represent sobriety (and, in Christianity, the virtue of temperance). Because it sinks to its knees to be loaded with its burden, Christian tradition approves of it as a creature that kneels before God, signifying both humility and obedience. Moreover, because it was said to be the mount of the Magi, it is a symbol of royalty and dignity, as well as of stamina.

Monkey *See The Animals Enter Noah's Ark, pages 156–57.*

Stag The stag is a universally positive symbol of life, wisdom and virility. Because of its branched antlers, it was equated by many cultures with the tree of life. By renewing its antlers annually, it is synonymous with renewal; furthermore, through their shape and height, the antlers can be identified with the sun's rays. In Christian tradition, as the enemy of the serpent (Satan), the stag symbolizes Christ, purity and solitude.

Above: The Virgin Mary lays a protective hand on a white rabbit in Titian's Madonna of the Rabbit *(1530). In medieval times, it was sometimes thought that does conceived their young without the aid of bucks, which is why female rabbits could be equated with the mother of Jesus.*

Wolf A creature of complex symbolism, the wolf can represent evil, cruelty, ferocity, avarice and the deadly sins of gluttony and covetousness, but also maternal love and valor—the latter attributes being derived from the she-wolf that suckled Romulus and Remus (*see* page 30). In medieval times, the wolf was regarded as a creature of Satan ridden by witches. In popular tradition, the wolf signifies the violence that underlies civilization. The fox is sometimes accorded similar meanings and is primarily a symbol of trickery.

Rabbit and Hare Because they are crepuscular, rabbits and hares symbolize the moon—indeed, in universal tradition, a rabbit can be seen on the face of the moon—and hence death and rebirth. Hares and rabbits share most other symbolic interpretations. They are creatures that burrow in earth and are prolific breeders and therefore represent fertility and good fortune. In Christianity, the rabbit's swiftness also led it to symbolize both the passing of life and diligent service. Their shy habits have led rabbits to epitomize timidity and sometimes cowardice. Through their procreative powers, both rabbits and hares were regarded as magical creatures in the Middle Ages.

Mouse An apparently harmless symbol of timidity and humility, the mouse can also signify hypocrisy (in Judaism) and destruction (in Christianity). In ancient times, the shrew was regarded as sacred in Egypt, while in Rome, the white mouse was a sign of good luck and an attribute both of Jupiter (Zeus) and Apollo. Because it is a rodent, for Christians, it can embody destructive power (it is sometimes depicted gnawing the tree of life), and thus Satan. "Plagues" of mice were regarded as a punishment from God.

Bat In an enduring traditional belief, the nocturnal bat is an agent of the powers of darkness, death and chaos. The combination of its mouselike body and black, webbed wings has incurred popular suspicion, as has its habit of roosting upside down. In medieval Europe, bats were considered witches' familiars; Satan was portrayed with bat wings, and bats were believed to play an incubus role, also sucking the blood of children, like a vampire.

Rat Rats have traditionally been regarded with mistrust as opportunist creatures scavenging off people's misfortunes, deserting sinking ships and accompanying death and decay. In addition, as rodents, they are often regarded as agents of destruction. In Christian allegory, the rat is a chthonic creature equated with Satan, witches and other sinister powers of darkness, but is also the emblem of Saint Fina, who lived in a rat-infested attic.

BIRDS

Eggs represent the womb, potential, hope and new life. Because most birds' wings give them the power of flight, and the skies have traditionally been regarded as the realm of the gods, and especially of sky deities, birds were once thought to act as messengers between the heavens and earth, and hence also to have the ability to prophesy future events. That some birds have a symbolism all of their own is usually due either to their idiosyncratic habits or to their striking appearance.

Below: One of the largest birds of prey to patrol the skies, its keen eyesight, deadly beak and powerful talons have caused the eagle to become a symbol of solar omniscience and overwhelming might.

Owl Although sacred to Athena (Minerva), the Greco–Roman goddess of learning, and a symbol of wisdom, the owl suffers negative associations in most traditions. In many cultures—including those of ancient Egypt and Christianity—this night bird once denoted death, misfortune and spiritual darkness. In medieval Europe, it was believed that witches could transform themselves into owls. The owl symbolizes blindness and is considered an unclean bird in Hebrew lore. *See* Athena/Minerva, page 22, and *Pallas Athene*, pages 50–51.

Birds of Prey The hawk, falcon and similar birds of prey have the conflicting symbolism of evil (*see* page 106) and death (*see* page 203), but also of solar light, sharing this significance with the eagle.

Vulture To the ancient Egyptians, the vulture was "pharaoh's hen" and symbolized exemplary motherhood: vultures were believed to be exclusively female and were said to feed their young on their own blood (a myth later applied to the pelican, see page 140). The vulture exemplified the female principle and the scarab, the male (in other cultures, the scarab was replaced by a hawk). In Greece and Rome, the vulture was sacred to Ares (Mars), Apollo and Herakles (Hercules). In the Middle Ages, the vulture's claw was believed to detect poison. For obvious reasons, the vulture is closely associated with death.

Dove The dove symbolizes peace in Christianity and other cultures, but has many further associations as well. Christianity's Holy Ghost is sometimes portrayed as a dove, as are each of the apostles. In Greco–Roman mythology, the dove was sacred to Athena (Minerva), signifying the renewal of life, to Zeus (Jupiter)—who was fed by doves—and to Aphrodite (Venus), as a symbol of love. The ancient Egyptians considered it representative of innocence and believed that it sat on the tree of life.

For **Eagle** see *The Air*, pages 158–61. For **Raven and Crow** see *The Chasseur in the Forest*, pages 154–55, *and La Pia dei Tolomei*, pages 190–91. *For* **Swan and Goose** *see The Air*, pages 158–61.

Above: Baldung has included an owl in his The Three Ages of Man and Death *(1539), perhaps on account of its medieval associations with darkness and the otherworld.*

Peacock The beauty and grandeur of the magnificently plumed peacock have given it a variety of associations. Its stateliness has often led it to be associated with royalty; Roman empresses and princesses had a peacock emblem. Further symbolism of the peacock derives directly from Greco–Roman mythology. *See The Creation of the Milky Way*, pages 38–39.

Ostrich and Emu Its idiosyncratic habit of burying its head in the sand causes the ostrich to symbolize primarily stupidity and the futile avoidance of truth. Historically, it has far more profound and positive significance. Its feathers were important symbols of justice and truth in ancient Egypt, helping to weigh the hearts of the dead in the underworld, as well as signifying the goddess Ma'at (*see* page 18). *See also The Air*, pages 158–61.

Stork Today, the stork is best known as the mythical bringer of babies to new parents, but it is also a more general good-luck symbol. The stork is a migratory bird—the emblem of the traveler—and represents spring, resurrection and new life (in the lands to which it migrated, it was often said to take on human form). This probably explains the origin of the stork's symbolism as the deliverer of children. Because it kills serpents, it is regarded in Christian tradition as an enemy of Satan and can epitomize Christ, as well as the virtues of chastity, purity, vigilance and prudence.

Right: The white crane represents longevity in Taoism, and is both the special attribute of Hsi Wang Mu, the Queen Mother of the West, and the bird that carries the Eight Immortals to the western paradise.

Pelican The pelican was once believed to feed its chicks with its own blood by pecking open its breast—thus trading its life for that of its young—and its primary significance is therefore of self-sacrifice, parental love and charity. In medieval tradition, it was said that the female bird smothered her young with love, but that the male revived them with blood from his side. Alternatively, the male killed them in anger and the loving mother revived them with blood from her breast—both myths, together with other variants, signify resurrection. Since the time of Dante, the pelican has been identified with Christ and additionally signifies piety and the Eucharist to Christians.

Above: *The rooster's ruddy plumage and habit of crowing at dawn associate it with the sun, and in Shinto belief, white cocks enticed Amaterasu from her cave. Thus the bird is an attribute of the solar goddess and is kept at her shrines.*

ancient Greece, it was believed to salute the sun by crowing at dawn and was sacred to Apollo and many other gods. In most cultures, this practice also caused it to represent both the victory of light over darkness (and hence good over evil) and guardianship. It was regarded as a symbol of fire by virtue of its fiery red comb. It is a universal fertility symbol, and in many cultures was a sacrificial bird, especially at harvest time. In Buddhism, the red cock symbolizes lust in the round of existence, while in Shinto Buddhism, it stands on the drum summoning the faithful to prayer. Because of its habit of strutting, it is also regarded as a symbol of conceit—particularly in men. In Christianity, because the cock crowed three times after Peter denied Christ, it became a symbol of Christ's Passion, but later came to signify a saint's repentance and papal vigilance, as well as being a resurrection symbol.

Magpie The black-and-white magpie has traditionally been distrusted in the West as a result of its perceived role in foretelling bad luck and death. Medieval Christians believed that the magpie signified evil, persecution or premature death. It may be depicted in scenes of the Nativity and can symbolize Satan, vanity and dissipated behavior.

Cuckoo In modern times, the cuckoo is probably best known for heralding spring and summer and for its bad parenting in abandoning its eggs in the nests of other species of birds. Yet it has a far more ancient and profound significance: in Greco–Roman belief, it symbolized marriage, as mythology relates that Zeus (Jupiter) once assumed the form of a cuckoo in order to seduce Hera (Juno), whose attribute it then became.

Swallow A migratory bird, the swallow's return in spring signifies hope, fertility and the renewal of life. Because it was once believed to hibernate (variously in mud, caves or water), it can symbolize resurrection. In common with most birds, it also represents light. In many ancient cultures, including the Egyptian (where it was sacred to Isis), it epitomized motherhood. A potent symbol in both ancient Greece and Rome, it was unlucky to kill a swallow as it embodied the spirits of dead children; it was also an attribute of Aphrodite (Venus). The swallow is revered in Islam as it is thought to make an annual pilgrimage to Mecca. In the Middle Ages, swallows were believed to feed their offspring on the sap of the celandine, which gave them the power of penetrating sight, so they became symbolic of God's illumination.

REPTILES, FISH & SEA CREATURES

Reptiles, fish and other sea creatures often have ambivalent symbolism, for while the long shapes of many link them with the masculine principle, some reptiles' habit of shedding their skins and emerging "renewed," and marine beings' watery, moon-influenced world, associate them with feminine generative power. Those that are venomous or vicious are furthermore clear symbols of danger and death, while those that are harmless, or edible, are regarded as symbols of either divine benevolence or of the bounty of the sea.

Cockerel The cockerel, cock or rooster generally signifies courage and vigilance, but also arrogance and conceit. In

Snake *See* opposite.

Snake

The snake, or serpent, is a universal symbol, one with the most complex and converse connotations. Ancient cultures believed that because the snake shed its skin, it symbolized immortality, and so it became associated with Asclepius, the Roman god of healing, and also with many Hindu gods. In Indian culture, the kundalini snake is believed to exist at the bottom of the human spine, symbolizing cosmic energy and life. The ancient Egyptians, Romans and Greeks regarded it as a protective spirit. Largely through its role in tempting Eve, thus bringing about the Fall of humankind (*see Paradise*, pages 94–97), the snake came to be seen as crafty and malevolent—the personification of the Devil and sin in Christianity (*see The Temptations of Christ*, pages 106–07). Its slithering movements, scaly skin and venomous, forked tongue inspired fear, while its lidless eyes denoted watchfulness and wisdom. Because it is born from an egg, the snake is sometimes regarded as androgynous, and because it often lives underground, it has been supposed to be chthonic, sharing the dragon's symbolism (*see* page 144). Its shape makes it a powerful phallic fertility symbol. When depicted coiled, it may signify dynamic potential. *See also* Nagas, page 64, and *The Gods Worship Devi*, detail, page 86.

Symbolic Associations
healing
immortality
the Fall/sin
the Devil
phallic symbol
fertility
dragons

As Featured In:
Tintoretto, *The Brazen Serpent*, 1575–76
Michelangelo, *The Last Judgment*, 1535–41

Above: Raphael's depiction of the Fall shows Adam accepting the forbidden fruit from Eve, who has been duped by the serpent, which has the head and torso of a woman.
Left: William Blake's Satan, Sin and Death: Satan Comes to the Gates of Hell, *from his illustrated* Milton's Paradise Lost. *The coiled serpents under Sin may symbolize her dual seductive and destructive forces.*

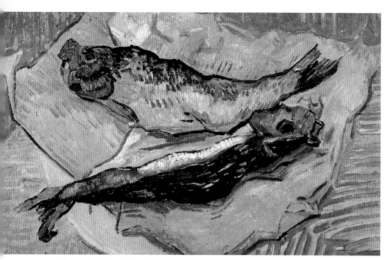

Above: Fish, such as the bloaters painted by van Gogh in 1889, can represent the faithful believers of many religions, including Judaism, Christianity and Buddhism.

Crocodile and Alligator

Crocodiles and alligators share the same mixed symbolism of death and destruction, as well as of life and renewal. Because the crocodile is a creature of both water and land, its significance is complicated beyond that of being a devouring animal. It was believed, in ancient Egypt, to have been born from the water and therefore represented the vicious chthonic and solar deity Sebek (Sobek), but it could also be the form of the earth god Geb, as the life force. Alternatively, the ferocious crocodile embodied fury and disorder and was the typhonic attribute of the evil deity Set. The hybrid crocodile Ammit ate the hearts of the sinful after judgment by Osiris (*see The Hall of Judgment*, detail, page 36), and the dead themselves were sometimes depicted as crocodiles of knowledge. Because it was believed to be tongueless, the Classical world regarded the crocodile as symbolic of silence. The Biblical Leviathan (*see* page 144) was linked with the crocodile, and in Christianity, it shares the symbolism of the dragon as the guardian of knowledge.

Fish

As well as being a potent symbol of Christianity, fish—aquatic creatures of elongated shape—represent male fertility (a good haul representing abundance) and also lunar deities. Because the depths themselves signify the unconscious mind, fish can denote creativity and inspiration. Fish can also symbolize female fertility. Fish, in Greco–Roman belief, were important to the goddess of love, Aphrodite (Venus), and to the god of the deep, Poseidon (Neptune). To Buddhists, the fish represents freedom of mind and faith, for, like Christ, Buddha was the fisher of men and women. The fish is heavenly food to the Jews, and can furthermore represent the faithful swimming in the waters of the Torah. *See also Matsya*, pages 88–89.

Whale

The huge whale was a symbol of power in the regenerative energy of the cosmic waters until it came to be regarded as the devourer of the Biblical Jonah, when it symbolized death, the grave and hell. In this context, however, it can also signify resurrection, because once Jonah had renewed his faith after three days and nights, the whale released him. The story can be compared with Christ's death, burial and resurrection. Because of their massive size, early sailors mistakenly tried to land on whales, and so they represented the Devil's lure and cunning.

Dolphin

A universally popular symbol, the dolphin signifies salvation, speed, love and diligence. The ancient Greeks and Romans regarded it as the king of sea creatures, and so it signified maritime power and pulled the chariot of Poseidon (Neptune). It was also the "woman of the sea," sacred to Aphrodite (Venus), as well as to the Babylonian Ishtar and Egyptian Isis. At Delphi, it was dedicated to Apollo, god of the sun, but, in association with Delphi, the dolphin (*delphis*) can also signify the womb (*delphys*). It is frequently depicted entwined with an anchor, "making haste slowly," representing prudence. It is a symbol of Christ on the cross when portrayed on an anchor or pierced with a trident; with a ship, it represents the Church being guided by Christ.

Below: A medieval engraving of Jonah and the whale that devoured him, thus saving him from drowning in stormy waters. The whale delivered Jonah miraculously to safety on the shore of Nineveh.

ARACHNIDS, INSECTS & MOLLUSKS

Certain arachnids, insects and mollusks may be included in paintings as a symbolic reference to a particular human characteristic or life metaphor that they are regarded as embodying.

Spider   Today, the spider is an unambiguous phobic symbol, yet through the spinning of its web, it symbolizes life and fate. Because its web radiates from the center and is generated from the spider's body, in some cultures, the web is a symbol of the sun and creation. In ancient Egypt (where the spider was sacred to Neith) and Greece, where it was a symbol of the Moirae (the Fates), Athena and Arachne, the web symbolized fate. In Hinduism, as in other traditions, the web signifies the cosmic order, with the spider as the center or *maya*—the weaver of illusion. In Christianity, the cobweb is symbolic of human frailty and futility, with the sticky web leading to the spider's identification with Satan and evil. Because it immobilizes and then pounces on its helpless prey, the spider represents the terrible Great Mother, who creates, but also destroys. Despite all of this, in popular tradition, it is unlucky to kill a spider, which can signify money or good luck (as it did to Romans).

Butterfly   Because it evolves from egg to caterpillar to chrysalis and then emerges in its full glory from an inert cocoon, the primary symbolism of the butterfly is that of the soul, transformation and rebirth—the creation of life from apparent death. Christian tradition accepts the butterfly as an emblem of resurrection (the caterpillar signifying life and the cocoon, death), but has additionally considered it a symbol of vanity and transience because it lives for such a short time. In ancient Greece, Psyche (*see* page 26) was represented as a butterfly because both shared the same name.

Bee   The bee is a communal, busy insect and thus symbolizes cooperative industry and diligence. Bees can also signify vigilance and purity (because they feed off blossoms and were believed to be parthenogenic). For this reason, the bee is associated

*Above: The shell is an attribute of Venus (see page 22), who was born at sea and came ashore at Paphos, Cyprus, in a scallop shell, as seen in this 1879 painting by William-Adolphe Bouguereau. **Left:** Psyche's identification with the butterfly is the origin of the association between this ethereal insect and the soul.*

with Christianity's Virgin Mary and, in ancient Greece, with virgin priestesses, or *melissae,* who were termed "bees" (the queen bee being the Great Mother). A bee and beehive represent the faithful and the Church in Christianity. *See also Napoleon on the Throne*, pages 198–99.

Shell   The shell is a universally positive, feminine symbol of birth, life, resurrection, love and good luck. Because of its hard casing, which protects life (and may contain pearls), the bivalved mollusk symbolizes the womb and fertility; as an aquatic being, it is also feminine, lunar and associated with virginity.

FANTASTIC CREATURES

Fantastic creatures are figments of humankind's imagination that, through their hybrid bodies, represent a combination of qualities. They may appear in faithful artistic illustrations of ancient myths, but may otherwise serve as symbolic vehicles of expression. (For details of more fantastic creatures, refer to the index.)

Dragon   The symbolic meaning of the dragon is sharply divided in Western and Eastern cultures. In the Orient, the dragon is seen as a positive symbol, with connotations of joy, health and fertility, protecting humankind from evil spirits. In the Western, Christian tradition, however, the dragon shares the negative and satanic symbolism of the snake, representing destructive power, the defiler of innocence and guardian of hidden treasure. *See also St. George, pages 178–79, and The Temptations of Christ, pages 106–07.*

Unicorn   A horn grows from the forehead of the horse-like unicorn. Usually white, it is said to have the legs of an antelope, the tail of a lion and the head and body of a horse, although it is sometimes represented in stag form. It can only be captured by a virgin, and, as such, symbolizes femininity, purity, chastity and the power of goodness *(see also Triumph of Chastity, pages 176–77)*.

Salamander   The salamander, which is sometimes equated with the lizard, can be portrayed in a number of ways. It can be a wingless dragon or a dog or human hybrid, but it is always pictured being engulfed by flames. Its primary significance is that of fire itself, of which it is both spirit and guardian. In medieval times, it additionally symbolized the heat of desire and, because it is sexless, chastity. In Christian iconography, the salamander represents faith and righteousness that survives the fire of temptation and evil.

Below: The mermaid is most commonly known in folk tales as the beautiful maiden who lures sailors to their deaths in treacherous waters.

The fierce Canaanite fish god, Dagon, who shares his name with an ancient Semitic corn god, is symbolized by his human upper half and fishlike lower half. According to the Bible, he was worshipped by the Philistines. It was during Dagon's festival that Samson (*see* pages 100–01) pulled down their temple.

In the Bible, Leviathan is the "crooked serpent," a huge and terrible fish that represents the primordial chaos of water. In addition, it is associated with the monsters of land and air, Behemoth and Ziz. Leviathan was subdued at the time of the Creation, but Job says that magic can revive the sleeping monster; it will be destroyed by Gabriel (or Behemoth) at the end of the world, however. According to Hebrew tradition, when the messiah comes, Leviathan will provide the food for the banquet of the righteous. It was said that its eyes lit up the dark sea and its foul breath caused the water to boil. This tradition is less clear on whether Leviathan is a crocodile, whale or sea serpent. In Islam, Leviathan is equated with Nun, and in Norse mythology, with the Mitgard serpent (*see* pages 58–59). In Christian belief, the gate to hell is symbolized by Leviathan's gaping jaws, and it can also represent lower life and worldly power. To Kabbalists, Leviathan is Samael, the prince of evil.

Phoenix   The phoenix, half-eagle and half-pheasant, is a universal symbol of resurrection and immortality. Its origins lie in ancient Egypt, where it was equated with the sun bird, Bennu. The dying phoenix is supposed to build a wooden funeral pyre and set itself alight by the sun's rays, then rising again from the ashes. Thus it epitomizes recreation from destruction. In Christian tradition, the phoenix denotes Christ's resurrection.

Mermaid   Half-woman, half-fish, the mermaid is a sea being symbolizing the unconscious (especially the feminine) aspect of the male psyche. By association with the Sirens (see page 32), the mermaid was once regarded as a harbinger of calamity, but came to represent elusive feminine beauty, as well as the less idealized characteristics of fickleness and vanity (represented by the mermaid's mirror).

This ancient Greek mosaic features spiral curves that resemble the motion of waves. This geometric pattern evolved into the "Greek key."

ABSTRACTIONS

SHAPES

Shapes can often be discerned in paintings, usually as background or compositional elements. Sometimes, however, they assume greater importance as part of a picture's message, which is why it is helpful to be familiar with their symbolism.

Circle   Although a simple shape, the circle is a universal symbol rich in meaning. The circle, which has neither beginning nor end, represents a never-ending cycle and is thus the primary symbol of eternity. It can also signify the cosmos, divinity, unity, perfection and life. In ancient Egypt, as well as in many other cultures, the circle, which echoes the solar disk in shape, represented the sun god and was a sign of the divine presence. In some interpretations, the central point in a circle represents the center of infinity, or the cosmic origin (and is also the symbol of the sun and gold). Inherent in its shape is an implication of a dynamic, endlessly turning motion, which equates the circle with the wheel, time, and with the relentless rules of cosmic law. The circle is also important as a meditational symbol in, for example, mandalas.

Spiral   The spiral is an ancient symbol redolent with profound symbolic interpretations. Because it resembles the movement of waves and water, it was once regarded as a symbol that emanated life and was a conduit through which all energy flows. The spiral can be both lunar and solar, for it signifies the phases of the moon and the rising, setting and generative power of the sun. As a result of all of these associations, the spiral was generally considered a potent fertility symbol. In common with the circle, the spiral shares the symbolism of continuity and cyclical move-

Above: The pentagram is primarily associated with Venus and Wicca, in which it represents the four elements and the spirit.

ment, but also signifies involution and evolution: while it contains elements of the old order, it branches out into new spheres and thus represents change and development.

Square   The static square signifies matter and earth. Because it is a perfectly balanced shape, however, it is a positive symbol. With its four equal sides, it can also signify stability—the collective balance of the elements, seasons and cardinal directions, otherwise always in opposition, are all associated with the number four. For this reason, the square is perhaps the most important of all Hindu symbols, signifying the anchor that assures the order of the universe—a function that it performs in the traditions of many other cultures, too.

Triangle   The triangle's symbolic importance lies in its three sides. Three is an important cosmic number signifying a multitude of triads, including birth, life and death; body, soul and spirit; father, mother and child. In Christian iconography, the equilateral triangle symbolizes the Holy Trinity. Linked to this concept is the isosceles triangle (the luminous delta) that represents the cosmos, at whose center is the omniscient eye of God. Two triangles make up the seal of Solomon, which represents the union of opposites; this is also a central feature of the Buddhist *sri yantra*, a complex meditational symbol (*see* Mandala, page 64).

Vertical Line   The vertical line may seem merely a simple stroke, yet it is full of symbolic meaning. It can be likened to the *axis mundi* that links the earth to the heavens and, indeed, to any other crucial link between lower and higher orders. In its similarity to the letter "I" and numeral "1" (*see* page 147), it represents the self and also paramount importance, thus representing authority and absolute power.

COLORS

Color symbolism is an important element in any painting, for colors, shades and hues create an atmosphere or evoke a mood at the very least. Most colors also have a variety of symbolic associations, ranging from the superficial or basic to the deeply abstract or profound. *See also* pages 162–63.

Purple Purple is regarded as denoting mystery and spirituality, for it often tints the sky at transitional, eerie times, such as twilight or during thunderstorms. Purple is also associated with nobility and authority, be it temporal or religious.

Blue and Green The color blue derives its symbolism from the undisturbed sky and tranquil sea, which is why it represents peace and a cool, unemotional head, as well as heaven and the watery realms, or air and water. Blue is also traditionally associated with young boys, and may occasionally signify depression. Being the color of leaves and shoots, green is associated with natural vitality and growth, especially in spring, but may alternatively represent naivety, jealousy or poison. *See also Round of the Prisoners* pages 164–65.

Yellow, Orange and Gold Yellow and orange both derive their positive significance from their symbolic association with the sun. Although these sunny hues generally signal a sense of contentment and cheerful, outgoing tendencies, yellow may sometimes identify a coward or traitor.

Below: The illumination and warmth that fire provides draw people to it and infuses them with a sense of well-being, as demonstrated by Gauguin in his Tahitian Dance *(1891). Fiery colors also indicate that people are "inflamed" with passion, whether love or anger.*

***Above:** By opting to shade Jesus's body in the color associated with vegetation and growth in his* Green Christ *(1889), Gauguin may have been signaling Christ's conquest of death and promise of eternal life.*

Gold signifies royalty and masculinity and is associated with solar deities, Zeus and Jesus Christ, among other figures (see, for example, pages 38 and 104).

Red and Pink Red denotes danger through its association with destructive fire and spilled blood, but fire and blood also link this color with warmth, the life force and overheated emotions, for when we are angry, we may "see red." Red has more positive symbolism as the color of hearts and red roses, when it signifies passionate or carnal love. Pink is associated with romance and young girls.

Brown and Black While brown is the color of the earth, and may therefore symbolize groundedness or matter-of-factness, black generally has negative associations with putrefaction, death and mourning, as well as with darkness and evil. *See also* pages 164–65.

White and Gray In total contrast to black, white represents spotless innocence and purity, and consequently also light, illumination and goodness. Being a mixture of white and black, gray can signify ambiguity, but also dullness.

NUMBERS

According to the Greek mathematician Pythagoras, who said that "everything is disposed according to numbers," and to the Greek philosopher Aristotle, who stated that they are "the origin and…substance of all things," numbers can be collectively regarded as agents that organize and regulate the universe. Although each number has its own, specific significance, in Western cultures, the numbers one to ten are regarded as the basis of numerological symbolism, while the Oriental tradition stresses the significance of the first twelve.

Zero The number of potential, zero is the starting point from which all other numbers spring. This significance is underscored by its similarity in shape to the seed, egg and womb, each of whose primary importance lies in its fertile possibilities. Furthermore, because the shape has no beginning or end, like the circle, it symbolizes eternity.

One One is the number of generation. As the point of the mystic center, it is the numeral of creative power or the supreme deity, and is thus a symbol of unity and enlightenment. It can also represent the human figure and the self.

Below: The four horsemen War, Pestilence, Famine and Death represent the Apocalypse of the Biblical Book of Revelation.

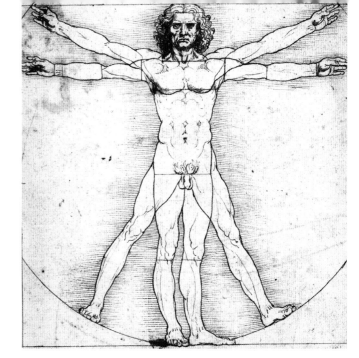

Above: Five is said to be the number of humankind because we have five senses, five digits on each hand and foot and five extremities (four limbs and a head).

Two In its association with the line, which has two points, the number two (the binary) represents both balance and the passage of time. The binary also represents the two sexes. In esoteric belief, the number two is an ambivalent symbol of duality, embodied in the alchemical androgyne (Hermes or Mercury), in the zodiacal sign of Gemini and in the two heads of the Roman god Janus. Both parts must be perfectly balanced in order to avoid disharmony.

Three The number three (the ternary) shares the significance of the three-sided triangle (*see* page 145). It is a self-contained entirety that represents all aspects of creation, therefore constituting a supremely important symbol of sacred trinities, such as those of Christianity and Hinduism. In most cultures it represents the underworld, earth and heavens; birth, life and death; the past, present and future; or the mind, body and spirit.

Four The symbolism of the numeral four (the quaternary) is related to the square (*see* page 145): it is a symbol of order, rationality and symmetry, and represents such quaternaries as the cardinal directions, the seasons, the elements and the phases of the moon.

Five According to Pythagoras, five is the number of the human being, who has five digits on each hand and foot and five senses, and whose body has four limbs and a head. The ancient Greeks identified five elements that make up a human: body, animal soul, psyche, intelligence and divine spirit. The number five is related both to the pentagram (*see* page 145) and the "golden number" or "divine proportion" that is believed to create architectural harmony.

Six The number six signifies universal harmony, stability and balance, as reflected in its relationship to the hexagon and Solomon's seal (or the Star of David, *see* page 72), which combines the triangles of fire and water. The Book of Revelation identifies six as the number of evil and says that the Beast of the Apocalypse bears the number 666.

Seven Because the number seven (the septenary) combines the ternary and quaternary—heaven or divinity, and earth or humankind—it unifies the macrocosm and microcosm and signifies perfectly integrated cosmic order. This association dates back to ancient times: in the Bible, for example, the septenary is described as representing entirety, and as governing time and space. In addition, the seven "planets" (the sun, moon, Venus, Mercury, Mars, Jupiter and Saturn) were believed to represent the powers of divinity and nature, to govern the seven days of the week and to symbolize the seven heavens through which the soul had to pass before attaining eternal life. The septenary is the number of hierarchies, for there are seven colors of the rainbow and seven musical notes. *See also* page 168.

Top: Giotto's exquisite depiction of the Last Supper, fresco, c. 1304–06, shows the thirteen figures at the inauspicious event.
Left: This ornate, sixteenth-century Islamic tile describes the shape of an eight-pointed star; eight is a significant number in Islamic symbolism, corresponding as it does, for example, to the eight divisions of space.

Eight In common with the number four, and because it combines the terrestrial square and eternal circle, the numeral eight (the octonary) is believed to be an agent of universal order. This is illustrated in the eight-spoked wheel of the Buddhist dharma chakra, the eight petals of the lotus, the eight symbols of good augury and the eight paths of Taoism. The octonary is associated with rebirth because it is the sum of the numbers one (representing divinity), three (signifying the soul) and four (symbolizing the body). Christian baptismal fonts are therefore usually octagonal in shape.

Nine As a triplication of the ternary triad, the number nine represents the powerful triplication of the three worlds, and of the body, intellect and soul. It therefore symbolizes eternity, completion and incorruptibility. *See also Apollo and the Muses*, pages 172–73.

Ten By combining the numbers one and zero—respectively representing divinity and potential—the number ten (the decad) signifies spiritual achievement and a return to unity. Because it contains all of its preceding numbers, it is also a cosmic numeral.

Thirteen In the Western world, thirteen represents death and is traditionally the unluckiest of numbers. The conventional explanation for its reputation as a malign numeral derives from Christianity's Last Supper (*see* pages 110–13).

HUMAN ALLEGORIES

THE LIFE CYCLE

Inherent in the cycle of life—which begins with birth and ends in death, and which, if we are lucky, allows us to experience childhood, marriage, or a similar partnership, maturity and old age in between this beginning and end—is a bittersweet inevitability that both fascinates and frightens humankind. Each of these stages, as well as the cycle as a whole, may be alluded to by allegorical means in art. They may also be depicted in reference to nonhuman parallels, so that a portrait of a bride and groom may refer to the alchemical union of mercury and sulfur, for example. *See also The Stages of Life*, pages 200–01.

Birth   A depiction of a newborn baby is a literal allusion to birth, but artists may use many other metaphors to represent the creation of a new life. These may include young animals and birds, as well as tightly furled flower or leaf buds.

Above: Gauguin's Sleeping Boy *(1881). Gauguin said: "In order to do something new, we must go back to the source, to humanity in its infancy."*

Childhood   Although the symbols that artists may use to represent birth and infancy are largely interchangeable—the color white, denoting innocence, and flower buds, for example—certain images signify the older child. These include the act of crawling, toys and childhood games. *See also* Pour Fêter le Bébé *(In Honor of the Baby)*, pages 192–93.

Marriage   The union of two people in marriage, or the loving pledge or commitment that they have made to one another to stay together for life, may be symbolized in a number of ways, and most traditionally by an engagement or wedding ring. Other symbols of love and marriage include red roses and hearts, a pair of lovebirds or doves, a dog (denoting fidelity), orange blossom, ivy and fruits (alluding to fruitfulness, or children). *See also Portrait of Giovanni Arnolfini and his Wife ("The Arnolfini Portrait")*, pages 187–89.

Maturity   Men and women who have reached physical maturity and are in the prime of life may be symbolized by such strong and vigorous-looking natural counterparts as trees or animals (a full-grown lion or lioness, for instance). The virility and fertility of maturity may also be represented aniconically, perhaps as a long, narrow shape or phallic symbol in the case of men, or as a rounded shape reminiscent of the womb or breasts in that of women.

Below: In art, marriage can symbolize the harmonization or reconciliation of conflicting qualities. Titian's An Allegory, Perhaps of Marriage *(1520), for example, depicts the marriage of Venus and Mars, and hence represents the union of opposites, of love and war.*

Old Age   Old age may be referred to in the allegorical language of art by the depiction of such natural parallels as fading flowers, withering fruits and the dying leaves of fall.

Death   Although the approach of death is implicit in many of the symbols of old age, it may be more explicitly conveyed, too, through coffins and gravestones, skulls and skeletons, for instance. In addition, black denotes death and mourning in the symbolism of color, while clocks, sundials and other timepieces are a reminder that every second that passes brings death closer. Other *memento mori*, or reminders of death, may be drawn from the natural or agricultural world, such as barren, wintry landscapes and the sickle or scythe that may be depicted in the hands of the Greco–Roman deity Kronos/Saturn, Father Time or the Grim Reaper. *See also The Triumph of Death, pages 202–03.*

Below: "How Queen Guinevere Rode a-Maying into the Woods and Fields Beside Westminster"—an exquisite watercolour by Arthur Rackham depicting Guinevere as an archetypal princess—though she is often portrayed as a siren, too.

Above: Goya's Las Viejas *("The Old Girls," 1810) graphically illustrates both the ravages of time and the blindness of human vanity. The winged older man in the background symbolizes death, and is about to sweep the old girls into the grave with his broom.*

MAJOR ARCHETYPES

There are certain personality types that appear time and time again in myths, legends and art—indeed, they crop up so frequently that they may be termed archetypal figures. The most important are four pairs of major female and male archetypes, each duo embodying positive and negative personality traits like two sides of a coin.

Princess/Siren   The princess represents the lovely young woman on the brink of maturity; she is innocent, unspoiled and full of promise, the fairy-tale prize of the noble prince. The seductive siren, by contrast, uses her sexuality to lure and test the prince in furtherance of her own selfish, heartless and destructive desires.

Mother/Terrible Mother   The mother is the loving, caring, empathetic and nurturing woman who always puts the wellbeing of her beloved children above her own needs and desires. Although she, too, is the fertile mother of offspring, the terrible mother is cruel, manipulative, dominating and often destructive in her ceaseless quest for personal gratification.

Amazon/Huntress The amazon is the independent woman who thinks for herself, fights her own battles and generally relies on no one but herself; she has a soft side, but keeps it well hidden. The difference between the amazon and the huntress is that the latter has a predatory taste for stalking, toying with, and ultimately emasculating, her favored prey—usually men.

Wise Old Woman/Witch Also known as the high priestess, the wise old woman uses her otherworldly spirituality and the wisdom of age to guide younger initiates and work for the collective good. Her dark counterpart, the witch, may share the same powers, but uses them for selfish or evil purposes. *See also* page 172.

Prince/Wastrel The prince is an idealistic young man who must make his own way in the world; despite being courageous and full of good intentions, he is somewhat naïve, and has much to learn. The wastrel, by contrast, is lazy, greedy, lacks moral fiber and is easily corrupted, for he is governed by his senses rather than by his conscience.

Father/Ogre The father protects and provides for his family and treats those who are younger and weaker than him with fairness, kindness and compassion, unlike the ogre, who neglects, bullies and maltreats those for whom he is responsible and generally abuses his position of power and authority.

Warrior/Villain The warrior is the powerful older man who uses his strength, bravery and martial prowess in order to defend or promote a common cause. Although also a man of action, the only interests that the villain will fight for are his own, and he will furthermore trample over or betray anyone who stands in his way.

Wise Old Man/Black Magician The wise old man, who is also known as the high priest, is the embodiment of wisdom and provider of sage and spiritual counsel to those who seek to counter the forces of evil and destruction with whom the black magician may, by contrast, identify, motivated as he is by an all-consuming desire for power.

Above: Caravaggio's Card Players *(c. 1595) illustrates the wastrel archetype.*
Below: The fresco Temperantia, *by Luca Giordano, illustrates the cardinal virtue of moderation and restraint.*

QUALITIES

Most of the world's major religions urge us to exercise self-denial in order overcome our selfish, animal instincts, represented by various vices, and to strive to live a moral, altruistic, worthy life by cultivating certain virtues. All of these qualities can be represented symbolically, as can the moral codes that proscribe or encourage them (the dharma chakra, or wheel of the law, of Buddhism, for instance).

Virtues and Vices In Christian tradition, there are four cardinal virtues—justice, prudence (or wisdom), fortitude and temperance—and three theological virtues: faith, hope and charity. Christianity furthermore identifies seven deadly, or cardinal, sins, which, if indulged in on earth, will condemn sinners to spending eternity in hell: lust, gluttony, avarice, sloth, anger, envy and pride. All of the virtues and vices have symbolic attributes. *See also The Seven Deadly Sins and the Four Last Things*, pages 168–171.

Fruit Garlands with Cybele

Jan Brueghel (the Elder) and Hendrick van Balen

1618, oil on wood, Mauritshuis, The Hague, The Netherlands

Such is the wealth of meticulously rendered detail that can be discerned in *Fruit Garlands with Cybele*, and so lush is the overall effect, that it almost goes without saying that this is a painting that symbolizes—and celebrates—Mother Earth's bounty. The two Flemish artists who collaborated in creating this luxuriant image have merged their respective, and related, talents (Brueghel being particularly acclaimed for his delicate depiction of flowers, animals and sylvan scenes, and van Balen being noted for his mythological subjects) to almost overwhelming effect.

Although the divine female focal point is named as Cybele in the painting's title, not only are the symbolic attributes of the Phrygian (or Anatolian) mother goddess—notably her castellated crown and attendant lions—absent, but this indolent goddess's corn-golden hair and ample curves are characteristically present in the depictions of many Greco–Roman goddesses of the earth, being especially equated with Demeter (Ceres), the goddess of corn and agriculture. It is furthermore significant that the goddess is portrayed enjoying the reverent attentions of the personifications of the four seasons, for in ancient times, when a meager harvest could mean famine and death, retaining the goodwill of Demeter was regarded as vital. According to the Greco–Roman mindset, winter was the period when the goddess mourned the temporary loss of her beloved daughter Persephone (to Persephone's husband Pluto, the ruler of Hades, the dark, underworld realm of the dead) so deeply that she withheld her gift of fertility from the world. It was thus considered crucial to propitiate Demeter properly so that in the spring, summer and fall, when she rejoiced in the company of her daughter, she would be certain to shower her blessings upon the earth, making it fertile and fruitful, the result being an abundant harvest. It is therefore likely that the "Cybele" portrayed here is actually a composite earth and mother goddess, and that the image of Demeter was at the forefront of the artists' minds when they painted her.

See also **Demeter/Ceres** (page 23), **Fruit and Flowers** (pages 128–30), **The Life Cycle** (pages 149–50).

An ancient Greek springtime rite involved clothing an effigy of Hera in bridal garments and garlanding her with flowers, in emulation of the role that the Horae (*see* page 29) were believed to fulfill. Yet the Horae were all female, and two of the four seasons portrayed here are clearly men, so artistic licence has obviously been used. The young man to the right, with the green leaves in his hair, represents spring, and the "sower of the seed," or male virility and fertility, perhaps in the form of the woodland spirit the Green Man, and the warmly dressed older man to the left, with his white-frosted beard, represents winter. The young woman who is about to crown the goddess with a floral coronet signifies summer,

while the female whose hairstyle incorporates ears of corn, who is presenting her mistress with an offering of ripe fruit, is fall, and harvest, personified.

Flowers represent feminine beauty and receptiveness, and can signify paradise, too.

As well as being an attribute of agricultural deities, ears of corn can represent birth, life and death (for corn is sown, grown and harvested), and also sustenance.

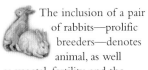

The inclusion of a pair of rabbits—prolific breeders—denotes animal, as well as vegetal, fertility, and the multiplication of the birds and the beasts (a variety of which are delightfully depicted here) in years of plenty, when there is enough food for all. Because they live in underground burrows, rabbits are also the creatures of Mother Earth.

Fish produce their offspring as eggs, and may therefore be linked with the fecund mother goddess. Fruits and vegetables of nearly every type signify natural fertility; because they contain seeds, they share the symbolism of the egg.

Putti, or chubby little cherubs with wings, often make appearances in High Renaissance and Baroque art, when they can denote the blessing of children (in both senses). They may have evolved from the *erotes*, in Greco–Roman mythology, Cupidlike scamps who attended Venus and acted as both divine messengers and "guardian angels" of human beings.

The painting's oval centerpiece recalls the shape of an egg, as well as that of the womb, both symbols of potential, conception and birth, as well as of femininity. The garland, or swag, that encloses it has the same significance the world over, being a symbol of honor and distinction, victory, salutation and festivity.

The *Chasseur* in the Forest

Caspar David Friedrich

1814, oil on canvas, private collection, Germany

Until the late eighteenth century, European artists tended to accord human subjects center stage in their works, relegating nature to the background, but the rise of the Romantic movement dramatically reversed this trend, to the extent that the natural settings depicted sometimes threatened to overwhelm the painted people who appeared to have strayed into the picture. For the Romantics, the emphasis was on imagination, intuition and instinct, and it was these subtle, yet powerful, internal forces that they aimed to arouse with their portrayals of the natural world. The German artist Caspar David Friedrich, in particular, found inspiration in the dark forests and misty mountains of his native land, and his paintings convey an almost pagan sense of spirituality, as well as evoking a profound psychological response to the unspoiled German landscape.

In Friedrich's *The* Chasseur *in the Forest*, it is the dark, dense trees that dominate the image, and that therefore create the atmosphere that influences the viewer's response. Trees have always had immense symbolism for humans, with many cultures envisaging the cosmos as a tree (the Norse Yggdrasil, for instance), and ancestries being charted by family trees. The "tree of life" may therefore shelter and nurture, which is why it is associated with the mother archetype, but may also represent the individual and his or her growth, along with the past in which that person is rooted, his or her present circumstances and finally, the direction in which that individual may potentially branch out in the future. And if a single tree signifies one person, a forest denotes a group of people. Another layer of meaning pervades this painting, for Friedrich created it in direct response to the invasion and occupation of Dresden, the city in which he lived and worked, by the Napoleonic Army in 1813. Look closely, and you can see that the solitary central figure is a soldier. In fact, it is a French *chasseur*, or cavalryman, who has been dwarfed by the mighty forest into which he has ventured, a forest that represents the German people.

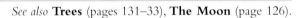

See also **Trees** (pages 131–33), **The Moon** (page 126).

The Celts worshipped their deities in sacred groves, and the trees that make up Friedrich's forest soar upward, toward the sky, as though emulating a Gothic cathedral or otherwise creating an environment that connects humankind with a higher realm. They are fir trees and, as evergreens (which retain their needlelike leaves in winter, when the boughs of deciduous trees look bare and dead), symbolize immortality. When interpreted in Friedrich's patriotic context, the suggestion is that the German people will survive, and rise above, any puny enemy incursions. As well as symbolizing the mother and community, the forest represents the unconscious mind: dark, unknown territory in which treasures—insights—may be found if monsters—fears—are faced and defeated.

The man stands at the center of a moonlit clearing. Its cruciform shape links it to the cross—could the Christian faith be this man's salvation? It is also strongly reminiscent of the crossroads: the *chasseur* must decide which path to take. Will he take his life into his hands and risk venturing into the forest? And if he does, will it prove as hostile as it appears? Or will he emerge "reborn" or wiser? His rigid stance, which hints that he is paralyzed by indecision, is echoed by the snow on the ground, which is variously a symbol of death, sterility, purity and frozen emotions.

The French word *chasseur* means "hunter," which can be taken to mean "seeker." Although he is in uniform, the *chasseur*'s sword remains sheathed and he has dismounted from his horse. His gleaming helmet draws the viewer's eyes to his head, underlining the sense that he has temporarily set aside his soldier's identity and is first and foremost an intelligent being in search of spiritual or psychological "gold."

The felled trees represent people who have been cut down in the prime of life on home ground, or the Germans who were killed defending their territory against French aggression.

Their black feathers cause crows, ravens and rooks to symbolize death, an association that is underlined by their carrion-eating habits and consequent tendency to frequent battlefields to feast on the fallen. Associated with such war deities as the Celtic goddess Babd, they were regarded as portents of doom and oracles of disaster. They do have positive symbolism, however, for their raucous croak sounds like *cras, cras*, which means "tomorrow, tomorrow," in Latin, so that some believe that they encourage us to hope for a better future.

Moonlight gently illuminates the cloudy night sky. Because the moon represents the feminine principle, which is in turn associated with the unconscious mind, when the clouds of confusion clear, lunar illumination may shed a little light on the mysteries that, until then, were cloaked in darkness.

The Animals Enter Noah's Ark

Kaspar Memberger

1588, oil on canvas, Residenzgalerie, Salzburg, Austria

As well as being a heraldic symbol of identity, the coat of arms that occupies the central ground at the top of this painting supplies a strong hint as to the symbolism underlying *The Animals Enter Noah's Ark*, a scene drawn from the Old Testament Book of Genesis (6–9). For these arms, which comprise a black rampant lion on a yellow ground adjacent to a red–silver–red set of horizontal bars (the arms of Salzburg), quartered with single cannonballs (the device of Wolf Dietrich von Raitenau), denote the prince–archbishop of Salzburg, which von Raitenau became in 1587, the year before he commissioned Memberger to paint a five-piece cycle of images based on the Noah's Ark theme. The patronage of this rich and powerful man, the leading Roman Catholic in Salzburg, means that we must keep a Christian interpretation at the forefront of our minds when considering this image.

The Old Testament relates that God was so displeased with the wicked behavior of the humans that he had created that he resolved to wipe them all out in a great flood—all, that is, except Noah and his family. He therefore instructed Noah to construct a wooden ark, or boat, and to fill it with a male and female representative of every species of living creature on earth. This Noah did, and so it was that he and his cargo survived the prolonged flooding of the earth. After the ark had come to rest on the mountains of Ararat, Noah sent out a raven on a scouting mission, and then a dove, which, on its second foray, returned with an olive branch in its beak, indicating that the floodwaters had fallen. When dry land was eventually visible, God instructed Noah and his passengers to leave the ark to "be fruitful, and multiply upon the earth" (Genesis 8:17).

According to the Christian viewpoint, the ark can denote the protection and salvation of either the Church or Christ in negotiating the dangerous waters of life, the Virgin Mary's womb, or else the world in microcosm, with its many and varied inhabitants representing the saints and sinners that inhabit it.

See also **Animals** (pages 133–38), **Birds** (pages 138–40).

In every culture, eggs are a symbol of the womb, of potential, of hope, and of the creation of new life. As the Easter egg, the egg represents the resurrection of Christ.

Monkeys, our closest relatives, generally have negative connotations in Christianity, probably because they are taken to represent that part of humankind's nature that is base, or "animal." They may thus symbolize such vices as lust, for instance, and sometimes even Satan. When monkeys are portrayed playing with a manmade artifact, such as the distaff depicted here, the combination may poke fun at human vanity, or generally send a demeaning message. As for the distaff itself, that may variously denote Clotho, one of the three Greek Fates, feminine activities, or—and this seems the most likely, given the context— Eve following the Fall.

Because it was this bird that provided the first tangible sign of life outside the ark following the flood, the dove (especially when portrayed with an olive branch in its beak) has come to denote God's covenant of peace with humankind, and hence peace itself.

The dove may also signify the Holy Ghost, one of the three components of the Christian Trinity.

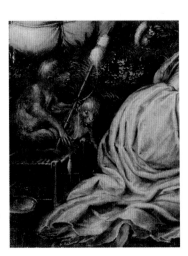

Apart from being a bird whose flesh is eaten on such festive occasions as Thanksgiving, the turkey has little sacred significance except in Native American belief, when it can denote fertility. Memberger may have included it here because it is said to become restless when it senses the coming of wet and stormy weather.

Christianity has an ambivalent attitude to cats, particularly black ones, which are traditionally the familiars of witches, associates of Satan. Some Christians smile upon them, however, on account of the furry "M" that can be seen above many cats' eyes, which they take to be a sign of the Virgin Mary's favor.

Purposes of composition apart, there may be a symbolic reason why Memberger has positioned a goat and sheep next to one another, for in Christianity, goats symbolize Satan and unbelievers (and lust), and sheep, members of Christ's flock (which is why Matthew 25:32 refers to Jesus, the shepherd, dividing his sheep from goats, which represent those who will suffer eternal damnation at the Last Judgment).

The Air

Johann Baptist Rudolf Byss

c.1718, oil on canvas, Sammlung Graf von Schönborn, Schloß Wiesentheid, Germany

The Swiss-born artist Johann Byss must have made umpteen sketches before setting to work on *The Air*, so many and varied are the birds that he has included in his allegory, one of a series of four entitled *The Four Elements* that was commissioned by his German employer, Lothar Franz von Schönborn, Archbishop of Mainz. Indeed, in one sense, it appears to be an encyclopedic inventory of birds, including such exotic specimens (to eighteenth-century European eyes, at least) as parrots, ostriches, flamingos and turkeys. In this manner, Byss has updated a centuries-old allegory, as well as setting himself the challenge of portraying all manner of feathered forms, and testing the viewers' avian knowledge, too.

The artist has retained some traditional touches, however, including, for example, the Greek goddess Hera (or Juno, as she was known in Rome), for according to a convention by which each element was personified as a Greco–Roman deity, Hera, the queen of heaven, represented the air. Byss has depicted her in a prominent position at the center of this image, wearing a sky-blue gown, with her crown and scepter signaling her authority and the golden chariot in which she traverses the sky acting as a temporary throne, while the peacocks that pull it wait alongside to resume their duties. In her role as the patron goddess of marriage and married women, the divine wife of Zeus (Jupiter) presides over a wedding ceremony, the implication being that this is truly a marriage made in heaven. Although Byss has not portrayed them here, the other three elements were similarly conventionally symbolized by Classical gods and goddesses: water, by Poseidon, or Neptune (he is, however, represented by a triton or merman and pair of fish-tailed water babies at left); fire, by Hephaestos, or Vulcan; and earth, by either Cybele or Demeter (Ceres). And while the birds and beings that populate this picture are primarily creatures of the air, their affinity with some of the other elements is subtly indicated here, too.

See also **Hera/Juno** (page 21), **The Seasons and Elements** (page 128).

The eagle was the attribute of Zeus (Jupiter), the Greco–Roman pantheon's chief god, and was, as such, deemed the king of the birds, which is why it became synonymous with power and victory and was adopted as the emblem of the Roman army and empire (and of many other subsequent bodies who aspired to be "top"). When the Roman emperor died, an eagle was released above his funeral pyre charged with carrying his soul to heaven to assume his immortal incarnation. The eagle was said to transport Zeus's thunderbolts in its claws, and similar associations with other sky deities led to it being associated with mythical, storm-bringing creatures like the Native American Thunderbird. As a snake-killer, the eagle, along with other birds that prey on serpents, can additionally be considered to represent the power of good, or light, vanquishing that of evil, or darkness.

The addition of wings to human bodies signifies their ability to fly swiftly around the world, unimpeded by earthly obstacles, above which they simply rise. The breath that this puffing cherub is visibly exhaling identifies him as a gust of air personified—maybe he will become a wind when he grows up. Air can also represent the breath of life, or the animating principle.

The ostrich may have wings, but can't fly, which is partly why it has earth-related symbolism. Another reason for its rather negative association with the earth is that it sometimes buries its head in the sand when distressed or confused, the upshot being that it can denote shutting one's eyes to the truth and preferring to remain in the dark rather than seeking enlightenment.

The Greeks considered the rainbow to be a manifestation of the goddess Iris, one of Hera's attendants. The ancient Egyptians and Babylonians, by contrast, believed that it adorned their principal goddesses, the former equating it with the seven stoles of Isis, and the latter, with the seven veils of Ishtar. Other cultures saw it as a bridge between heaven and earth, so that in Norse mythology, the rainbow Bifröst connected Asgard, the realm of the gods, with Mitgard, where the mortals dwelled.

Ducks represent marital fidelity and happiness in China, for once paired up, drake and duck are said to swim through the waters of life together, rarely straying from each other's side.

Their wings, and consequent ability to take flight and soar high above the earth, cause most birds to be symbols of the air, which is in turn considered to denote all things lofty and enlightened, such as an elevated state of consciousness, spiritual thoughts and noble aspirations. And because they were thought to travel effortlessly between heaven and earth, birds were said to act as messengers from the gods, carrying news and signals through the airwaves. Many belief systems additionally held that human souls took the form of birds, including that of ancient Egypt, where the *ba*, the immaterial essence of a person, was conceived of as bird with a human head; alternatively, certain birds were thought to carry the souls of the recently deceased to heaven.

The swan's symbolism is not clear-cut, and that it is interchangeable with that of the goose complicates matters even more, so it is appropriate that this bird is especially associated with transformation. Because it can fly, it is linked with the masculine, solar principle, but because it spends much of its time gliding through the water, it has feminine, lunar qualities, too. And because its plumage is white, and it often swims alone, it denotes sincerity and solitude. As the bird that pulled the Roman sun god Apollo's chariot, it was also associated with the Muses Erato and Clio, and was thought to embody the souls of poets. It was said only to sing when about to die, which why we refer to artists' final works or performances as their "swan-songs."

The goose had cosmic significance to ancient Egyptians, for one of their creation myths held that Hathor, the mother goddess, took the form of a Nile goose before laying either the world egg or the sun disk, the symbol of the sun god, Re. In Hinduism, the goose serves as the vehicle of the creator god Brahma.

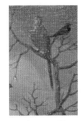

Westerners may admire parrots' talent for mimicry, but believe that these birds generally "parrot" anything they hear without understanding or insight. In Hinduism, by contrast, which considers the parrot to be the bird of Kama, the god of love, the parrot is said to utter prophetic phrases.

The crane was once thought to live for a thousand years, and therefore signifies immortality in China. Its one-legged stance gives it the reputation of being both vigilant and contemplative, for it would fall over if it stopped concentrating or fell asleep. Like many long-billed birds that poke their beaks into muddy riverbeds, it can also signify probing curiosity and the search for wisdom.

Falcons, hawks and other birds of prey are primarily associated with the piercing, all-encompassing vision that gives them an unbeatable "birds'-eye view" of the world. The falcon was considered the embodiment of Horus, the leading ancient Egyptian god who was master of the skies, and was associated with Re, too.

Landscape with House, Dog and Cow

Franz Marc

1914, oil on canvas, private collection, Switzerland

Eons of exposure to our natural environment has hard-wired an automatic response to different colors into the human brain. Thus the color yellow may remind us of the sun and warmth, thereby inducing feelings of sunny well-being, for instance, while red may evoke memories of blood and violence, and may consequently make us feel aggressive and unsettled. Through their work in the early years of the twentieth century, the leading lights of the German Expressionist movement—of which Franz Marc was one—sought to harness this primitive and innate language of color symbolism to express their emotions. And Marc was just one of the artists who went farther in developing their own vocabulary of color, the bare bones of which he sketched in a letter to his friend August Macke in 1910.

"The untouched instinct of animals for life struck a chord of all that is best in me," wrote Marc, in retrospective mood, to his wife in 1915. The cofounder (with Macke and Wassily Kandinsky) of the *Blaue Reiter* ("Blue Rider") group in 1911 felt an almost spiritual empathy with animals that roused him to try to express how it felt to be a horse, for example, through the medium of color. And when, on a visit to Paris in 1912, he saw French artist Robert Delaunay's abstract, vibrantly colored Orphic Cubist works, he, too, was inspired to experiment with crystalline shapes. All three elements—color, animals and fragmented forms—can be seen in *Landscape with House, Dog and Cow*, but one has to look at the image searchingly in order to discern the building and animals. Indeed, by 1914, Marc no longer regarded animals, or even nature, as pure, ideal subjects, and his style was consequently becoming increasingly abstract. We will never know how it would have evolved, however, for World War I broke out in the year in which Marc created this thought-provoking canvas, and two years later he was killed in action.

See also **Colors** (page 146).

The image's pointed components are reminiscent of shards of glass, or of fingers of rock crystal, both of which symbolize transparency of matter and penetrating and purposeful clarity of vision. As such, they represent knowledge and spirituality, while crystal has additional significance as a stone of healing, as well as an instrument of clairvoyance.

According to Marc, "yellow is the female principle, gentle, cheerful and sensual," and it is apt that the crescent moon should be pale yellow: it is regarded as a feminine symbol in most cultures. But is it waxing or waning, that is, gaining in strength or dying? Either way, change is signified.

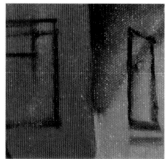

The house may represent Marc's home—his haven and place of security—but may alternatively denote the artist himself, for according to Jungian psychology, the house can symbolize the self, or "the mansion of the soul," with the basement, ground story and upper level respectively representing body, mind and spirit. It may therefore be significant that part of the upper wall is shaded blue, for "blue is the male principle, astringent and spiritual," declared Marc.

Dogs traditionally signify fidelity, protection, comradeship and friendship, and are furthermore associated with the masculine principle, which is why this canine may also represent the artist. It may be that Marc has depicted the dog investigating a patch of grass, whose green hue is associated with new growth, to emphasize, or encourage, these qualities in himself, or else, perhaps, to convey a sense of trusting naivety.

The cow represents the archetypal mother because it produces milk and because the shape of its horns resembles that of the crescent moon. Cows lie down when rain approaches —could Marc be warning of stormy times to come, and of the female response to them?

Marc considered that the purpose of life was to "reveal unearthly life dwelling behind everything, to break the mirror of life so that we may look being in the face." The fragmented appearance of this picture indeed resembles a smashed mirror, in which case is the "being" that we see the essence of the artist? Or is this a kaleidoscopic vision of his home circumstances, which have shattered, and are now constantly shifting? Is Marc expressing his sense of nostalgia, his current state of flux or his desire for future change?

"Red is matter, brutal and heavy, and always the color to be opposed and overcome [by blue and yellow]," stated Marc, who continued, "green always needs the help of some more blue (the sky) and yellow (the sun) in order to silence matter (red)." Marc also equated red with the earth, and in view of the impending war, it may be that he had a vision of blood-soaked battlefields.

Round of the Prisoners

Vincent van Gogh

1890, oil on canvas, Puskin Museum, Moscow, Russia

*R*ound of the Prisoners conveys exactly how low the artist was feeling when he painted it, thereby giving those who may never have experienced this soul-sapping condition a powerful insight into how it feels to be depressed.

When the Dutch artist Vincent van Gogh created this canvas, he was nearing the end of a year of voluntary incarceration in Saint-Paul-de-Mausole, Saint-Rémy-de-Provence, a psychiatric hospital in southern France to which he had been admitted after his mental health—always precarious—deteriorated dramatically (a few months earlier, he had cut off part of his left ear). Here, he continued to paint at a manic rate, producing around 150 oils alone, some of whose subjects emanated from his own imagination, while others, including *Round of the Prisoners*, were interpretations of copies of other artists' works sent to him by his brother, Theo. This painting's inspiration was an engraving by the French illustrator Gustave Doré (1832–83), entitled *Newgate: The Exercise Yard*, that appeared in his book *London: A Pilgrimage* (1872), Newgate being a prison in London. It may be that van Gogh simply considered reworking this image an interesting challenge, but given his circumstances, it is more likely that the original resonated with him in some way, perhaps because it mirrored the monotony of life in hospital or maybe because it echoed his sense of being a prisoner of his illness. Either way, through the use of little more than colour and shapes, he painted a picture that is at once dispiriting, claustrophobic and nightmarish, as well as utterly devoid of hope. Van Gogh produced *Round of the Prisoners* (which is also called *Prisoners Exercising*) in February 1890; in May, he was discharged and moved north, to Auvers-Sur-Oise; and on July 29, 1890, he took his own life. It is a chronology that helps us to understand that for van Gogh, his illness was a life sentence from which death was the only escape.

See also **Circle** (page 145), **Colors** (page 146).

Van Gogh (this is his self-portrait) looks directly at the viewer as he trudges around in the circle that he and his fellows have formed as a way of taking exercise. Like the wheel of life that constantly turns, describing an endless cycle of birth, life, death and rebirth, the moving circle is a symbol of the world, time and especially of eternity, which is clearly not always to be welcomed, judging by the defeated manner in which the men are traipsing in single file around their invisible circle, each isolated in his personal hell, but united by their endless suffering. Their circumambulation is aimless and futile, for although they are constantly on the move, they are getting nowhere. The empty circle can also denote a vacuum, void or emptiness.

The high brick walls symbolize human industry and manufacture, as well as constraint. The surface message is that the prisoners are being punished by society; the underlying suggestion is that the psychiatric patients' problems, and loss of freedom, are of their own making, or are all in their own minds. The bricks' terra-cotta color is furthermore that of the earth from which they were baked, and while the element of earth symbolizes matter, shades of brown represent the degradation of natural matter in fall, and consequently death and decomposition. These walls therefore denote a melancholy preoccupation with death, as well as imprisonment.

Some men stand to the side, watching the prisoners. The central figure's blue coat marks him out as a figure of authority and a dispenser of justice, this being a color that is associated with sky gods, many of which, like the Greek Zeus (or Roman Jupiter), meted out punishment by hurling thunderbolts at transgressors who breached their stipulated code of conduct.

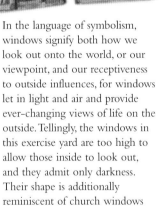

In the language of symbolism, windows signify both how we look out onto the world, or our viewpoint, and our receptiveness to outside influences, for windows let in light and air and provide ever-changing views of life on the outside. Tellingly, the windows in this exercise yard are too high to allow those inside to look out, and they admit only darkness. Their shape is additionally reminiscent of church windows —was van Gogh alluding to a spiritual "nothingness," or his loss of religious faith?

"Instead of trying to reproduce precisely what I have before my eyes, I use color more arbitrarily so as to express myself more forcibly," wrote van Gogh. The blue–green shades that predominate evoke both poison and mold, both of which can invade, and eventually overwhelm, healthy organisms, resulting in death and decay.

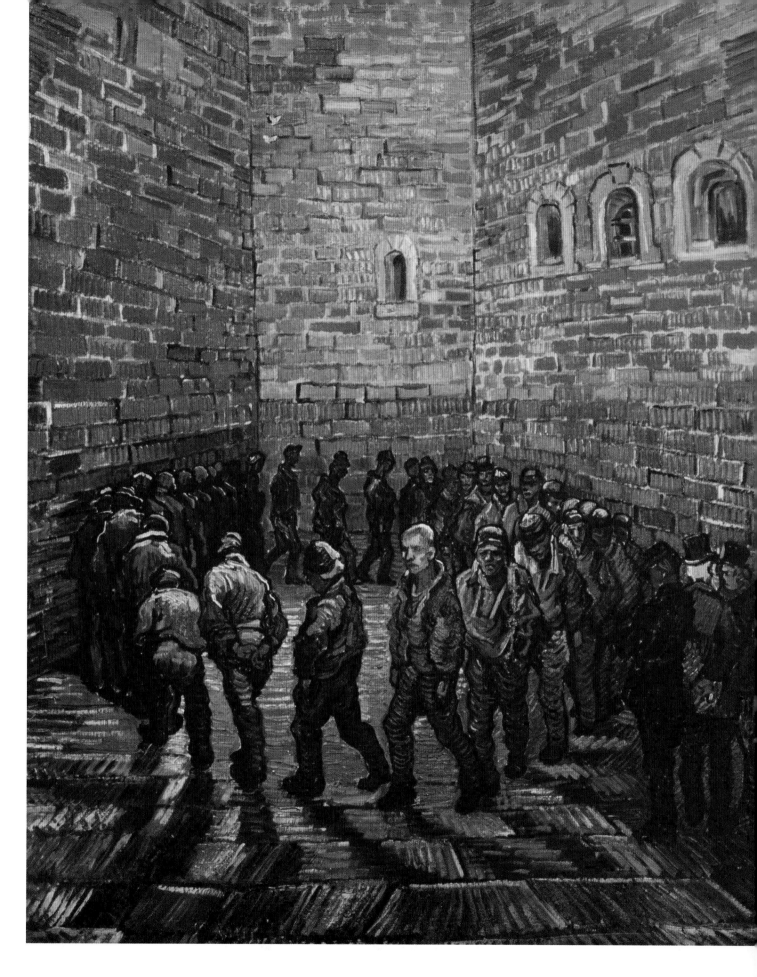

Blue may be the color of blue skies, but is also associated with depression, or "the blues," while thriving vegetal life may be green, but this is a color indicative of putrefaction, too. By mixing and applying these shades, was van Gogh expressing his feeling of having been terminally tainted by a terrible, toxic disease of the mind?

Round Table with the Holy Grail

artist unknown, from the *L'Estoire de Saint Grall*, by Robert de Boron

c.1450, manuscript illumination, Bibliothèque Nationale, Paris, France

As well as signifying eternity, the circle can represent completion and perfection, be it physical, psychological or spiritual, or all three. Because its shape is similar to those of the sun and planets, it can also symbolize the cosmos. In addition, in science, a circle with a dot at its center denotes the sun and gold, both of which, in their own way, represent radiant preeminence. The image of the Round Table of Arthurian lore, with the Holy Grail at its center, metaphorically corresponds to all of these concepts, while the numerous Grail-quest romances that have been told over the centuries attest to the near impossibility of attaining the "Holy Grail" of total perfection.

Symbolically, the Holy Grail has its origin in the Celtic cauldron, a mythical provider of plenty that, being equated with the womb, is in turn a symbol of the feminine power of procreation. It was the French poet Robert de Boron, who lived during the twelfth and thirteenth centuries, who, in his poem *Joseph d'Arimathie*, is thought to have been the first to "Christianize" this ancient Celtic symbol by linking it with Christ. Indeed, de Boron's romance provides the foundations for what has become an archetypal tale that relates that the Holy Grail was the cup that Christ filled with wine, which he called his blood, and exhorted his disciples to drink from at the Last Supper. Then when, at the crucifixion, the centurion Longinus pierced Christ's side with his lance (in this context, known as the "bleeding lance," and possibly a phallic symbol), Joseph of Arimathea caught Christ's blood and water in the Holy Grail. Joseph later traveled to Glastonbury, in England, where, before his death, he entrusted the Grail to Bron and his descendants. Said to have miraculous powers of healing, renewal and redemption, as well as being a source of never-ending nourishment, the Grail—like paradise, now lost to humankind—is sought by many, but appears only to the worthiest, the purest of heart.

See also **The Last Supper** (pages 110–13), **Circle** (page 145).

The courageous knight Lancelot was the father of Galahad. He was King Arthur's most trusted lieutenant until his affair with Guinevere jeopardized the Round Table fellowhip.

Historians agree that King Arthur—*Le Roy Artus* in Old French—did exist, albeit as a sixth-century Celtic warlord. Considered symbolically, however, it is likely that he represents a chief Celtic god, and his knights, lesser deities.

In some versions of the Grail quest, Galahad ("the Chaste") is the perfect knight, the last descendant of Joseph of Arimathea who is predestined to win the Grail. Not only has the artist depicted him as being head and shoulders above the rest here, but the canopy above him is reminiscent of the "T"-shaped *tau* cross, which early Christians inscribed in the Roman catacombs to symbolize immortality.

The Round Table, which was created by Merlin, represents the "roundness and rightness of the world." There being no "head" or "foot," those who sit at it have equal status; as a result, it can signify unity and perfect balance. When Grail lore specifies that the Round Table was modeled on the one that hosted the Last Supper, reference is made to a place identified with that of the traitorous Judas Iscariot, which is consequently left unoccupied. Only the "perfect knight" may sit at the "siege perilous," or "perilous seat," without incurring disaster, and when he does, totality is achieved.

In the illustration, the names visible around the table read: GAWAIN, VNEL, BORT, LANCELOT, GALAAD, PERSEVAL, LE ROY ARTVS, DELIAS, TRIST..., LE ROY RYONS, LE ROY CARADOS, LE ROY VOIER, LE ROY BANDEMA...

Supported by a pair of ethereal beings, the golden Grail radiates divine light from the heart of the Round Table. According to some accounts, when Galahad occupied the "siege perilous" at Pentecost (the feast day that commemorates the Holy Ghost's descent on the apostles), it made itself manifest, filling the surrounding knights with a sense of well-being and providing them with their favorite foods. Often represented as an ornate chalice of the type used to contain communion wine, the Grail may be more simply represented as a downward-pointing triangle, a symbol of life-giving water and femininity. An alternative name, Sangraal, is derived from *Saint Graal*, the Old French for "Holy Grail," but some claim that it is derived instead from *Sang Royal*, or "Blood Royal." According to this theory, the Holy Grail represents the womb (said to be Mary Magdalene's, whose traditional attribute is similarly a vessel) that perpetuated Christ's bloodline through the birth of his progeny.

The Seven Deadly Sins and the Four Last Things

Hieronymus Bosch

c.1480–1500, oil on wood, Museo del Prado, Madrid, Spain

Although the number seven generally has positive symbolism, denoting, for example, entirety (there being seven days in the week and, in ancient astrology, seven planets or heavens), in one particular Christian context, at least, it has negative connotations. For ever since their codification during the sixth century by Pope Gregory the Great, Christians have been warned against succumbing to seven deadly, or cardinal, sins, which, if indulged in in life, will incur eternal damnation in the afterlife. These are lust (*luxuria* in Latin), gluttony (*gula*), avarice (*avaritia*), sloth (*acedia*), anger (*ira*), envy (*invidia*) and pride (*superbia*).

In his decorated table-top, which the Roman Catholic King Philip II of Spain installed in his bedroom at the Escorial palace, Netherlandish painter Hieronymus Bosch has depicted scenes of people engaged in each of the seven deadly sins, arrayed around the radiant, all-seeing eye of God, in whose "pupil" Bosch has painted a portrait of Christ rising from the grave, displaying some of the wounds that were inflicted on him at his crucifixion—a reminder that he gave his life in order to redeem humankind's sins. And if that weren't enough to prick a transgressor's guilty conscience, Bosch has furthermore included representations of the "Four Last Things"—death, the Last Judgment (top right), heaven (bottom right) and hell—as a *memento mori*, or a reminder that death comes to us all, and that how our behavior on earth is judged will decide whether we end up spending eternity in a state of heavenly bliss or infernal torture. And if we are deemed guilty of committing any of the deadly sins, a really hideous fate awaits us, as Bosch has illustrated.

The number seven is not only associated with sin in Christianity, however, for seven cardinal virtues—chastity, moderation, generosity, zeal, meekness, charity and humility—counterbalance the seven deadly sins.

See also **The Last Judgment** (pages 116–18), **Death** (page 150), **The Triumph of Death** (pages 202–03).

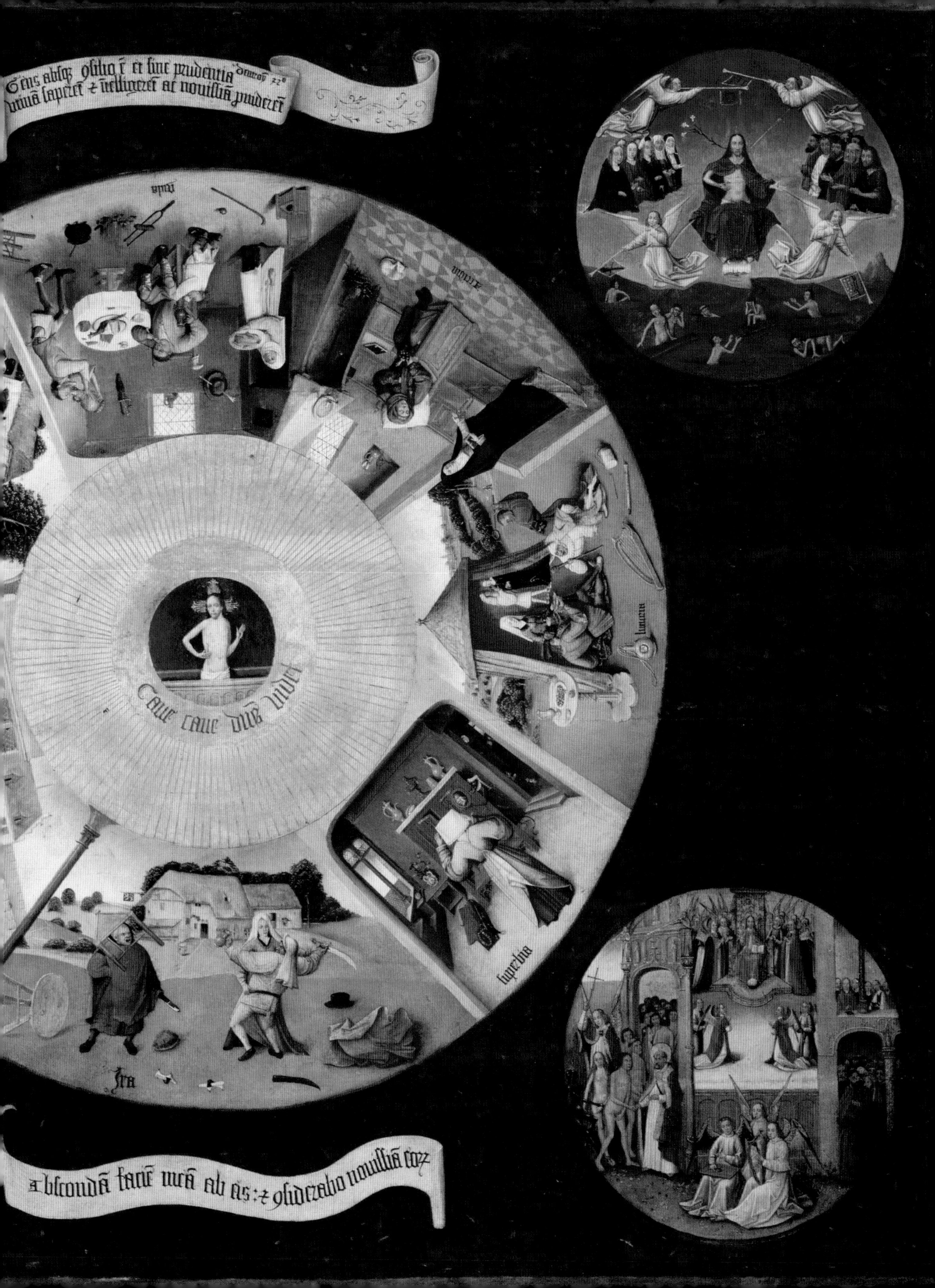
superbia
Ira

In the first of the "Last Things," a skeleton—death—points his arrow at the man on his deathbed, confirming that his time has come. A demon (a symbol of temptation) and angel are in attendance, ready to fight over the dying man's soul.

A demon encourages a lady who has donned her finery to admire herself in the mirror. For her deadly sin of pride (*superbia*), she may be broken on a wheel in hell, or maybe the little devil has a more imaginative punishment in store for her. The toad that crawls over her in the infernal afterworld signifies that the devil has entered into her, while the infernal, tailless peacock that pecks at her appalled companion symbolizes vanity.

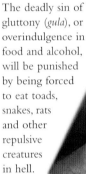

The deadly sin of gluttony (*gula*), or overindulgence in food and alcohol, will be punished by being forced to eat toads, snakes, rats and other repulsive creatures in hell.

Whosoever is culpable of the deadly sin of envy (*invidia*) in this world may find that their jealousy is frozen out by immersion in ice-cold water in the next.

Those guilty of the deadly sin of sloth (*acedia*), or idleness and time-wasting, will pay the price in hell, where they will be made horrifically jumpy when they are cast into a pit full of slithering, sharp-tongued serpents.

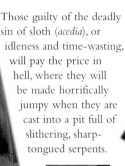

Rather than fanning the flames of their passion, those who succumb to the deadly sin of lust (*luxuria*) will find that hell quenches their carnal desires in red-hot fire and brimstone.

Those who cannot control their anger (*ira*) and resort to violence when in the prime of life may find that the tables are turned on them in death, and that they are destined to spend eternity being cut to pieces by pitiless demonic butchers.

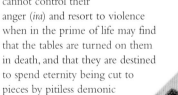

If people cannot conquer their avarice (*avaritia*) when on earth, they may be boiled in the best-quality oil forever after in hell.

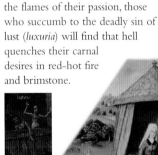

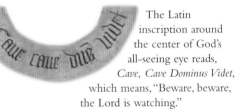

This Latin text is taken from the Old Testament Book of Deuteronomy, 32.28–29, and its English equivalent is: "For they are a nation void of counsel, neither is there any understanding in them. O that they were wise, that they understood this, that they would consider their latter end!"

Another verse from Deuteronomy (32:20) reads, when translated from the Latin, "I will hide my face from them, I will see what their end shall be."

Below this Biblical inscription can be discerned the artist's signature, "Hieronimus Bosch."

The Latin inscription around the center of God's all-seeing eye reads, *Cave, Cave Dominus Videt*, which means, "Beware, beware, the Lord is watching."

Apollo and the Muses

Maarten de Vos

1580, oil on wood, Musées Royaux des Beaux-Arts, Brussels, Belgium

Not only is nine a number of great symbolic resonance in many cultures, it overwhelmingly transcends global differences of interpretation as one that has huge significance to all humankind. For nine months is the period of human gestation, during which an embryonic person is conceived, incubated and nourished until the infant is ready to embark upon life's journey and emerges into the world. Therefore a number of creation and completion, as well as of ends and beginnings, nine is also the number of the Classical Muses (from *mousai*, "mountain spirits" in Greek), Greco–Roman goddesses who together represented the sum total of human knowledge, also acting as patrons, encouragers and inspirers of the arts, and thus symbolizing ends and beginnings, too.

Although different ancient Greco–Roman sources give conflicting accounts of the Muses' number, parentage and individual responsibilities, it eventually came to be accepted that there were nine of these accomplished sisters, who were born to Zeus and the Titan Mnemosyne ("Memory") on nine consecutive nights at Pieria, below Mount Olympus. Calliope ("Beautiful Voice"), who spoke for the sisters, was the Muse of epic poetry; Clio ("Proclaimer"), that of history; Erato ("Lovely") was the Muse of lyric and love poetry; Euterpe ("Joy") was music's Muse; the responsibility of the Muse Melpomene ("Lamenting") was tragedy; Polyhymnia ("Many Songs") was the Muse of sacred songs; Terpsichore ("Lover of Dance") presided over dance and song; Thalia ("Good Cheer") was the Muse of comedy; and astronomy's Muse was Urania ("Celestial").

Apollo, who, it is told, was a talented player of the lyre, as well as a prophetic pronouncer of oracles, often led the Muses in song on Mount Parnassus (where his Delphic Oracle was situated), on such occasions being called Apollo Musagetes. And when they weren't making music with Apollo, the Muses spent their time singing and dancing on mountainsides, taking part in, or judging, musical competitions and tending the waters of poetic inspiration that flowed from the fountains of Hippocrene and Aganippe, on Mount Helicon, and Castalia, on Mount Parnassus.

See also **Apollon/Apollo** (page 23), *Apollo and Mercury* (pages 44–45), **Numbers** (page 147–48).

Portrayals of Polyhymnia may have her playing a keyboard, or sometimes a lute, or else simply looking thoughtful. The "F.MDVOS" that can be seen on the side of her instrument, which is decorated with the famous Greek-key motif, is the artist's signature and stands for *fecit* ("made by" in Latin) Maarten de Vos.

Soberly dressed Melpomene is often depicted holding a Greek tragedian's mask or a dagger, but has, perhaps, picked up a violin in order to play a haunting lament.

Thalia, the Muse of comedy, seems to be suppressing a smile as she strums her lute. Artists may alternatively portray her holding a Greek comedian's mask or a shepherd's crook.

Although Erato shakes a tambourine here to provide rhythm, she is an equally adept player of the lyre, violin and many other instruments.

Calliope's "big-sister" status is indicated by her seated, center-stage position. She is typically depicted holding a manuscript and a stylus, or else a trumpet.

As is traditional, Euterpe is shown playing a flute, for her particular preference is for wind instruments.

Clio appears engrossed in her manuscript; perhaps she is reading about the Greek heroes' exploits.

Terpsichore plucks the strings of a harp, but may, on other occasions, generate dance music on a lyre or violin or accompany her sisters on a pair of cymbals.

Urania is typically shown studying either a globe or the starry heavens, but has put away the compasses that she often holds in order to coax a melodious tune from her lute.

The tenth figure amid this nonet of Muses stands out on account of his masculinity. He is Apollo, the Greco–Roman god of light, prophecy, music and order, who makes such sweet music with his golden lyre that all of nature stops to listen. There is a sad story attached to his laurel wreath, for it is a reminder of Daphne, the nymph who rejected his love so emphatically that she begged her father, the River Ladon, to save her from Apollo's determined advances, whereupon she was transformed into a laurel tree.

El Aquellare (The Witches' Sabbath) Francisco de Goya

c.1797–98, oil on canvas, Museo Lazaro Galdiano, Madrid, Spain

In Christian belief, Satan, or the devil, and his forces of evil wage a constant war against God and goodness, and miss no opportunity to tempt and corrupt susceptible humans with alluring promises of personal gain and gratification (in this life, at least, and typically at a terrible cost to others). In art, as in the Bible, the Devil and his black-hearted demons have been portrayed as serpents and dragons, as other types of monstrous hybrids and as cunning shape-shifters who may even assume human form in their quest to win as many souls for hell as possible. In folklore, they may be aided in their fiendish mission by malevolent human helpers, or witches, whose magical powers are the gift of their dark master, whom they worship in desolate spots on moonlit nights. And because much of the symbolism associated with all things satanic is derived from the notion that Satan, once a rebel angel named Lucifer, covets God's power, many aspects of Devil-worship recall Christian rites, albeit with a perverted twist. Thus witches' covens are said to be made up of thirteen, precisely because that number arouses a superstitious shudder in Christians, there being thirteen at the Last Supper, when Satan entered into Judas Iscariot (John 13:27), prompting him to betray Jesus. Similarly, their midnight meetings, known as "witches' sabbaths" or "sabbats," are the infernal equivalent of the Judeo–Christian Sabbath, the traditional day of rest and worship of God.

History has shown that belief in witchcraft, and the persecution of women branded witches—many of them harmless eccentrics, practitioners of herbal medicine, cat-lovers or merely those whose neighbors had experienced a run of bad luck—often increases during times of social upheaval, for which scapegoats are sought, and nowhere more so than in Spain, where thousands accused of heresy and witchcraft were put to death by the Spanish Inquisition. It may therefore be that Goya's painting (one of six commissioned by the Duchess of Osuna) arose from social dissatisfaction or that it satirized Spain's ruling regime.

See also **Satan and His Demons** (page 82), **Dionysus/Bacchus** (page 25).

In Greco–Roman mythology, certain goddesses were linked with the moon, the most feared being Hekate, or Hecate, the Greek goddess of the underworld and mistress of the arts of black magic who had three faces, each representing a lunar phase. Placated, worshiped and invoked by women in night-time rites, Hekate was regarded as the goddess of witches.

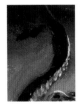

Bats are associated with Satan in Christian art, partly on account of their Devil-like black wings. They were regarded as being unnatural crosses between mice and birds; they hang upside down while sleeping, and they only emerge from their roosts to hunt at night. Considered to be agents of darkness, destruction and death, bats were feared as the vampiric familiars of witches.

The Devil is sometimes depicted as a goat, in part because the New Testament equates goats with the damned, and also because this animal is regarded as an incarnation of the deadly sin of lust. This Satanic goat may have been modeled on the goatlike Pan, the Greek god of flocks who was equated with the Roman Faunus, but the vine or ivy leaves that garland his horns (themselves phallic symbols) suggest Dionysus, or Bacchus, the Greco–Roman god of wine, whose attendants, the satyrs, were half-men and half-goats. Dionysus was said to roam the world teaching the vintner's secrets to select initiates, the mixed-sex bacchantes, whose rowdy, intoxicated night-time orgies of celebration (called dionysia or bacchanalia) may have been at the root of tales of Devil-worship, just as the maenads, Dionysus's female followers, may have inspired the idea of witches' covens.

Satan sits at the center of a circle of hags, his fiery eyes glowing as a plump baby is offered to him. Witches were said to sacrifice children to the Devil in cannibalistic rituals ("black masses") that parodied the Eucharist and Christ's self-sacrifice.

Triumph of Chastity

Jacopo del Sellaio

c.1480–90, tempera on wood, Museo Bandini, Fiesole, Italy

Del Sellaio's *Triumph of Chastity* is based on the *Trionfi* ("Triumphs"), an allegorical cycle of verses by a fellow Italian, the fourteenth-century poet Petrarch, that describes how Eternity, Time, Fame, Death, Chastity and Love—each personifications of their respective qualities—vanquish one another in turn, leaving Eternity the ultimate victor. The concept of a triumphal possession in which a conqueror's chariot is pulled through the streets (in Chastity's case, by unicorns) in order to receive the people's plaudits, rather in the manner of a carnival or parade float, was not invented by Petrarch, however, instead being a customary way of fêting triumphant generals in Rome.

Just as her "triumph" was inspired by ancient Rome, so Italian Renaissance artists modeled the figure of Chastity on such Roman virgin goddesses as Diana (Artemis), the deity of the moon and hunting, and Minerva (Athene), the goddess of wisdom and war, often furnishing her with their attributes, such as a crescent moon or bow, or a shield. Chastity is also one of the three monastic vows (the other two being poverty and obedience), or "counsels of perfection," and in an exclusively Christian context, is typically depicted successfully fighting off a snake or wild boar, or any other creature associated with uncontrollable lust.

On the face of it, the unicorn—a fabulous creature said to have the body of a diminutive white horse or antelope, whose name is derived from the Latin description of its distinguishing feature, *unum cornu*, the "one horn" that grows from its head—has straightforward symbolic significance as the pure and noble companion of virgins, notably Christianity's Virgin Mary. Although its traditionally spotless white coat and the supposed ability of its horn to neutralize poison are largely responsible for its association with virtue and purity, if one considers its horn a phallic symbol, its equine body to represent animal passions and potency, and its goatee ("goatish") beard to signify lust, the notion that only a virgin could capture it and quell its libidinousness by appealing to its higher nature, or ability to reason, adds a deeper layer of meaning.

See also **Eros/Amor/Cupid** (page 26).

Among the virginal figures accompanying Chastity is Tuccia, a vestal virgin who, in Roman legend, was accused of having committed adultery (for which she would have been buried alive if found guilty), but who proved her innocence by carrying water from the River Tiber to her temple (in Rome's Forum) in a sieve. The sieve has consequently become a symbol of all virgins.

The victorious lady's triumphal banner is decorated with the image of an ermine, or rather, a stoat, which, in wintry northern European climes, exchanges its dark coat for a white one (although the tip of its tail remains black). White is the color of innocence, purity and virginity, which is why the ermine is the emblem of Chastity.

Having described how Love, who is usually depicted as Cupid or Amor (the Roman god of love whose ancient Greek counterpart was Eros), failed to conquer Chastity, Petrarch goes on to describe how Lucretia and Penelope (each of whom, in lore, famously resisted men's lustful advances) broke his arrows, threw away his quiver and plucked the feathers from his wings, thereby rendering their prisoner impotent and incapable of either letting loose his "shafts of love" or flying away.

Chastity is usually represented as a young, serious-looking woman, who is veiled or modestly dressed. The golden object that she is holding may be a section of Cupid's shattered bow, and may thus be a trophy, a tangible symbol of her victory over carnal love. Alternatively, it may be a palm leaf or branch, a symbol of military triumph that champions carried in ancient Rome, and that was adopted by Christians to denote victory over death.

Flowers, the symbol of fresh, unsullied beauty, strew the path of the virtuous victors, and Petrarch singles out roses and violets for special mention: in the language of flowers, white-petaled roses and violets denote virginity, while roses in general signify beauty, and violets, modesty.

Petrarch names the Sabine women, who were raped by the men of Rome, as being among the troop of women parading alongside Chastity's chariot as they enter Rome.

St. George

artist unknown

Nineteenth century, tempera on wood, private collection, Frankfurt, Germany

On the face of it, this vibrant painting is exactly what it seems, namely, a depiction of St. George killing the dragon. But there is far more to it than that, not least because it is a Russian icon (a word derived from the Greek *eikon*, "likeness"), which, in accordance with the traditions of the Greek-influenced Orthodox, or Eastern, Church, means that it is regarded by believers as a sacred aid to meditating on, praying to, and ultimately communing with the holy or saintly personage portrayed, rather than simply a piece of piety-promoting representational art, as is more characteristic of the Roman Catholic Church.

Legend tells us that St. George was a Christian born in Cappadocia, Asia Minor, who joined the Roman Army. He would eventually die an agonizing martyr's death in Palestine around AD 300, a victim of the Roman Emperor Diocletian's persecution of Christians, but before then, while riding one day, George encountered a princess weeping beside a lake. When he enquired about the cause of her distress, she explained that a dragon living in the lake had been terrorizing her town. It had started by killing citizens with its poisonous breath, and although it had stayed away when offered two sheep daily, the town's supply of livestock had now run so low that lots were being drawn each day to decide which young man or woman would be sacrificed to the beast. Now it was the princess's turn to die, and she pleaded with George to go before he, too, was devoured. George, however, resolved to save her, and when the dragon appeared, made the sign of the cross, and then attacked and wounded it. Before delivering the *coup de grâce*, George ordered the princess to tie her girdle around its neck and lead it into the town; this awe-inspiring demonstration of the power of Christ so impressed the citizens that they all converted to Christianity.

In symbolic terms, St. George represents Christianity, or the power of goodness, vanquishing Satan, or evil, and this icon encourages believers to wage war on, and conquer, the sin within themselves. Because it has striking parallels with such more ancient myths as that of the Babylonian Marduk and Tiamat, and the Greek Perseus and the sea monster, this conquest may also represent the defeat and demonization of the divine, lunar feminine by a masculine, solar, hero figure. And finally, when decoded, its secular symbolism may denote the victory of reason over ignorance.

*See also **Andromeda** (pages 56–57), **Dragon** (page 144), **Colors** (page 146).*

The artist has indicated the sanctity of Christ, the angel and St. George by portraying them with haloes.

Screened from earthly view by a bank of clouds, Christ is on the side of St. George as he watches the champion of Christianity do battle against the dragon. The book that Jesus holds in his hands may be the *liber mundi* (Latin for "book of the world") or *liber vitae* ("book of life"), but in either instance, represents God's universal knowledge and ineffable wisdom.

The crosses at the top of George's lance (which can represent a solar ray or shaft of light) and emblazoned on his armor symbolize the aggressive and protective power of Christianity in the war against the Devil, wickedness, paganism and heresy.

The crown that the angel—a messenger of God—is about to place on the saint's head symbolizes his victory over the dragon, but may also refer to his impending martyrdom, a martyr's crown signifying victory over death.

If George himself denotes the spirit of Christianity, or soul, his horse represents the animal energy, or body, that is under the control of this overriding spirit, its white color additionally symbolizing light, spotless purity, and spiritual illumination.

The horse's hoof tramples on the dragon's tail, heralding the creature's defeat, a message that is also conveyed by the knot that the dragon's tail is forming (it was said that a dragon's might was concentrated in its tail, and that a knotted tail therefore symbolized the "tying up" of this strength, or impotence).

Just as the Virgin Mary's girdle may symbolize her chastity, so the princess's girdle may denote virtue, which, in a maiden's innocent hands, has the power to neutralize the dragon's evil-doing instincts.

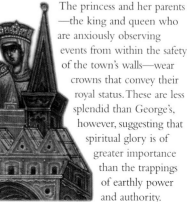

The princess and her parents —the king and queen who are anxiously observing events from within the safety of the town's walls—wear crowns that convey their royal status. These are less splendid than George's, however, suggesting that spiritual glory is of greater importance than the trappings of earthly power and authority.

The dragon's scarlet head and wings are the color of blood and battle, while its black body is associated with darkness and death, corruption and evil. The fantastic creatures described as dragons can vary greatly in form, but are generally said to have a crocodilelike head, a lion or bird of prey's limbs and talons, a bat's wings, a lizard or fish's scaly body, and a snake's tail; some may also have multiple heads and fire-exhaling lungs. Although they are said to prefer living in dark places, such as underwater habitats or caves, as hybrid beings, they are also at home in the open, on land or in the air.

Minerva Tames the Centaur

Sandro Botticelli

1482, oil on wood, Galleria degli Uffizi, Florence, Italy

In recent years there has been some disagreement about the identity of the beautiful woman Botticelli has depicted coolly stopping an unhappy-looking centaur in his tracks by grasping him by the hair. For many centuries she was considered to be Minerva, the goddess of wisdom and war and the Roman equivalent of the Greek Athene, but recent research suggests that she is actually Camilla, who is described, in ancient Roman texts, as being a daughter of Metabus, king of the Volsci, and a virgin huntress with martial tastes who dedicated herself to the service of Diana (Artemis).

In fact, in an allegorical painting like this, it is not who she is that is important, but what she represents, and in this respect it matters not whether she is a mortal or a goddess. For all three suggested subjects have virginity in common, which, in the Renaissance period during which Botticelli worked, was much admired, being equated with virtue, purity and the ability to reason clearly and logically without having one's clarity of judgment clouded by messy, illogical animal passions. The superiority of rational thought over a confused state of libidinous irrationality is underlined here by Botticelli's inclusion of the centaur, a wild, strange and potentially dangerous creature that has submitted to the lovely, but firm, lady and is on the verge of being tamed. Indeed, with the exception of the wise and accomplished Cheiron (Chiron), who acted as a mentor to many young Greek heroes, Greek mythology asserts that centaurs were notorious for their lustful, violent, drunken rampages, the nadir of their "animal" behavior being when they ran amok at the wedding feast of King Pirithous of Lapith after one of their number, Eurytus, had tried to rape Hippodamia, the bride. No such fantastic beings exist in reality, of course, and, symbolic considerations apart, it is likely that fleeting, bruising encounters with an uncultivated tribe of accomplished nomadic horsemen inspired the Greeks' tales of brutish centaurs.

See also **Minerva Competing with Neptune for the Possession of Attica** (pages 46–49).

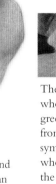

When Botticelli painted this allegory, the halberd —a staff with a spearhead surmounting an ax and a pick—was a weapon wielded by sentries. It therefore denotes vigilance, and the means with which to defend against aggressive incursions. By including it in this image, Botticelli may have been suggesting that although the heroine has some serious hardware to fall back on if necessary, the mere touch of her hand is enough to subdue the centaur that has encroached into the territory that she is guarding, the message being that even the strongest of beasts is no match for moral authority.

The centaur's hybrid body fuses the head, arms and torso of a man with the legs and body of a horse, and therefore combines both human and equine qualities. Because he has a human brain, he is equipped with the ability to think lucidly, to reason and to rein in his animal instincts. But because he has an animal's powerful nether regions and energy, these usually prevail, especially when alcohol dissolves any human moral inhibitions.

The lady is garlanded in foliage whose small, narrow, grayish-green leaves identify it as coming from an olive tree. The olive is a symbol of Minerva (Athene), who created it in order to enrich the lives of the people of Athens, which boosts the case of those who claim that Botticelli was depicting this goddess. Yet it also signifies peace, knowledge, purification and victory, all of which have resonance in this situation.

The three interlocking rings that are woven so decoratively into the lady's diaphanous dress are an emblem of the wealthy Florentine de' Medici family, a leading member of which commissioned this painting from Botticelli. As well as acknowledging Lorenzo's financial part in the image's creation, this device recalls the Holy Trinity, Botticelli thereby subtly introducing a Christian symbol into an ostensibly pagan image at a time, and in a place, that was exclusively Roman Catholic, and aligning it with virtue. On the sleeve, the symbol morphs into a quartet of rings, and in this instance

Although the centaur's bow and arrow can signify power and control when wielded by the intelligent and judicious Cheiron, in this, more general, context, the arrow should be read as a phallic symbol on account of its rigid shaft and penetrating tip.

it may be significant that the number four represents rationality and balance.

A Tryst at a Riverside Café

James Tissot

c.1869, oil on canvas, Sotheby's, London, England

"Every picture tells a story," as the saying goes, and although there is no mythical tale or historical legend connected with this couple that can tell us more about their identity or the precise nature of their relationship, their creator, the French artist James Tissot, has provided us with plenty of clues with which to piece together a likely story.

Tissot (whose signature can be seen beneath the trellis on the left), paid such meticulous attention to the details of his female subjects' apparel that his paintings have become an important source of information for those researching Victorian costumes. Here, however, he has chosen to dress his glamorous couple in bygone fashions inspired by the French *Directoire* (Directory) period (1795–99). Indeed, the voluminous folds that cascade softly from the high waistline of the lady's dress, along with her beau's cocked hat, contribute to the sense that they have stepped straight out of the pages of a historical romance or romantic novel. That said, the key to decoding the story underlying this picture can be found in the pair's body language, which conveys the intimacy, sensuality, excitement and secrecy involved in an illicit affair, or one that may soon be embarked upon, at least, for the dashing man appears to be whispering a seductive proposition to the pretty young woman. By turning her back on him, she, it seems, is either attempting to hide her rapt, expressive face, and consequently her tender feelings, from him or is pretending to disassociate herself from him lest they be spotted together, perhaps by a jealous husband or fiancé or else by a disapproving mother or society matron. Whatever their exact circumstances, the powerfully romantic aura that they project appears to have infected the dreamy-faced waitress, who seems to be lost in a world of her own as she starts to set the tables for lunch.

See also **Colors** *(page 146).*

The whiteness of the young lady's dress signals her innocence, although it is unclear whether this refers to her naivety, chastity or pure morals. Being the color of baptismal gowns and wedding dresses, white is also the color of initiation, rites of passage and embarkations on new phases of life. Yet the touches of black in her outfit not only show that she has a sophisticated flair for accessorizing, but furthermore suggest that she harbors characteristics that are the complete opposite of "whiter than white."

The lady's lapdog may be a fashion statement, but in the language of symbolism, represents marital fidelity. Perhaps it is no coincidence that its outstretched paw is in line with the ring on its mistress's left hand—an engagement or wedding ring, perhaps? And if so, does the ring, which is a symbol of unity and eternity, bind her to another man?

The debonair suitor cuts a dash in his flamboyant outfit, but it is the scarlet hue of his coat that gives him such a rakish air. Red sends contradictory signals, being the color of blood and fire, and therefore of the life force, of danger and destruction, of masculinity, impulsiveness and aggression, and of sexual arousal, heated emotions and red-hot passions. Being the color of hellfire, it is additionally a hue linked with Satan and temptation, also being associated with revolution and the overthrow of the old order, which is not always a bad thing.

All things considered, it appears as though this vital, virile man is trying to talk the passive object of his desire into making a life-changing choice, but will it be for better or for worse?

Bridges are symbols of transition and change because they enable us to cross from one place, or stage, to another in a journey, including the journey of life. Water, and consequently the river that flows beneath the bridge, is a feminine symbol, being linked with the moon and the unconscious, but do the solid-looking family homes on the other riverbank represent the young lady's future or her past?

A mysterious object lies on the otherwise clean-swept ground. Could it be a sausage that neither the waitress nor dog have noticed, or have otherwise chosen to ignore? If so, could Tissot have intended it to be read as a phallic symbol? Could he have been alluding to the carnal potential in the couple's relationship?

The Merchant Georg Gisze
Hans Holbein the Younger

1532, oil on oak, SMPK, Gemäldegalerie, Berlin, Germany

Although it was painted in London, England, neither the sitter nor the artist were English, and, indeed, they probably conversed in Middle Low German while *The Merchant Georg Gisze* was taking shape. It was important to both men that it had the "wow factor," Gisze wanting to impress his fiancée back home, as well as his business associates, with a portrait in which he appeared both authoritative and prosperous, and the German-born Holbein, who had recently arrived in England from Basle, in Switzerland, in search of work, hoping that it would trigger a flood of lucrative commissions. The portrait must have fulfilled all expectations, for it is recorded that Gisze was married three years later in his Baltic hometown, and that Holbein was employed by King Henry VIII of England in 1536. *The Merchant Georg Gisze* is a rewarding picture for the twenty-first-century viewer to study, too, partly because its photographic quality is as impressive today as it was in 1532, partly because the everyday objects that surround him make the long-dead Gisze (1497–1562) seem more of a real person, and partly because it gives us an extraordinary insight into how offices looked nearly six hundred years ago.

As a merchant from Danzig—today known as Gdansk—a town that belonged to the Hanseatic League (a powerful, northern European trade confederation), Gisze's business was international, and by 1532, it had taken him to London, where he lived and worked tax-free with other German merchants in the Thames-side Steelyard complex. Being based in London for a few years must have been good for trade, but can't have been a particularly comfortable existence, not least because only bachelors were permitted to reside at the Steelyard. This explains the presence of the Venetian-glass vase filled with flowers—an otherwise rather incongruous touch in a trader's office—for according to the conventions of the time, carnations denoted engagement, leading one to surmise that Gisze had his likeness painted as a gift for his bride-to-be, and that Holbein included the flowers as a tribute to her.

See also **Flowers** (pages 129–30).

A pair of scales and a signet, or seal, counterbalanced by a ball of amber (for which the Baltic region is renowned) hang from a shelf. Holbein has included Gisze's personal motto to the left: *Nulla sine merore voluptas*, or "No joy without sadness" when translated from the Latin, which may refer to his separation from his fiancée.

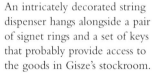

An intricately decorated string dispenser hangs alongside a pair of signet rings and a set of keys that probably provide access to the goods in Gisze's stockroom.

A number of red seals have been tucked behind a batten, alongside the letters whose contents they once kept private. Some of the writing is legible, such as *In Jurge zu Basel 1531*, or "From George in Basle 1531" (could this have been a letter recommending Holbein to Gisze?)

Pinned to the wall, as though it were an office memo, is an important statement written in Latin (then the international language of both business and posterity) and a little Greek. *Distichon I Imagine Georgii Gysenii Ista, refert vultus, qua cernis, Imago Georgi Sic oculos viuos, sic habet ille genas Anno aetatis suae xxxiiij Anno dom 1532*, it says, which means: "Look at the portrait of George Gisze. What you see here shows his features and figure; his eyes and cheeks look exactly as they do in life. In his thirty-fourth year, in the year of our Lord 1532."

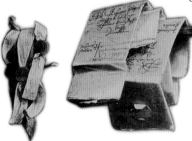

continued overleaf

The document that Gisze is holding is a letter addressed to *Dem Erszamen Jorgen gisze to lunden in engelant mynem broder to handen* (the Middle Low German for, "To the honorable George Gisze in London, England. To be given into his hands.")

During this period, carnations in a vase represented engagement (the underlying symbolism was probably to do with future children, for a water-filled vase can signify the fertile womb, and pink flowers, the babies that it sustains). Rosemary, a few sprigs of which can be discerned here, symbolizes remembrance—an appropriate floral message to send to Danzig.

Arrayed on the expensive Oriental carpet that serves as a tablecloth are a brass timepiece, which suggests both that time passes quickly and that its owner, like it, is well-regulated, or disciplined; a signet; writing implements, sticks of sealing wax, a sand-shaker with which to dry wet ink and a pile of loose change (or wax disks) in a pewter stand; and a pair of scissors.

One of Gisze's numerous signet rings also lies on the table: used to imprint a symbol of personal or corporate identity on molten sealing wax, it may be that Gisze handed them to his representatives to use, or that he himself acted as the agent for many different concerns, whose seals he was therefore entrusted with as a sign that authority had been delegated to him.

Giovanni Arnolfini and his Wife ("The Arnofini Portrait")

Jan van Eyck

1434, oil on wood, National Gallery, London, England

The question mark that casts doubt upon the identity of the man portrayed in the painting perhaps provisionally entitled *Portrait of Giovanni Arnolfini and his Wife ("The Arnolfini Portrait")* is by no means the only query that art historians have raised in relation to this image. Indeed, the more one delves into the theories that it has generated, the more of an enigma it becomes, so that in the end, the only certainty is that this Early Netherlandish masterpiece was painted by Jan van Eyck, who positioned his brush above the round mirror and signed his work with a flourish. Or did he? For rather than following artistic convention and using the conventional Latin wording *Johannes de Eyck fecit*, or "Jan van Eyck made this," the artist instead wrote *Johannes de Eyck fuit hic, 1434*, or "Jan van Eyck was here, 1434," which does not necessarily mean the same thing.

Although it was thought to depict a married or betrothed couple, little was known about this painting until a sixteenth-century inventory, written in French, was discovered that appeared to refer to it as "A big panel painting, Hernoult le Fin with his wife in a room." Van Eyck was working in Bruges, one of the most important ports in the duchy of Burgundy (and, indeed, the world), in 1434. Searches of the city archives revealed two potential candidates for the fur-draped man: the brothers Arnolfini (the Italian equivalent of the French "Hernoult le Fin"), namely Giovanni di Arrigo, or di Nicolao, and Michele, scions of a wealthy merchant and banking family from Lucca, Italy, who had taken up residence in Bruges to conduct business with Philip the Good, Duke of Burgundy (who was also van Eyck's patron). The records reveal that Giovanni married Giovanna Cenami, the daughter of another Italian financier, and the wealth inherent in such a union, along with the evident prosperity of the bedchamber depicted in such intricate detail by van Eyck, has led scholars to claim that the painting commemorates their wedding. Others, however, insist that it is simply a double portrait of a well-to-do husband and wife. The debate will no doubt continue, but for the moment it seems safe to say that the symbolic messages contained in this image allude to the ideal Christian marriage.

See also **The Virgin Mary** (page 76), **Margaret of Antioch** (page 80), *Crucifixion of Christ* (pages 114–15), **Dog** (page 136).

That only one candle is burning in such a handsome chandelier, and in such a well-ordered household is a mystery. Art historians' best guess is that the single flame conforms to Christian convention in symbolizing Christ's divine illumination, or all-seeing eye, or else may signify faith, one of the three theological virtues.

The brush hanging by the bed would have been used for dusting, and thus signifies a disciplined housekeeper and a clean, well-run household.

The lady may appear pregnant, but a comparison with other northern European paintings of this period reveals that even saintly virgins were portrayed with protruding abdomens, indicating that this body shape was then considered the ideal for young women, as were voluminous gowns fashioned from heavy fabrics.

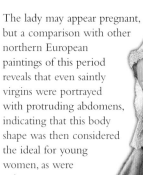

A rosary (or two) hangs on the wall. Rosaries aid the memory when at prayer, and consequently denote piety. And because rosaries can represent the Virgin Mary, the "rose" of heaven, they may also refer to Christianity's ideal feminine, a role model to which fifteenth-century women were encouraged to aspire.

Ten medallions, each portraying a scene from Christ's Passion, with the Crucifixion at the top, surround a convex mirror, again suggesting piety, as well as feminine purity, for the Virgin Mary was often likened to a "spotless mirror." Zoom in on the mirror, and we can see the reflections of two additional people (witnesses to a wedding, maybe?), a male figure in red and a turbaned man in blue, who may be van Eyck himself.

The wooden finial on the bedhead has been carved into a representation of St. Margaret of Antioch and the dragon. The saint's escape from the dragon's stomach caused her to be invoked by women in childbirth, who prayed for an easy labor at a time when children were almost invariably born in the marital bed.

Like all canines, the little dog symbolizes faithfulness, and because, being a lapdog, it belongs to the lady of the house, wifely fidelity in particular.

Oranges imported from the Iberian Peninsula would have been expensive luxuries in fifteenth-century Bruges, so their inclusion in the painting emphasizes the household's wealth. In symbolic terms, oranges can denote fertility, while orange blossom represents virginity and blushing brides.

It appears that the man has kicked off his pattens (the wooden clogs that protect his stockings while out and about in the filthy streets on business), while the lady's red slippers can be seen lying higgledy-piggledy in the background. Because they strike such untidy notes in an otherwise formal composition, supporters of the wedding theory have speculated that they refer to God's Old Testament injunction to "put off thy shoes from off thy feet, for the place whereon thou standest is holy ground" (Exodus 3:5), their argument being that because marriage is one of the sacraments of the Church, it takes place on sacred ground.

La Pia dei Tolomei

Dante Gabriel Rossetti

1880, oil on canvas, Spencer Museum of Art, Lawrence, Kansas, USA

The English artist Dante Gabriel Rossetti paid homage to two of his great loves in his painting *La Pia*: the work of the poet Dante Alighieri (1265–1321), from whom he derived his first name and whose Italian heritage he shared; and Janey Morris (née Burden), the wife of his Pre-Raphaelite "brother," William Morris.

Dante Alighieri immortalized the character of La Pia (Italian for "the pious woman") in Part II, *Purgatorio* ("Purgatory"), of his epic poem *Divina Commedia* ("Divine Comedy"), of 1321. In the fifth canto (lines 130–6), Dante relates that when he encountered the soul of La Pia in purgatory (for she had died without absolution), she implored him to "Remember me who am La Pia, me from Siena sprung and by Maremma dead. This in his innermost heart well knoweth he, with whose fair jewel I was ringed and wed." Dante's Italian contemporaries would have been familiar with the true story of La Pia, of the family of Tolomei, a noblewoman from Siena whose husband, Nello della Pietra dei Pannocchieschi, was responsible for her death in 1295, some say due to his jealousy on account of her adultery, and others, so that he would be free to marry the Countess Margherita degli Aldobrandeschi. Although there is also some disagreement as to the exact manner of La Pia's death—one version of the tragic tale telling us that illness killed her, another asserting that she was thrown from a window to her death—it is agreed that she met her untimely end in the unhealthy, marshy region of the Sienese Maremma, in Tuscany, and specifically at the Castello della Pietra, or Pietra Castle, where her husband had imprisoned her. In portraying the unhappy, rejected La Pia with the features of Janey Morris, Rossetti may have been hinting that he was longing to act as Janey's knight in shining armor in liberating her from a marriage that, he felt, had become her prison, and from a husband who had become her jailor.

See also **Plants** (pages 130–31), **Birds** (pages 138–40).

The bundle of weapons over which her husband's standard is draped represents the violence that could be used against La Pia should she try to escape. They could furthermore be interpreted as phallic symbols on account of their elongated forms, or, because they are tridents, as the pitchforks wielded by Satan's demons in hell.

A clamor of rooks (birds of the crow family) flies through leaden skies past the brooding La Pia. Like all noisy, black, carrion-eating birds, rooks are said to portend death. Scholars believe that by depicting these birds, Rossetti was also referring to the section in his poem *Sunset Wings* (1871) that starts, "And now the mustering rooks innumerable / Together sail and soar, / While for the day's death, like a tolling knell, / Unto the heart they seem to cry, Farewell, / No more, farewell, no more!"

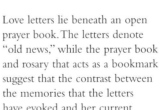

Like all instruments that measure the passage of time, the sundial alludes to the passing of human life, which moves closer to death with every hour that passes. The gnomon is decorated with a wheel of fortune, a symbol of the fickleness of fate that can reverse the fortunes of anyone and everyone in a matter of seconds.

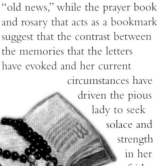

Love letters lie beneath an open prayer book. The letters denote "old news," while the prayer book and rosary that acts as a bookmark suggest that the contrast between the memories that the letters have evoked and her current circumstances have driven the pious lady to seek solace and strength in her faith.

Lost in thought, La Pia toys with her wedding ring, the "fair jewel" with which her husband "ringed" her, or claimed ownership of her, on the occasion of their marriage.

The fig leaves to the lonely lady's left represent potential fruitfulness, which is doomed to remain unfulfilled, while the evergreen ivy on her right may symbolize the memories to which La Pia clings, or else her undying fidelity (because it attaches itself to solid structures, ivy was once regarded as a symbol of married women who depended on their husbands for support).

The bell in the castle's belfry adds to the ominous atmosphere, suggesting that it won't be long before it tolls a funeral knell for La Pia. The fortress of which it is a part is a place and symbol of imprisonment, but in other contexts, castles can denote defensiveness, security and protection from hostile aggressors. In psychology, a princess languishing within a castle can represent both long-sought-after enlightenment and an object of sexual desire. In addition, a black castle in which a solitary occupant is incarcerated may represent hopelessness, failure and hell. Towers, too, have symbolic significance: as watch-towers, they denote vigilance, and, as soaring structures, spiritual or intellectual elevation; their shape can also cause them to be phallic symbols, while in Christian iconography, they may signify chastity.

Pour Fêter le Bébé (In Honor of the Baby)

Henri Rousseau

1903, oil on canvas, Kunstmuseum Winterthur, Winterthur, Switzerland

Often dismissed as "primitive," naïve art may be created by artists who are unskilled and unschooled in the references, techniques and styles employed by many a polished "professional," but it is mainly thanks to Frenchman Henri Rousseau that it has been accepted not only as a *bona fide* genre, but as a meaningful one, too. Indeed, some would say that because its images are transferred to the canvas directly from the painter's imagination, without first passing through any sort of artistic filter, it has a simplicity and honesty that makes its symbolism especially powerful.

Nicknamed *Le Douanier Rousseau*, or "Rousseau the Customs Officer," on account of the day job that he held down with the toll-collecting body of Paris from 1871 until 1893, Rousseau began painting in middle age, and then only as a hobby. He began to make a name for himself from 1886, however, when he started to show his paintings at the recently founded *Salon des Indépendants* (an annual exhibition of the works of artists unattached to the official *Salon* in Paris), and although his untutored style and childlike vision attracted much ridicule and derision, by 1893, he was sufficiently encouraged to devote himself to his art full-time. Rousseau may not have had a sophisticated style, nor an in-depth familiarity with artistic conventions, but as a father of nine children, he certainly understood both how a child regards itself as being the most important person in its world and how unconditional, overwhelming love can turn parents into putty in their children's hands. And how better to express these understandings than, on the one hand, to portray a giant-sized infant as a symbol of a young child's outsized ego (as well as of the enormous importance with which mothers and fathers imbue their offspring) and, on the other, to depict it in control of a puppet with an adult's features?

See also **Colors** (page 146), **Flowers** (pages 129–30).

The child's golden hair and white dress denote the innocence of infancy.

Puppets are toys, and are therefore symbols of childhood. Just as puppet-masters represent those with control over others, so puppets signify those who are being manipulated, maybe against their will, when they may lack the mental strength to resist. Rousseau had a very similar mustache to the one sported by this puppet—perhaps he has therefore depicted one of his children "pulling his strings." Alternatively, maybe his intention was to contrast the freedom of childhood with the constraints of adulthood, when the many responsibilities mean that the power to act entirely autonomously is lost, so that as a grown-up, one is no longer truly a free agent.

 Not only do the daisies' golden centers and white petals echo the colors of the toddler's hair and clothing, these flowers in particular symbolize childhood. This association is partly due to their color symbolism, and partly due to the daisy chains that children have traditionally enjoyed making through the ages. Their simple, unaffected charm also links daisies with children, who are typically equally straightforward and lacking in artifice.

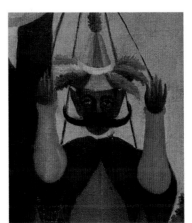

Buds and flowers that have just started to bloom can represent children, who are not only in the "flower of youth," but can be compared to the beautiful fulfillment of the potential hinted at by seeds, or embryonic life. Blooms can also denote the transitory nature of life, however, for their time in full flower is brief, and they will soon wilt and die. Decoded this way, floral symbolism can hint at a parent's bittersweet sense of melancholy that death awaits their precious child, who has only just embarked on life's journey, when he or she reaches the end of the road. Their colors can add an additional nuance of meaning, for while white flowers signify purity, red flowers can denote blood, and hence vitality (but again, also death), and blue blooms can symbolize the imagination and dreams.

The Battle of Issus

Abrecht Altdorfer

1529, tempera on wood, Alte Pinakothek, Munich, Germany

Committing the details of a resounding battlefield victory to canvas serves a number of purposes, including the glorification of the victor for propaganda purposes. But why depict a battle that took place nearly two thousand years ago, and at the behest of a patron—Duke William IV of Bavaria—whose socio–political position was not only secure, but who was more interested in art (this being one of a cycle of sixteen paintings that he commissioned) than in martial matters? If one considers that, in art, many battle scenes are symbolic portrayals of the clash between the perceived forces of good and evil, or "us and them," and one then takes the situation in central Europe at the time that this picture was painted into account, a compelling explanation soon presents itself.

The battle that the German artist Albrecht Altdorfer has rendered in paint was fought at Issus (in the part of Asia Minor that is now Turkey) between King Alexander III of Macedonia (356–323 BC) and King Darius III of Persia (c.380–330 BC) in 333 BC. In this, the second of the two kings' encounters, Darius and his army were routed, just as they had been at the Granicus River, and would be again at Arbela, Alexander subsequently marching as far east as the Punjab region of the Indian Subcontinent. Over the millennia, the heroic Macedonian warrior and strategist—now known as Alexander the Great—gained almost mythical status, eventually being as revered for his nobility of character as for his military prowess. And at a time when the army of the Ottoman sultan Suleiman the Magnificent was sweeping ever westward from Turkey into the heart of Europe, evoking the memory of this ancient champion of the West's famous victory over the forces of the East was almost certainly intended to hearten all those who saw it. Courage was certainly needed, for in the fall of 1529, the Ottoman Turks besieged Vienna, the capital of the Holy Roman Empire that, like the artist's hometown of Regensburg, lay on the River Danube. With the rapacious Turks now far too close for comfort, Altdorfer, in his capacity as a town councillor, was charged with reinforcing Regensburg's defenses.

See also **The Sun** (page 126), **The Moon** (page 126).

The Macedonians have pitched camp outside a town that looks remarkably like a German or Austrian city. Its church spires are prominent, maybe to emphasize that an Eastern (Muslim) victory would spell disaster for Christian Europe.

The swirling clouds and depiction of both the moon and the sun in the sky give the battlefield an apocalyptic atmosphere. The crescent moon is a symbol of the East and the Ottoman Empire, and is on the verge of being eclipsed by the rising sun that is a symbol of the West, and of Alexander the Great.

When translated from the Latin, the text framed by the plaque suspended above the battle scene reads: "Alexander the Great defeats the last Darius. Of the Persian army, 100,000 foot soldiers were killed and more than 10,000 horsemen. Darius's mother, wife and children were taken prisoner and also 1,000 Persian horsemen." Altdorfer has also included smaller labels giving details of the opposing forces at various points in the thick of the battle, perhaps to underline that although Alexander and his men were greatly outnumbered (Alexander had 32,000 infantry and 4,000 cavalry, while Darius boasted 300,000 foot soldiers and 10,000 horsemen), they nevertheless prevailed.

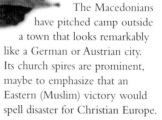

Alexander is at the center of the battlefield, directly below the ring that hangs from the plaque. His white horse is the legendary Bucephalas. By portraying Alexander as a sixteenth-century knight, complete with lance, and by giving his soldiers the uniforms, weapons and heraldic banners of his own era, the artist may have been drawing an explicit parallel between the all-conquering Macedonians and his European contemporaries, who were now threatened by Turkish aggressors.

Some smartly dressed ladies can be discerned amid the Persian throng. Presumably they are Darius's womenfolk, who will soon be taken prisoner by Alexander (history relates that he treated them courteously).

Darius has turned his chariot around and prepares to flee the battlefield. His soldiers' turbans resemble those worn by the Ottoman Turks.

Scholars believe that the body of water on the left represents the Red Sea; that the large island is Cyprus, in the Mediterranean Sea; and that the Nile Delta can be seen to the right.

The Third of May 1808

Francisco de Goya

1814, oil on canvas, Museo del Prado, Madrid, Spain

Although *The Third of May 1808* is a history painting that graphically illustrates the violence and horror of the events that occurred on that date on the Montana del Principe Pio in Madrid, Spain, it should not be regarded as a piece of reportage, or the equivalent of a twenty-first-century newspaper photograph, partly because it was painted six years after the event, and partly because the artist had a point to prove.

The painting depicts a bloody episode that took place during the Peninsular War (1808–14), or War of Independence, as it is called in Spain. The French emperor having ordered Marshal Joachim Murat and his army to enter Spain ostensibly to restore order following a *coup d'état* that replaced King Charles IV with his son, Ferdinand VII, Napoleon I then took advantage of the situation and had his brother, Joseph, "elected" king instead of either Bourbon. Uproar ensued among certain elements of Spanish society, and on May 2 (*Dos de Mayo* in Spanish), 1808, the citizens of Madrid rose up in rebellion against the French occupiers, only to be brutally suppressed. It is the summary execution of the rebels on the orders of Murat on May 3 (*Tres de Mayo*), 1808, that Goya has depicted. Implicit in his portrayal is the goodness, innocence and helplessness of the Spaniards facing the firing squad; some say that it was vital that the artist presented the French in as black a light as possible when he was authorized by the Regency Council to create two images (the other being *The Second of May 1808*) in honor of Ferdinand's restoration to the throne in 1814. Indeed, because he had retained his position as court painter during the French occupation, he was regarded as *afrancesados* ("Frenchified" in Spanish) at best, and as a collaborator at worse. This is probably why Goya eventually thought it prudent to move to France in 1824, where he ended his days. As for Murat, whose loyalty Napoleon had rewarded with the kingdom of Naples later in 1808, he died at the hands of a firing squad in 1815.

See also **Colors** (page 146).

Goya has presented the French soldiers who make up the firing squad as a robotic collective, a faceless, ruthless, heartless and inhuman killing machine. Toting their guns and festooned with swords, their wealth of weapons stands in stark contrast to the unarmed, defenseless Spaniards, and their proximity to their victims also suggests "overkill." The packs strapped to their backs signify that they are on the march, that they are merely passing through, and that they are therefore not bound to this city—or country—by ancient ties of time and blood, unlike their victims.

Those nearby hide their eyes, being either unable to witness the horrors that are unfolding before their eyes or to face their executioners, for they are next in line to be shot. One cannot tear his eyes away from the dreadful tableau, however, and stands transfixed, his glassy stare betraying his terror.

The crimson of the dead man's spilled blood and the yellow of the next victim's breeches are reminiscent of the colors of the Spanish flag—a subtly patriotic touch on the part of the artist, perhaps?

A tonsured Franciscan friar, in his gray habit, clasps his hands tightly in prayer.

Monks, priests and other representatives of the Roman Catholic Church had encouraged the popular uprising, for French-sponsored rule not only promised to liberalize Spanish society, but to abolish the heresy-suppressing Spanish Inquisition—the Church therefore had much to lose under King Joseph.

The man's white shirt appears to glow in the light of the lantern that illuminates the dreadful scene. Everything about him suggests innocence and martyrdom, from the spotlessness of his shirt to his outstretched arms, which appear to signal his surrender, yet, at the same time, almost to invite death. His right hand bears a wound like stigmata, or the wounds that were inflicted on Christ when he was nailed to the cross, and his pose echoes that of the crucifixion, reinforcing the impression of self-sacrifice and martyrdom.

The executions of May 3, 1808, were carried out at night, and the saturated quality of the black sky serves both to highlight the painting's symbolic white elements and to emphasize that this was a black night, associated with evil, death and mourning.

Napoleon on the Throne

Jean Auguste Dominique Ingres

1806, oil on canvas, Musée de l'Armée, Paris, France

Rulers tend to make use of the dark art of propaganda (or "spin," as it is today also known) during periods of political or military transition or turbulence, when, in order to eliminate any threats to their position and power, it is vital to stamp out any internal dissent, as well as to intimidate any potential foreign aggressors. Suggesting, for example, that a ruler has the sanction and protection of the supreme being, and, indeed, has even been blessed with quasidivine qualities, will, it is hoped, deter any would-be rebels from attempting to launch a *coup d'état* similar to that with which the Corsican-born soldier Napoleon Bonaparte (1769–1821) overthrew the *Directoire*, or Directory, as the body of five directors that had governed France since 1795 was known. From 1799, first consul (chief magistrate) of France, Napoleon was elected consul for life in 1802, and then, on May 18, 1804, emperor; he was crowned as such on December 2, 1804.

This portrait of Napoleon in his coronation robes could be regarded as a collaborative effort in the projection of might and majesty between Ingres, an up-and-coming young French artist, and his newly imperial subject. In planning his piece, Ingres drew inspiration from ancient Roman and Byzantine—imperial—art and, in particular, from the magnificent portrayal of God the Father in Jan van Eyck's *Ghent Altarpiece* (c.1432). When it was exhibited, his portrait was condemned as being both a bad likeness of Napoleon, and too stiff and iconic a representation of a man of the people. But was Napoleon this anymore? For by staging his coronation at the cathedral of Notre-Dame de Paris, inviting Pope Pius VII to consecrate him as emperor and commissioning a stunning set of regalia replete with autocratic, dynastic symbolism, Napoleon I had signaled that he was no longer a commoner, but the rightful successor of Charlemagne, the Frankish king whom Pope Leo III had crowned Holy Roman emperor in Rome on Christmas Day 800. Fifteen years after the Revolution, and eleven years after King Louis XVI was guillotined, France had now exchanged its hard-won democracy for despotic rule.

See also **The Air** (pages 158–61), **Zeus/Jupiter** (page 20).

The golden wreath that Napoleon wears is a gilded replica of the laurel wreaths with which military victors were crowned in imperial Rome when they entered the city in triumph. Not only did laurel leaves symbolize victory and immortality (being evergreen), but the plant from which they were plucked was sacred to Jupiter (the Romans' supreme god, whose counterpart in Greece was Zeus), so that whoever wore a laurel wreath was believed to be blessed with the god's approval and protection. The halolike effect imparted by the curved back of the throne reinforces this association with the glorious, the sacred and the divine.

"Pxit" is short for pinxit, the Latin for "painted this."

A model of Charlemagne surmounts the scepter in Napoleon's right hand, symbolizing the new emperor's inheritance of the first Holy Roman emperor's authority. Charlemagne (742–814) was the greatest scion of the Carolingians, the dynasty that succeeded the Merovingians as rulers of France.

An ivory "hand of justice," whose fingers form the sign symbolizing the Holy Trinity, signifying blessing, tops the scepter in Napoleon's left hand; it is said to have been Charlemagne's. Scepters are attributes of supreme authority whose symbolism lies in their phallic shape. Like swords, they also resemble petrified solar rays or the *axis mundi* that keeps the world stable and connects earth and heaven. Like magic wands, scepters are also said to concentrate and discharge blasts of pure energy, much like the thunderbolt that Jupiter wielded.

Roman emperors wore bright-red robes, while costly ermine fur has been associated with nobility since medieval times. The sumptuous velvet is embroidered with wreaths enclosing Napoleon's monogram—"N"—and numerous bees, Napoleonic symbols. As social insects that work together to create honey, bees represent cooperation, industry and prosperity, and were also royal emblems in ancient Egypt and Chaldea. Napoleon selected them to represent him and his dynasty primarily because hundreds of small, golden, winged, decorative objects, which were thought to represent bees, had, in 1653, been found in the Tournai tomb of Childeric, a Merovingian monarch. Stylized bees therefore linked Napoleon with another regal French dynasty.

A sword purporting to be Charlemagne's hangs by Napoleon's side; according to the eleventh-century epic poem *The Song of Roland*, this sword had mystical properties. As part of a ruler's regalia, the sword denotes justice, as well as the wearer's authority.

The eagle on the rug is the "king of the birds" that was sacred to Jupiter and that adorned the standards of the Roman Army, making it a symbol of supreme authority, sovereignty and military might. It lies at the center of a zodiac, denoting the god's mastery of the universe and transcendence of time as Jupiter. The scales of Libra at left represent judgment and justice.

The Stages of Life
Caspar David Friedrich

1835, oil on canvas, Museum der Bildenden Künste, Leipzig, Germany

Caspar David Friedrich was sixty-one when he painted this haunting image, and maybe the German artist sensed that his creative career, and, indeed, his life, were drawing to a close, for it seems especially poignant that he should have chosen to focus on the subject of aging and mortality shortly before suffering a severe stroke, and only five years before he died.

The theme of the stages of life is an age-old one, and recalls the riddle that, in ancient Greek myth, the Sphinx asked Oedipus, Prince of Thebes: "What goes on four feet, on two feet, and three, but the more feet it goes on, the weaker it be? Oedipus answered correctly, the solution being "man"—or rather, "humankind"—and it is in this spirit that Friedrich has depicted himself and his family. In *The Stages of Life*, Friedrich leans on a cane, or "goes on three feet," while his three children (he married relatively late in life), Gustav Adolf, Agnes and Emma, amuse themselves on the ground, evoking the "four feet" metaphor of crawling, these personifications of old age and childhood being linked by the gesticulating hands of maturity, in the shape of Friedrich's nephew, who stands upright, on his "own two feet." There is no set number denoting the stages of human life in the language of symbolism, which can range from three (childhood, adulthood and old age) to twelve, when the passage of the years in someone's life is likened to the passing of the months of the year. When the stages are specified as being four, these represent childhood, youth, maturity and old age, and can be symbolized by the four seasons: respectively, spring, summer, fall and winter. And although it is not usually a number associated with the stages of life, five is regarded as being the number of humankind, for we have five senses, five digits on each hand and foot and, if the head is included, five "limbs," which may be one of the reasons why Friedrich included five people in his very personal allegory.

See also **Numbers** (pages 147–48), **The Life Cycle** (pages 149–50).

Three sticks create a makeshift tripod that supports an object resembling a skull, which Friedrich may have intended as a *memento mori* alluding to the inevitability of death. While the three limbs of the tripod refer to the "three feet" of old age, as personified by the old man to the right—and may also refer to the Christian Trinity—the stick that has been jammed into the sand next to him looks like a crutch, a symbol of infirmity and the need for support.

A barrel that is usually used for storing live fish is empty, suggesting that the time of plenty is now over, and that since life can no longer be sustained, death awaits.

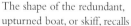

The shape of the redundant, upturned boat, or skiff, recalls a burial mound, or grave, perhaps the next destination for the old man, who stands well back from waterline, where the younger people have positioned themselves.

It is sunset, a time of day that is traditionally linked with old age (dawn denoting birth; morning, childhood; noon, adulthood; afternoon, maturity; and night, death). The crescent moon that can just be seen above the horizon may denote waning powers leading to death, but may hint at rebirth, too, for the monthly lunar cycle can be compared to the human life cycle. The crescent moon can also symbolize the boat that carries the soul safely through the darkness of night, or death, into the light of dawn, where it experiences rebirth.

Ships sail to and from the German shore on the Baltic Sea. They can represent the vessel—the human body—that carries the soul through the waters of life, in a journey that may sometimes be plain sailing, and sometimes terribly turbulent. In Christian belief, boats may also represent the Church, or even Christ himself.

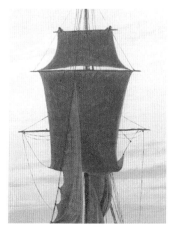

Three crosses can be discerned at the center of the painting: the cross formed by the largest ship's mast and yard; the cross created by the combination of the incoming water and the sandy spit; and the cross on the Swedish flag that the children are holding aloft.

All may refer to the artist's Christian faith, which teaches that those who believe in Christ will enjoy a spiritual rebirth and eternal life after death. Friedrich may have depicted the Swedish flag partly because Sweden was then the most dynamic national power on the Baltic, and partly because its composition, if not its colors, are reminiscent of the flag of the Resurrection that, in art, sometimes accompanies Christ.

Because the sea and land merge here, the strand, or beach, denotes a staging post between the elements of water and earth, or between life and death (or vice versa). In addition, the grains of sand found on a coastline can be equated with the sand that flows through traditional hourglasses, and can thus signify the passing of time, as well as impermanence.

The Triumph of Death

Lo Scheggia

1450, tempera on wood, Pinacoteca Nazionale, Siena, Italy

As Benjamin Franklin famously commented in 1789, "In this world nothing can be said to be certain, except death and taxes," and this truism must have seemed especially pertinent during the fourteenth century, when the terrible bubonic-plague pandemic called the Black Death swept through Asia and Europe, leaving an estimated 50 million people dead. This was also the century in which the Italian poet Petrarch wrote his *Trionfi* ("Triumphs"), a series of allegorical verses telling of how Chastity conquered Love, Death overcame Chastity, Fame subjugated Death and Time got the better of Fame, before being vanquished in turn by Eternity. In such existentially bleak times, it may therefore have been no coincidence that Petrarch seemed to emphasize that although our reputations may live on long after the grave has claimed our bodies, in the end, time will obliterate our memory, and even time is as nothing in the face of eternity.

Yet when you consider that Petrarch was writing in a time and place that was exclusively Roman Catholic, as well as plague-prone, his contemporaries may not have considered this message chilling, for the Christian Church teaches that God is Eternity, and that after the Last Judgment, the virtuous will enjoy eternal happiness in the new heaven and earth, while sinners will suffer eternal misery in hell. Such paintings as *The Triumph of Death*, which is based on Petrarch's *Trionfo della Morte* (in Italian), or *Triumphus Mortis* (in Latin), can therefore be regarded as doing viewers a service in acting as a *memento mori* (the Latin for "remember, you must die"), namely in reminding them that death is inevitable, and may strike at any moment, so that it would be advisable to mend any wicked ways immediately, lest eternity be spent in torment. Although this may initially appear a macabre image with which to decorate a *cassone*, an Italian wedding chest, by including it, "Lo Scheggia," or "the Splinter," as the Italian painter Giovanni de Ser Giovanni was nicknamed on account of his predilection for painting on wood, was therefore offering sound and pious advice.

See also **Death** (page 150), **Winter** (page 128).

Skeletons and skulls are among the most commonly used devices for *memento mori*.

Petrarch tells us that the Death that he encountered was "a woman shrouded in a dress of black," but skeletons are sexless, as are the skulls—booty—depicted here at Death's feet. That said, the Grim Reaper, who turns the living into the dead by scything them down, or harvesting them, is conventionally thought of as being male because the figure is based on the Greek god Kronos, who castrated his father, Ouranos (Uranus), with a sickle, and who was in turn associated with the Roman god Saturn, who, being a god of agriculture, carried a scythe.

The snow-covered mountains suggest that it is winter, the season traditionally associated with death, when all of nature seems lifeless (apart from the evergreen trees that are hope-giving symbols of immortality and eternity).

As Death's chariot moves inexorably onward, it leaves corpses strewn in its wake. The golden crown and miter of two of the recently deceased identify them as a king (or emperor) and bishop (or pope), while the rest are young men in the prime of life, thereby illustrating that Death is no respecter of status, power, riches, youth or health.

In the background, a funeral procession enters a church. This reminds the viewer that the dead will be resurrected, and the righteous will then begin their glorious life in Christ.

The chariot was a symbol of victory on the battlefield in ancient Rome, and the chariots of victors were pulled in triumphal processions through the Roman streets to the temple of Jupiter on the Capitoline Hill. Death's chariot makes something of a mockery of the triumphal chariot's traditional splendor, and thus of human vanity,

however, for its richly embroidered covering doesn't quite conceal the wooden wheels of a rustic ox cart, and it is being dragged along by a pair of undernourished-looking oxen, rather than a pair of prancing horses. In this context, the wheels may symbolize the cycle of life and the passing of time, but also eternity.

The oxen denote patience because they plod along steadily in the fields (and consequently Death's willingness to wait until a soul is ready to be reaped) and also death, partly because their horns form the shape of a crescent moon (which can also signify rebirth), and partly because the color of their coats is that of death.

Some of those preceding Death are hunters carrying birds of prey, whose hawkish eyes, brutal beaks and cruel claws spell instant death to their furry victims.

INDEX OF ARTISTS

INDEX

BIBLIOGRAPHY

Aldred, Cyril, *Egyptian Art*, Thames and Hudson Ltd., 1985.

Alexander, David and Pat (Eds.), *The Lion Handbook to the Bible*, Lion Publishing, 1983.

Ann, Martha, and Imel, Dorothy Meyers, *Goddesses in World Mythology*, Oxford University Press, 1993.

Bauer, Wolfgang, Dümotz, Irmtraud, and Golowin, Sergius, *Lexikon der Symbole*, Marix Verlag GmbH, 2004.

Bäumer, Angelica, *Gustav Klimt: Women*, George Weidenfeld and Nicolson Ltd., 1985.

Becker, Udo (Ed.), *The Element Encyclopedia of Symbols*, Element Books Ltd., 1994.

Bell, Robert E., *Women of Classical Mythology*, Oxford University Press, 1991.

Benét, William Rose, *The Reader's Encyclopedia*, Guild Publishing, 1987.

Bulfinch, Thomas, *The Golden Age of Myth & Legend*, Wordsworth Editions Ltd., 1993.

Carr-Gomm, Sarah, *The Secret Language of Art*, Duncan Baird Publishers Ltd., 2003.

Chetwynd, Tom, *Dictionary of Symbols*, The Aquarian Press, 1993.

Chevalier, Jean, and Gheerbrant, Alain, *The Penguin Dictionary of Symbols*, Penguin Books, 1996.

Chilvers, Ian, *Dictionary of Art & Artists*, Grange Books, 2005.

Cirlot, J. E., *A Dictionary of Symbols*, Routledge, 1995.

Comini, Alessandra, *Gustav Klimt*, Thames and Hudson Ltd., 1978.

Cooper, J. C. (Ed.), *Brewer's Book of Myth & Legend*, Cassell Publishers Ltd., 1992.

Cooper, J. C., *An Illustrated Encyclopaedia of Traditional Symbols*, Thames and Hudson Ltd., 1978.

Craven, Roy C., *Indian Art*, Thames and Hudson Ltd., 1993.

Crompton, Samuel Willard, *Gods & Goddesses of Classical Mythology*, Barnes & Noble Inc., 1997.

Dictionary of Classical Mythology, Brockhampton Press, 1995.

Douglas, J. D., & Tenney, Merrill C., *NIV Compact Dictionary of the Bible*, Hodder & Stoughton, 1989.

Dube, Wolf-Dieter, *The Expressionists*, Thames and Hudson Ltd., 1979.

Duchet-Suchaux, Gaston, and Pastoureau, Michel, *The Bible and the Saints*, Flammarion, 1994.

Farmer, David Hugh, *The Oxford Dictionary of Saints*, Oxford University Press, 1996.

Fisher, Sally, *The Square Halo*, Harry N. Abrams, Inc., 1995.

Fontana, David, *The Secret Language of Symbols*, Pavilion Books Ltd., 1993.

Frédéric, Louis, *Buddhism*, Flammarion, 1995.

Gibson, Clare, *Sacred Symbols*, Saraband Inc., 1998.

Gibson, Clare, *The Secret Life of Dreams*, Saraband (Scotland) Ltd., 2003.

Gibson, Clare, *Signs & Symbols*, Saraband Inc., 1996.

Gibson, Clare, *Symbols of the Goddess*, Saraband (Scotland) Ltd., 2004.

Hall, James, *Illustrated Dictionary of Symbols in Eastern and Western Art*, John Murray (Publishers) Ltd., 1994.

Hariri-Wendel, Tanja Al, *Symbols of Islam*, Sterling Publishing Co., Inc., 2002.

Haworth-Maden, Clare (Ed.), *The Glory of the Nativity*, Saraband (Scotland) Ltd., 2004.

Haworth-Maden, Clare (Ed.), *The Passion of the Christ*, Saraband (Scotland) Ltd., 2004.

Holy Bible, The, Authorized King James Version.

Julien, Nadia, *The Mammoth Dictionary of Symbols*, Robinson Publishing, 1996.

Kreijger, Hugo E., *Kathmandu Valley Painting*, Serindia Publications, 1999.

Laneyrie-Dagen, Nadeije, *How to Read Paintings*, Chambers, Harrap Publishers Ltd., 2004.

Lewis, Bernard (Ed.), *The World of Islam*, Thames and Hudson Ltd., 1994.

Littleton, C. Scott (Ed.), *Mythology*, Duncan Baird Publishers, 2002.

Lodwick, Marcus, *The Gallery Companion: Understanding Western Art*, Thames and Hudson Ltd., 2002.

Mackenzie, Donald A., *Indian Myth and Legend*, the Gresham Publishing Company Ltd.

Mackenzie, Donald A., *Teutonic Myth and Legend*, the Gresham Publishing Company Ltd.

Mannering, Douglas, *Great Works of Biblical Art*, Parragon Book Service Ltd., 1995.

McLeish, Kenneth, *Myths and Legends of the World*, Bloomsbury Publishing plc, 1996.

Mühlberger, Richard, *The Bible in Art: The Old Testament*, Moore & Moore Publishing, 1991.

Murray, Alexander S., *Who's Who in Mythology*, Studio Editions Ltd., 1995.

Murray, Peter and Linda, *Oxford Dictionary of Christian Art*, Oxford University Press, 2004.

Oesterreicher-Mollwo, Marianne, *Herder-Lexikon Symbole*, Verlag Herder, 2004.

Oswalt, Sabine G., *Concise Encyclopedia of Greek and Roman Mythology*, Wm. Collins Sons & Co. Ltd., 1969.

Ovid, *Metamorphoses*, Penguin Books Ltd., 1979.

Radice, Betty, *Who's Who in the Ancient World*, Penguin Books Ltd., 1973.

Read, Herbert (Ed.), *The Thames and Hudson Dictionary of Art and Artists*, Thames and Hudson Ltd., 1994.

Robins, Gay, *The Art of Ancient Egypt*, British Museum Press, 1997.

Rynck, Patrick de, *How to Read a Painting*, Thames & Hudson Ltd., 2004.

Sacred Symbols: Ancient Egypt, Thames and Hudson Ltd., 1995.

Sacred Symbols: Mandala, Thames and Hudson Ltd., 1995.

Sala, Charles, *Caspar David Friedrich*, Éditions Pierre Terrail, 1994.

Shearer, Alistair, *Buddha: The Intelligent Heart*, Thames and Hudson Ltd., 1992.

Sommer, Robin Langley, *The Wonder of the Miracles*, Saraband (Scotland) Ltd., 2004.

Thomas, Annabel, *Illustrated Dictionary of Narrative Painting*, John Murray (Publishers) Ltd., 1994.

Voragine, Jacobus de, *The Golden Legend*, Penguin Books, 1998.

Walker, Barbara G., *The Woman's Dictionary of Symbols and Sacred Objects*, Pandora, 1995.

Whitford, Frank, *Gustav Klimt*, Brockhampton Press, 1995.

Wimmer, Otto, *Kennzeichen und Attribute der Heiligen*, Tyrolia-Verlag, 2000.

Zerbst, Marion, and Kafka, Werner, *Das Große Lexikon der Symbole*, E. A. Seemann Verlag, 2003.

ACKNOWLEDGMENTS

The publisher would like to thank Ute Krebs, Kate Tasker and Lucy Scrivener of akg-images, London, and also Fiona Fox for their help in the preparation of this book.

Grateful acknowledgment is made to the following individuals and institutions for permission to reproduce illustrations and photographs:

© **2006 JUPITERIMAGES:** 7, 8 t, 9 b, 10 t, 14 t, 16 b, 17 bl, 18 tl & tr, 20 b, 21 bl, 23 c, 24 b, 25 tl & b, 27 b, 29 b, 31 tl, c & b, 32 c, 33 b, 63 c & br, 64 tr, 66 c, 66–67, 67 tr & br, 71 cl, 81 br, 136–137, 140 b, 141 b, 142 b, 143 b, 144 b, 145, 147, 148 b; **akg-images, London:** 1, 2, 3 (Jean-Louis Nou), 5 (Erich Lessing, t & m, Rabatti-Domingie, b), 12 (Cameraphoto), 36–37 (Nimatallah), 38–39 (Erich Lessing), 40–43, 44–45 (Erich Lessing), 46-49 (Cameraphoto), 50–53 (Erich Lessing), 54–59, 60, 69 cl (Erich Lessing), 72 tl (Cameraphoto), 86–89 (Jean-Louis Nou), 90–91 (Gérard Degeorge), 92–93, 94–97 (Erich Lessing), 98–99 (Cameraphoto), 100–01 (Joseph Martin), 102–03 (Rabatti-Domingie), 104–05 (Erich Lessing), 106–07, 108–09 (Cameraphoto), 110–13, 114–15 (Erich Lessing), 116–18, 119–21 (Erich Lessing), 122–23, 124, 126 cl & br, 130 tl (Jean-Louis Nou), 131 tl (Erich Lessing), 152–55, 156–57 (Erich Lessing), 158–67, 168–71 (Erich Lessing), 172–73, 174–75 (Joseph Martin), 176–77 (Rabatti-Domingie), 178–79, 180–81 (Erich Lessing), 182–83 (© Sotheby's/akg-images), 184–86, 187–91 (Erich Lessing), 192–95, 196–99 (Erich Lessing), 200–01, 202–03 (Rabatti-Domingie); **CorelDraw:** 13 l, 14 b, 16 t, 17 t, 18 b, 24 t, 63 tr, 64 tl, 65, 76 b, 139 b, 150 b; **Library of Congress, Prints and Photographs Division:** 73, 131 tr & b; © **Jay Olstad:** 15 b; **Planet Art:** 6 t & b, 8 b, 9 t, 10 b, 11, 17 br, 18 c, 19 t, 20 t, 21 t, 22–23, 25 tr, 26, 27 t, 29 t, 30, 31 tr, 32 t, 33 t, 34 b, 61, 63 bl, 68 l, 69 t & b, 70, 71, 72 tr & b, 74–75, 76 t, 77–81, 82 t, 84, 85 t, 125, 126 t & br, 127 t, 128 t & b, 129, 130 tr & b, 132–133, 134 t, 135, 136 b, 137, 138, 139 t, 140 t, 141 t, 142 t, 146, 148 t, 149, 150 t, 151 t; **Saraband Image Library:** 6 c, 13 r, 15 t, 19 c & b, 21 br, 28, 32 b, 34 t, 35, 62, 64 c & b, 66 tl, 67 c & b, 82 c & b, 83, 85 b, 127 b, 128 c, 134 b, 136 t, 143 t, 144 t & c, 151 b.